THE PAUL JENNINGS READER
COLLECTED PIECES 1943–89

Paul Jennings began his career as a humorist with a piece published in *Lilliput* in 1943, and by the end of the war had acquired cult status among readers of *Punch* and *The Spectator*. His celebrated column, 'Oddly Enough', ran in *The Observer* from 1949 to 1966. Thereafter he remained prolific, contributing principally to *The Times, The Telegraph Magazine* and *Punch* until shortly before his death on Boxing Day 1989. Two days before he died, with publication of this volume in mind Paul Jennings made a selection of his work from 1978 onwards, none of which has previously been anthologised. That selection forms part of *The Paul Jennings Reader*. The remainder is drawn from the complete Jennings *oeuvre*. It includes his early work, old favourites from his *Observer* days and much that has not previously been published in book form. *The Paul Jennings Reader* is a lasting tribute to the man whom his *Times* obituarist called 'the most consistently original comic writer of our century'.

THE

paul jennings

READER

COLLECTED PIECES

1943-89

Introduction by
Griff Rhys Jones

BLOOMSBURY

First published in Great Britain 1990
Bloomsbury Publishing Limited, 2 Soho Square, London W1V 5DE

A CIP catalogue record for this book
is available from the British Library

ISBN 0-7475-0664-7

10 9 8 7 6 5 4 3 2 1

Typeset by Hewer Text Composition Services, Edinburgh
Printed by Clays Ltd, St Ives plc

CONTENTS

Introduction

There is a purpose to this introduction, which was clearly outlined to me by the publisher. 'Research suggests that there is a generation of intelligent reading people under the age of about thirty-five who are on the whole not aware of Paul,' he wrote. 'I am sure they are aware of you, though.'

Well. Quite. I'm glad somebody researches these sorts of things, aren't you? So, my impressionable and well-researched juniors (it was well calculated flattery – I am about thirty-six in fact), allowing for the fact that it is possible that there exists such a thing as a generation of intelligent reading people under the age of thirty-five, let me introduce you to Paul Jennings.

(If you are over thirty-five you can skip all this. First, because you will, as intelligent reading people of advanced years, be fully aware of Paul Jennings and his genius. And secondly, because, for the same reason, if I understand the publisher correctly, you will be entirely unaware of me.)

But, for ignoramuses of tender years who happen to have got this far, let me first of all assure you that you will not regret having picked up this book. (Even if you might be having second thoughts at this moment.) 'It can confidently be said of Jennings,' *The Times* obligingly intoned in his obituary, 'that no one who troubled to read him thought him unfunny.' I should add that he really is no trouble to read either, so you are safe enough so far.

Paul Jennings is a man I unhappily list under the category of great funny men I might almost have met, but didn't. Alas, he died on Boxing Day 1989, in Suffolk. During his last months he struck up an acquaintanceship with my parents. They also live in Suffolk. (It's a lovely place Suffolk. I live in Suffolk too. There's a lot about Suffolk in here as well. Another good reason for reading it.) My parents never got round to arranging an introduction to Paul Jennings. Such is the way with parents. They introduced me to the retired schoolmaster from Basildon, the woman who has psychic messages from her nephew and the man who does their garden on Tuesdays, but not to Paul Jennings, foremost comic muse of the post-war generation. If my parents had shared a beach hut with the Marx Brothers it would have slipped their minds.

But as Raymond Chandler wrote, 'Never meet a writer if you liked his book.' So it's probably better that I write as a fan, or perhaps like some tiresome bore trying to foist a private passion on a perfect stranger, but not as someone who knew his subject intimately. We are never at our best with paragons are we?

Here is Jennings on a literary party held in an L-shaped room:

'He sits with his wife on a settee in the smaller part of the L. People are introduced to him. Soon it will be our turn. What shall I say? *You have formed my soul?*

'How absurd to be towering over him – he sitting, I standing. He cups his ear, I talk loudly. We are as if on a tiny white stage. Thousands, half seen in the blurred dark background, are listening. We are introduced. I hear myself speak.

' "I bet I am the only man at this party who has to catch the 8.30 from Liverpool Street." '

He's allowed to say that T. S. Eliot formed his soul, of course. Not something we are encouraged to think about humorists, of which Jennings himself was only too aware. 'You've only got to try and imagine a piece called *The Creative Agony of Paul Jennings* to see what a marginal position is occupied by us jokers.' But I remember pinching *The Jenguin Pennings* from my godmother when I was about eleven and getting stuck into pure comedy in handy bite-sized chunks. Marginalia? Quite possibly. I was snorting too much to make an assessment.

It was the sort of collection of which he wrote 'all that publishers and booksellers want to do with our books is actually to get the people into the shops, once they're there they can get them with the real stuff, with the endless, endless talk about sex, betrayal, neurosis, doom, murder, despair; with *writing*.' But you sense through this guarded whinge that Jennings knew he was writing Writing though perhaps not that he was capable of forming souls, at least not the same sort of souls as T. S. Eliot.

It was one of his virtues that there is no such thing as the typical Jennings piece, although aficionados recognize that he was the absolute master of what we might call advanced bath-writing, the warm-water peregrination that starts with an idle notion drifting through the steam, sets off down the plumbing and ends up somewhere in the main drainage system, disgorging the midget factories of Birmingham, Hoggin Inspectors, Ilford's touring dustmen, the negative relaxation piano and other grunts and rumbles on the way. (There's a lot about the pleasures and terrors of baths in here too.) He is not entirely the 'wouldn't it be funny if' sort of writer, nor the 'isn't it funny that' man. He is something unique, somewhere in between.

For seventeen years he wrote a column called 'Oddly Enough' in the

Observer. It was one of the few columns that lived up to its title. Unlike the great Beachcomber, who teased and primped rather than actually combing, Paul Jennings had an enviable capacity for sniffing out the peculiar and improbable where it lay, in signs, instructions, labels ('the overcoat which I once saw marked OF LORDLY APPEARANCE'), machinery and patented inventions: 'a rocking-chair with bellows that worked a carpet cleaner, reversible trousers, a wristband to absorb crayfish juice, and an anti-seasickness deck mounted on a huge bellows into which the ship's boilers blew steam when the ship was in a trough, letting it out when the ship rose on a crest, so that the deck remained level. I swear I am not making these up.'

Others discover the same sort of thing, and send them on postcards to Esther Rantzen. What makes the difference is the relish with which Jennings sets about what he has found in brilliant extended, self-perpetuating, de-ravelling, fantasy pieces.

'Until recently my favourite world's biggest thing was the organ in the Municipal Auditorium, Atlantic City.' He strikes out positively, laying the subject before us with a whiff of boyish enthusiasm, before discreetly promoting the notion that somewhere within the mighty organ there exists a caretaker's flat. There follows a touching vignette: the organist at home, a friend to call 'when, suddenly, the room would begin to shake with sound'. Pausing to clear up the furniture he moves on to consider big things generally and gargantuan paper bags in particular, before finishing with the awful vison of the largest housewife in the world swinging her handbag astride the unimaginable hills, and all in under a thousand words. It is febrile stuff. He ferrets things out. His comic voice is one of the perpetually puzzled, amazed. The world really is odd. There are strange things out there: peculiar, disturbing and, if pursued to their logical ends, daft. Jennings goes in pursuit of them with excitement, wariness and one pregnant eyebrow. It is this that gives his writing such vigour.

The way some fools write about comedy you might think it was a matter of choosing the correct subjects (literature, gardening and cricket, or a combination of the three) and noting their peculiarities. But most great comic writers have that wholly enviable thing, a 'voice'. As with good comedians, the address is all. Jennings is the antithesis of the standard *Punch* waffler. No 'coves' 'troll up', 'heave into view' or 'sally forth'. The style is always brisk. Sometimes he abandons grammar altogether and resorts to what appears to be a furious notation. AND HE IS STILL FUNNY. This is because, unlike the average humorist, who has nothing to say but struggles to say it funnily, Jennings invariably has several funny things to say and a pressing urge to get them down for us hot and strong. It makes for that sort of bubbling excitement and understated relish you expect from a really expert storyteller. He is never ponderous. He revels in words. He wallows in them. His writing is alive with the joy of discovery. 'I have gritches at the bottom of my garden!' Instead of a barrage of loopy vocabulary, his ear or eye alights on the deliciousness of a single word or phrase and hangs it up in all its chunkiness. 'Nevertheless, I breathlessly instructed the dotard to drive furiously down Wigmore-street . . .' It has a poetic ring, don't you think, that 'dotard'? Or try rolling this round your tongue: 'The station is filled with the hiss of steam and the blooping and twanging of harps.'

Mind you, language, like life, is full of the inconsequential, the misleading and the downright peculiar. German in particular. It was apt that he should be drawn to this guttural, lip-smacking, vowel-strangling langauge with all its bolted-on extra bits. Some of the funniest pieces in the book are his attempts to wrestle meaning from his own smattering of German while trying to play Halma. 'At this Game 2 or 4 Persons can betake themselves and each of these wears a Colour and damn it, when 2 Persons play, a big House with 19 Stones, when 4 Persons play, he besets a little House with 13 Stones.'

He summed up his philosophy early on, in his 'Report on Resistentialism.' While other philosophers are concerned about what men think about things, resistentialism is the philosophy of what Things think about us.

'"Things are against us" is the nearest I can get to the untranslatable lucidity of Ventre's profound aphorism, "*Les choses sont contre nous*".'

Despite the fact that this startling existentialist observation found its way into the *Fontana Dictionary of Modern Thought*, Jennings is not a Wittgenstein Blues writer, dropping his learning on us from a great height. It's there all right, but undercut: 'In one of Malraux's books (what am I saying? I've only read one . . .)' Or 'Schiller is in the same class as skiing for me. I should love to be good at it, but it's too late now.' For he has also that sublime gift of the funny writer, candour. Somewhere between the confessional and the bar stool he takes us into his confidence. He admits things, gets frustrated by things, enjoys things, fails utterly to understand things, laughs at things, yes, there are brilliant parodies of Beckett and Joyce, but there is also nonsense. Sometimes, gloriously, he lets go altogether and the pure excitement of silliness overcomes him. There are whole pieces in babblespeak, great little nonsense poems, crazy lists, mad theories and daft observations littering these pages like beacons of inanity.

'I myself suffer from Laughter Fits of. But I am calmed to dignified normal silence, outwardly indistinguishable from Boredom when I consider the sad Sophomaniac, a long-haired fellow who is mad about wisdom.'

I should not be writing this introduction. There is only one person for the job – Harblow, the tireless companion who is never brought down by *les choses* being *contre nous*, who can be relied upon to expect rationality to apply to things and for whom it generally does. Where is Harblow when we really need him? I don't know. But as Paul Jennings himself said, in an earlier collection of his work, 'It seems to be the done thing for a book of essays, especially humorous essays, to be preceded by a preface telling you what the stuff is like. I can't think why. After all if you've picked this book up in the shop it'll only take a minute or two to read one of the actual pieces.' I totally agree. Get reading. Your only problem might be putting it down again, not after two or three minutes but after two or three hours.

Griff Rhys Jones

Moses Was a Sanitary Officer

HAVE YOU EVER watched a soldier marching, and wondered what he was thinking about? If he is a species known as A Young Soldier, I can tell you! He is thinking about a little booklet, excitingly titled 'Army Form B. 51.'

I don't know whether they would let civilians have a copy, but if you want one you can try at H. M. Stationery Office, giving them the reference (799) Wt. 25958 – 1000. 600M. 9/39. W. C. & S. Ltd. Gp. 394. T. S. 9825. Forms/B/51/25. And don't forget the (799) or they'll probably give you a dehospitalisation (Other Ranks with Ague) Certificate instead.

Whoever wrote Army Form B. 51 believes in Applied Psychology. The idea is that we should go around muttering health slogans, such as: '. . . *my usefulness depends on the state of my feet*' or ' . . . *my skin is a covering for getting rid of waste in the form of sweat.*' '*Hard clean feet*' seem to have fascinated the author: feet occur everywhere, like a theme in music. '*Flies*,' he says, '*carry minute portions of filth on their feet.*'

As a matter of fact, I am rather saddened by this. I had always imagined that flies did things conscientiously: I used to imagine them carrying little sacks labelled FILTH over their shoulders and emptying them with a smirk on to the butter. But they only do it unintentionally with their six little feet.

A. F. B. 51 gives Young Soldiers the funniest reasons for doing or not doing things. '*The spittle or saliva is intended to keep the mouth soft . . . such substances as bread, biscuit, rice and pastry require to be well mixed with this saliva . . . in order that they may be perfectly digested. By the habit of spitting you waste this useful substance.*'

On page 6 it says, '*If you feel too much air or draught in a room, wear your woollen cap.*' I like to think of the Young Soldiers sitting on their beds, waiting for Lights Out, looking like goblins in their woollen caps.

But the climax occurs on page 20: – '*At night it is very important to protect the belly by extra covering. If no blankets are available, any impro- vised covering will do, such as a belt, an old bag, some straw or a puttee.*'

I dislike the scornful implication of '*an old bag*'. That's right, any old thing will do for these Young Soldiers. Keep those extra blankets and the nice new bags for the sergeants' bellies, and afterwards, perhaps, you might dig up some straw, or a puttee for them.

1

I would like to tell the bit about Moses being '*an able sanitary officer*', but I haven't got time. I am off to the Q.-M. Stores on my hard clean feet to get one of those Woollen Caps.

❧

Who is This That Cometh?

I HAVE OFTEN wondered why it is that second-lieutenants always go on the piano. Sergeants go on the mantelpiece, majors hang in the drawing-room with their horses, and pilot-officers are on a special little table. But the day after I was commissioned I got an air-letter asking for a photograph to go on the piano.

That meant formal, because the only time people ever see the piano in our house is when it is being played at a party or when the man about the garage has to be shown into the drawing-room because we don't want to switch off the Brahms in The Room and you know how people look at photographs in a strange drawing-room, especially if they are musicians and can tell there is a long wait before even the end of the slow movement.

'Formal' in India means mess kit. Well, of course things aren't what they were, and we don't hang our swords up outside the mess these days; but even so my mess kit is pretty terrifying. It was made for me by a man who loomed on my doorstep one night and produced about a hundred letters signed by brigadiers and people in 1917 (this seems to have been a peak year) saying that in their opinion Lal Boomla was the best tailor in India, if not the Empire.

Mr. Boomla was a determined man. All I wanted was a khaki drill jacket – just a simple little thing with sticking-out officer's pockets and no, repeat NO, brass buttons.

'I have been making for the sahibs for thirty-two year,' he said, 'and they *all* have brass buttons.'

'Maybe the brigadiers did,' I said feebly, 'and anyway times have changed sinced 1917.' But I knew I was beaten.

When the thing came it was even worse than I thought. They weren't brass buttons so much as brass *knobs*. I felt like a bedstead in it. At first I hid it away in a drawer until the day when *I* should be a brigadier.

2

Until this photograph. Very well, they shall have it, I thought, good enough to go on a four-manual organ (with sixty-four-foot pipes and a *tuba mirabilis*). I went down to the bazaar to make an appointment. Anything other than toilet articles that you want to buy in our bazaar, unless you are particularly interested in a nest of tables or a little Taj Mahal or a large tin box, has to be specially ordered from Bombay, and photographic plates are no exception.

'Any day after next Saturday,' he said. 'We close at six.'

I thought rapidly. 'Four-thirty next Sunday,' I said. At that hour the bazaar is usually deserted. I would nip in and out in my embarrassing finery while everyone was still asleep.

At four-fifteen on the following Sunday the casual observer would have seen a heraldic figure on a bicycle pedalling stiffly towards the bazaar, because its trousers were starched. As a matter of fact several observers did, and they were far from casual. To be exact, they were about three hundred British Other Ranks. It seems the first house of the Garrison Cinema had been put forward to four-thirty.

There have been a lot of notices in this area about slackness in saluting. I didn't notice it this Sunday. I suppose being dressed like that was asking for it. It seemed to electrify them. One arm after another shot up with a precision which at any other time would have been commendable. At this time, however, I was wearing one of Mr. Boomla's poplin shirtings (he never called them shirts) under my jacket. Now, it is a peculiarity of India that they *always* make the sleeves of shirts too long. Perhaps they think it doesn't matter anyway because most people wear K. D. tunics which button at the wrist. Well, this tunic of Mr. Boomla's didn't; and if there is one gesture more than another which will make one's shirt-sleeve fall down it is the salute. When they were down to my knuckles I was trying to pull the wretched right sleeve up from the armpit with my left hand and I foolishly attempted to return a salute with my right. My cycle is not very well balanced. Even the B.O.R.s who picked it up for me saluted first.

It is still very hot at four-thirty, and what with the starch and the collar and tie (the only one for miles around at this hour) and the violent saluting I was not quite so heraldic by the time I reached the bazaar. It seemed to contain the rest of the B.O.R.s, having tea out. Heads turned in the windows of all the Chinese restaurants as I progressed down the main street. My intention must have been obvious as I slunk into the photographer's with my arms folded (*damn* those cuffs).

When I reached the blessed dark of the studio the man said 'Side or full face, sahib?'

'Either,' I said, 'as long as the uniform is in.'

'This is a fixed camera,' he said – it certainly was, on an enormous

3

concrete slab. The camera itself was about the size of a tea-chest – 'and we can only take your face.'

The first person I met when I came out was the C.O. I saluted him carefully. He didn't seem very pleased to see me. 'Read Standing Order No.42,' he said.

I did when I got back, having met all the B.O.R.s going to the other cinema on the way. It said: 'Mess kit will NOT be worn before 1800 hours.

Ça Marche Bien

WHEN THE PEOPLE at the garage in which Harblow's car seems to spend most of its time said that they couldn't provide him soon enough with a reconditioned engine or a back axle or whatever it was this time it was rather a judgement on him. We had originally planned to go to France in his car – or, rather, *in* France, since the ability to go across water is one of the few attributes he has never claimed for it – because Harblow said, 'If we go in UB the French will laugh at us (UB is the name of my car which was made in 1926). It was useless to point out to him that the only cars worth having these days are those made before 1930 or after 1946, because the ones in between have the benefit neither of the divine simplicity of UB, with its wire cable brakes, gravity petrol feed, unadorned dashboard and high sidescreens, nor of the one-year period of grace which elapses before the extraordinary and, to my mind, retrogressive complications on the modern car bring it to a standstill. Harblow's car was made in 1935, an absolutely fatal year when they were just beginning to build all those baroque bulbous-looking things round the carburettor, but he still goes round telling everyone with foolish pride what a good year it was.

So we went in UB after all. From the practically deserted quayside at Newhaven, with its silent electric cranes, their grabs disdainfully shortened to cope with UB after the S.S.s and Daimlers, the boat took us slap into the middle of Dieppe on what appeared to be market-day. The majority of the passengers were French, and they were being met by

4

an average of five relatives each. Before this vast assembly the cars were being lifted out by the noisiest and most insecure-looking steam crane I have ever seen. I don't suppose it *was* insecure really, any more than those incredible wire railways in the Alps on which people go on not getting killed year after year. But since childhood, when I observed that the best model steam engines were the ones with horizontal boilers, I have always distrusted the ones with the boiler standing on its end. (For one thing, the fire can't heat so much of the water, can it?) The piston, which was only about a foot long, whizzed round at an enormous speed when the crane was making a wobbly turn on its axis or the thing was out of gear, but whenever it picked up a car it emitted a sort of slowing-down, groaning noise which suggested that it could only just make it.

The crane seized UB with obvious relief after a long row of shiny new cars labelled '*Export. Sportcar A. G. Zurich,*' and deposited it with a flourish in the midst of the cheering spectators. The French did not exactly laugh at UB. I think they were too amazed. But they did shake my faith in their famous logic. Harblow had already remarked on the extraordinary number of French cars on the roads; many of these, it is true were modern cars with bumpers and, delightful phrase, *avertisseurs sonores*. (UB's advertiser, one of those ancient klaxons which seem to go through a couple of gears before they reach a steady note, we had left behind because age had so reduced its sonority as to make it practically inaudible.) But there were also a considerable number of what I can only call jalopies even older than UB – strange jalopies with bodies like boats, only with the sharp end at the back, old high jalopies with vertical steering columns; and we even saw one jalopy with solid tyres. I do not think the arrival of UB seriously lowered the average age of cars in France. Yet, for some reason, it was greeted on the quayside and wherever we went with cries of '*le petit tank anglais!*' except for one wonderful moment in a dark garage when a man said, '*Qu'est-ce que c'est que vous avez là? C'est un jeep, hein?*' Almost every time we went into a garage the man would slap it casually and say, '*Cinq chevaux, hein?*' and my reply, '*Non, monsieur, sept-point-neuf. Presque huit,*' always produced a sensation. The economical French would make any engine with 8 *chevaux* power a car about 15 feet long (and, by a quaint reversal, carry about 40 *hommes*).

It was just after Chamonix, as I now tell my 1935 friends casually, that UB suddenly and unaccountably began to boil after every kilometre and shed glorious light on one of my two pieces of exotic French. I suppose everyone keeps a few outlandish words in addition to his basic vocabulary. Thus, just as I know that the German for accelerator is *Geschwindigkeitsumschaltungshebel*, I also know that the French for a swarm of bees is *un nid d'abeilles*. When we went into a garage and explained that *l'eau boullit toujours* the *mécanicien* (mechanic) looked at the *radiateur* (radiator) and shook his *tête*, saying, '*Ah, c'est un vieux nid d'abeilles*' (an old nest of bees).1935 motorists like Harblow have never heard of honeycomb radiators, and it took me some time to convince him that this was not just a quaint Gallic oath.

The *mécanicien* was very thorough. He replaced the lozenge in the cylinder head which we had blown out with the steam. He tested the ignition, the oil pressure, the gearbox and the brakes. He blew up the tyres and came out for a ride with us (or with me anyway, as there wasn't room for Harblow as well) to see the water boil for himself, which it did with a fierce glub-glubbing noise before we had even got out of the town. He didn't do anything to the old nest of bees or in fact to any part of the actual water system, contenting himself with telling us that the *radiateur* was blocked up, and he gave us some *pastilles* (pastilles) which he said would *déboucher* it. We took this to mean that they would dissolve the rust and other blockages in the water.

For the next two days we amazed the inhabitants of the Jura mountains by driving through their villages with a huge bulging red rubber bag dangling at the back of UB. It was a groundsheet filled with about two gallons of water and tied up, after stupendous efforts, with rope. Every five kilometres or so we stopped. There was no sound except the water glub-glubbing away and the tinkle-tonkle of the mountain cow-bells. We waited for the glub-glubbing to cease (the tinkle-tonkle never ceased, not even at two in the morning. I had no idea cows were so restless) and then we filled a very ornate jug, which Harblow had bought in Chamonix, from this great bladder *without undoing the rope*. It's quite easy if you don't mind it going up your sleeve. We stuffed *pastilles* into the *radiateur* until it was full of a thick brown liquid and we were afraid that any more would dissolve the *radiateur* itself. Slowly and patiently we increased our range before boiling to six, seven, ten kilometres.

Just outside Dijon we discovered what was wrong. The rubber tube from the *radiateur* to the engine (*moteur*. They *would!*) was absolutely solid. It had perished inside. In a rash moment I passed on to Harblow my other piece of exotic French – *caoutchouc*. As anybody in the Fourth Form will corroborate, this fantastic word actually means rubber. (Where *did* they get it from? To my mind anything, even *snerl*, or *pingleboob*, sounds more like rubber than *caoutchouc*.) When Harblow rushed into a nearby garage and informed it that '*le caoutchouc est mort dedans*' it was one of the occasions when they did laugh.

Report on Resistentialism

HATRED OF ONE'S father at Victoria. Clapham, a nightmare of cream-painted plumbing and baths in the sky. Sorrow and *Angst* over the fish in the dining-car. Then Dover, looking guiltily northwards at the death of the spirit. After the suicidal WI. milk-bars, the red-haired men on the trams, what hearts-ease to be in Paris once more – to see the *familistères*, the *cyclisme*, the *Métro*; to hear the *grand cri sangloté du monde*; the insouciant talk of the *pâtisseries*, the badinage of the *épiceries*, and above all the bubbling creative activity of the little resistentialist cafés where the disciples of Pierre-Marie Ventre meet to discuss this fascinating new philosophy. Listening to Ventre for several evenings, I perceived that Paris still brandishes the sword of European thought, flashing brightly against the dull philistine sky.

Resistentialism is a philosophy of tragic grandeur. It is difficult to give an account of it in text-book English after hearing Ventre's witty aphorisms, but I will try. Resistentialism derives its name from its central thesis that Things (*res*) resist (*résister*) men. Philosophers have become excited at various times, says Ventre, about Psycho-Physical Parallelism, about Idealism, about the I-Thou Relation, about Pragmatism. All these were, so to speak, pre-atomic philosophies. They were concerned merely with what men think about Things. Now resistentialism is the philosophy of what Things think about *us*. The tragic, cosmic answer, after centuries of man's attempts to dominate Things, is our progressive losing of the battle. 'Things are against us' is the nearest I can get to the untranslatable lucidity of Ventre's profound aphorism, '*Les choses sont contre nous*'.

Of course, resistentialism represents to some extent a synthesis of previous European thought. The hostility of Things has been dimly perceived by other philosophers. Goethe, for instance said that 'three times has an apple proved fatal. First to the human race, in the fall of Adam; secondly to Troy, through the gift of Paris; and last of all to science through the fall of Newton's apple' (*Werke*, XVI, 17). This line was, of course, pursued by Martin Freidegg in his monumental *Werke* (Leipzig, 1887) and, of course, Martin Heidansieck (*Werke*, Leipzig, 1888). The latter reached the position that man could not control Things, but although there are flashes of perception of the actual hostility of Things in his later work, it was left to Ventre to make the

7

brilliant jump to the resistentialist conception of the planned, numinous, quasi-intellectual *opposition* of Things as a single force against us.

One reason for the appeal of resistentialism to the modern mind is its bridging of the gulf between philosophy and science. Indeed, some of Ventre's followers go so far as to claim that resistentialism is just a transcendental version of modern physics. Some examples may make this clear. For instance, readers of this journal will recall the interesting account that appeared some time ago of the experiments in which pieces of toast and marmalade were dropped on various samples of carpet arranged in order of quality from coir matting to the finest Kirman rugs; the marmalade-downwards incidence was found to vary directly as the quality of carpet. More recently researches in the American field by Noys and Crangenbacker, two Americans, have involved literally thousands of experiments in which subjects of all ages and sexes, sitting in chairs of every conceivable kind, dropped various kinds of pencil. In only three cases did the pencil come to rest within their reach. Gonk's Hypothesis, formulated by our own Professor Gonk of the Cambridge Trichological Institute, states that a subject who has rubbed a wet shaving-brush over his face before applying the cream cannot, however long and furiously he shakes the brush, prevent water from dribbling down his forearm and wetting his sleeve once he starts shaving. Gonk has also, of course, carried out some brilliant research on collar-studs, shoelaces, tin-openers, and the Third Programme atmospherics.

Ventre, however, scorns the false positivism of the scientists with their fussy desire to dominate. Things *cannot* be dominated. Resistentialism is a tragic philosophy. It sees that man is doomed by Things the moment he attempts to achieve anything outside his own 'mind' which, like Disney's flying mouse is Not A Thing At All. To the resistentialist man is no-Thing, or rather a pseudo-Thing (the nearest I can get to Ventre's subtle expression *pseudo-chose*). Things are the only reality possessing a power of action to which *we* can never aspire. The resistentialist ideal is to free man from his tragic destiny of Thing-hauntedness by refusing to enter into relation with Things. Things always win, and man can only be free from them by not doing anything at all.

This brings me to the aesthetics of resistentialism. Readers of this journal are already aware of the profound effects of the new philosophy on Art and Literature. We have already seen Ventre's play *Puits Clos*, which expresses resistentialism in a dramatic parable in which three old men walk round ceaselessly at the bottom of a well. There are also some bricks in the well. These symbolise Things, and all the old men hate the

8

bricks as much as they do each other. The play is full of their pitiful attempts to throw the bricks out of the top of the well, but they can, of course, never throw high enough, and the bricks always fall back on them. In the musical field there is already a school of resistentialist composers among the younger men, notably Dufay and Kodak. Recognition of the Thing-ness of musical instruments – the tendency of the French horn to make horrible glubbing noises, the tragic mathematical fact that if music goes at more than a certain critical speed the friction of the violinist's bow will set fire to the strings – is behind Kodak's interesting sinfonietta for horns, trumpets, strings, sousaphones and cymbals without any players.

At one of the resistentialist cafés Agfa, one of the painters in Ventre's entourage, told me that he is contemplating an exhibition of his work in London. If this bold venture succeeds it will be a great day for the readers of this journal. But of course it won't be the same thing as here, in Paris, among the insouciant talk of the *pâtisseries*, the badinage of the *épiceries* . . .

Activated Sludge

IT IS NOT often one has a chance to dawdle in Victoria-street, S.W.1. For one thing, one is usually on one's way to Victoria. For another, it is always cold there, except in deep July and August. There is a curious air of a perpetual Sunday morning in an Edinburgh suburb about those gaunt black buildings. Victoria-street is a kind of geological formation, a miniature Grand Canyon, with a restless, dusty sirocco of its own. One stops to look in some excellent shop window, and this evil wind, blowing sand and bits of old Government posters, drives one shiveringly on.

Most people, if they think at all about the offices in Victoria-street, probably have a confused general picture of civil engineers, the Conservative Bookshop, and a great number of Societies for This and That. If they have never dawdled – and on the non-Victoria side at that – they will never have noticed the most interesting address of all. For I am prepared to testify on oath that on the portico pillars of one building there is a bronze office sign which simply says:

ACTIVATED SLUDGE.

I have not inquired too straitly into the nature of Activated Sludge. For it is an expression which has the authentic ring of a fundamental mathematical problem, the kind of classical antinomy that has always beguiled ancient philosophers, like Squaring the Circle, or Zeno's Paradoxes, or finding the Philosopher's Stone. In this concept of Activated Sludge two perfectly opposite forces are held in perfect equilibrium, like all those electrons, mesons, neutrons, protons and morons in the atom.

For consider the word 'sludge'. The Shorter Oxford Dictionary defines it as 'thick mud'. That is not quite right, but it will do. There are advertisements in American oil journals for beautiful strong machines, painted green, and called sludge pumps. One imagines the end of the hose buried in this sludge, or thick mud, drawing it up from the bowels of the earth with a horrid sucking noise, forcing it, like some lewd toothpaste, into a sludge pond, on an old part of the oilfield not wanted for anything else.

One imagines sludge as a kind of ultimate unwanted, the liquid, or at any rate viscous, equivalent of a slag heap, only capable of usefulness again after millions of years of organic change have assimilated it into the living earth once more. Sludge, one would think, is the best word in the English language to describe something inert, *unactivated*.

But there it is, with an office in Victoria-street. Activated Sludge is probably one of the countless obscure but necessary things without which our careful civilisation would fall to pieces, something which makes tremendous headlines when it is in short supply. (One remembers all that fuss about wolfram during the war). Perhaps any municipal engineer can tell you about the great deposits of activated sludge in Merionethshire. Perhaps Britain leads the world in sludge. Perhaps even now a party of British experts is on its way to investigate an enormous vein of sludge just discovered in Rhodesia, a vein which will bring us two million pounds' worth of orders for sludge-buckets, and separators, and rotary activators.

Indeed, now that I think of it, there was a picture in my first (and last) chemistry book, called 'John Dalton Collecting Marsh Gas'. It showed a Constable-looking scene, with tall summery trees, and John Dalton, surrounded by curious glass vessels, leaning over the bank of what appeared to be a stream. But when you looked closer you saw that it wasn't a stream at all. It was – O horrible! – a noxious black pond – a *sludge* pond, on which monstrous black bubbles formed of some hellish

10

gas brewed in its evil depths were winking with heavy lechery in the slimy ooze. . .

Perhaps, as well as evolving his theory of the atom, Dalton also discovered Activated Sludge. One can imagine the scornful laughter of the Royal Society when he read his first paper, *On the Natural Activation of Sludge*; the years of struggle; the final triumphant vindication of his views; then the great expansion period as Britain's great sludge mines were developed; the threat to our trade by the invention in 1893, by the German chemist Tumpf, of a synthetic activated sludge process; and then there followed Britain's answer with the Duplex rotary activator . . . Ah, they could tell you a fine tale at Victoria-street. But it might not be so interesting.

How to Spiel Halma

THE OTHER DAY, when I was in one of those shops that sell old lithographs and Profpects, and boot-trees, and tiled pictures and 1920-ish faded yellow dresses, and old copies of the 'Saturday Evening Post', and little lead shoes, and clocks of green marble shaped like Birmingham Town Hall, I found a dusty old box containing a game of Halma. In German.

I bought it, because the instructions looked so fascinating. I am not what you would call fluent in German. I know just enough for me to bumble along in a half-understanding daze, feeling comfortably that by knowing just a few more words I could speak it like a native. I desist from actually learning these few more words because I know that in fact this would be a dreary process extending over several years while I found out about things like *schicksal* and *empfindsamkeit*; and because I also know that during the first half of this period the pleasant sense of comprehension which I feel now would diminish rather than increase.

My friend Harblow doesn't really know any more German than I do. But he is never content to allow a German sentence to remain merely a matter for pleasant speculation. As soon as he discovered my Halma, nothing would please him but that we should evolve a theory of the game from the extremely explicit-looking set of instructions on the lid of the box, and actually play.

Neither of us had played Halma before, but Harblow pointed out that the board seemed straightforward enough, like a chessboard seen through a telescope the wrong way round, and with zigzag enclosures in each corner. 'Now, let's try the first paragraph,' said Harblow briskly, and he read on: –

An diesem Spiel können sich 2 bis 4 Personen beteiligen, von denen jede eine Farbe wählt, und damit, wenn 2 Personen spielen, einen grossen Hof mit 19 Steinen, wenn 4 Personen spielen einen kleinen Hof mit 13 Steinen besetzen.

The only difficult words here seemed to be *beteiligen* and *wählt* (I just happened to know that *Farbe* is 'colour'). Our (mainly my) translation ran thus: 'At this Game 2 or 4 Persons can betake themselves and each of these wears a Colour and damn it, when 2 Persons play, a big House with 19 Stones, when 4 Persons play, he besets a little House with 13 Stones.'

It was clear enough for me. It conjured up a pleasant picture of these Persons wearing their Colours and heraldically besetting each other's Houses like something in a Book of Hours. 'Damn it' I took to be an idiomatic way of saying that the real way to play this Game is with 4 Persons. Of course, if you must, you can play with 2 Persons, but damn it, it's a pretty poor show. Harblow, however, insisted that *damit* means 'with that ' or 'therewith', so I allowed this, to pacify him; although it didn't seem to make any more sense.

The next sentence said: 'The Players now try so quickly as possible with their Stones to beset the House of the Against-man (*Gegner*) and he is the self-same Winner (*Gewinner*) who the first *gelingt*.' Even Harblow had no theory for *gelingt*, so we went on to the main paragraph, a magnificent jumble of instructions of which we could not translate any particular sentence except one; but the general sense was that you got to the Against-man's House by the process of *überspringen* or overspring-ing, as in draughts. The sentence we did understand was *Es kann auf diese Weise eine ganze Reihe von Steinen übersprungen werden* – in this way it can a whole Row of Stones be oversprung.

We started to play, with 19 Stones (damn it), and we moved one at a time to beset each other's Houses until our forces met in the *Mittel* (Middle) of the *Feld* (Field). Suddenly Harblow, by a most curious progression involving horizontal, vertical and diagonal moves, over-sprang five of my Stones and arrived behind my zigzag thing. To my protests at the obvious irregularity of this he replied: 'Well, it says here

12

that you can move *auch seitwärts oder rückwärts,*' as if that settled it.

'Well, what does that mean?' I said.

'Either sideways or – well, *rückwärts*. I am sure 'forwards' is *vorwärts*, and you couldn't want to move backwards, so *rückwärts* must be one of these untranslatable words for the silly way a knight moves in chess.'

'What way is that?'

'Er – two forwards and one sideways.'

'I'm sure it's two sideways and one forwards.' (We don't know much about chess either.)

In the end we agreed that you could overspring a Stone that was next to you in *any* direction. When I jumped over some of my own as well as Harblow's Stones to beset his House he objected, but I pointed out to him that it was possible *über eigene und fremde Steine fortzuspringen* – over own and strange Stones to jump strongly. I had him there.

As the game progressed, if you can call it that, it began to dawn on us that we were not clear what was meant exactly by *besetting*. At the beginning we had agreed that when you oversprang the Against-man's Stone you did not remove it from the board, as in draughts, because if you did this neither *Spieler* would have any Stones left to beset the Against-man's House *with*. On the other hand, if there were not some system of being sent back to base how could this sentence be construed?: –

der Gegner muss natürlich wiederum danach trachten, diesen Stein womöglich in dem eigenen Hof des Spielers einzuschliessen.

The obvious meaning of this was that the Against-man must naturally again after that treat, this Stone how possibly in the own House of the Player to shut in. It obviously implied arriving before the Against-man's House with pretty large forces, a thing quite impossible to achieve by either party, however cunning, if being oversprung meant the loss of a Stone every time. And another thing that rather militated against anybody shutting anybody else in was the fact that it was perfectly easy for both *Spielers* to evacuate their Houses completely long before the Against-man arrived anywhere near the scene.

So the game rather petered out. Harblow's view, for which he can offer no proof, is that the rules we evolved would work all right with 4 Persons. But, of course, the difficulty is to find 2 other Persons whose knowledge of German is exactly the same as our own.

The Curbing of Merrie England

WHIPPENDELL WOODS ARE a second-class beauty spot on the northern fringe of London. In this uneasily rural district one is always slightly surprised to find oneself merely walking, among the tufty grass and untidy undergrowth. One usually clatters past it all on an embankment, staring down at the white suburban roads ending suddenly in potato fields, the older townships with their red clock towers, the unpromising lakes with enormous gawky dredgers moored on them. (There is no sign of a dredger shipyard on the reedy marge, but surely they couldn't have brought those things on lorries?)

Not many people go to Whippendell Woods, and you hear nothing in their thick depths except distant boys and motor-cycles. It is only when you read the by-laws that you realise how Whippendell Woods, before the Puritans who obviously drew up these fantastic restrictions, must have been the gayest, busiest place in all Merrie England.

'Into the pleasure ground known as Whippendell Woods,' say the by-laws disapprovingly, 'a person shall not bring or cause to be brought (a) any beast of burden, or any cattle, sheep, goats or pigs; (b) any barrow, truck, machine or vehicle, except a WHEELED bicycle' (their capitals).

'A person shall not, in the pleasure ground (a) play, or take part in any game of football, quoits, bowls, hockey or cricket; (b) play or take part in any game with a golf ball.'

'No persons shall deliver any public speech or address in any part of the pleasure ground, or hold or attempt to hold any public meeting therein for the purpose of delivering any public speech or of passing any resolution or of holding any discussion.'

What a hive of activity the place must have been! One sees it populated by a vast throng of these Persons, engaged in a marvellous pageant of all the human crafts and sports, formally displayed as in a mural painting. Here are the simple peasants with their goats and pigs; here is the entrepreneur from London, causing to be brought in large herds of oxen; here the high-spirited lads from Rickmansworth and apprentices from Watford in doublet and hose, playing quoits; here housewives cleansing their druggets; here men with primitive, lumbering bicycles having squares of oak instead of WHEELS; and here others are wheeling a curious *machine* on a low wooden platform. It looks rather like an ancient Roman ballista.

14

Whippendell Woods are very thick nowadays, and it would take a bulldozer a long time to clear a cricket pitch, but clearly it was different then. And how fascinating to speculate as to the nature of those other 'games with a golf ball' which get a paragraph all to themselves. What a pity that golf itself is the only one that has come down to us. What fun it would have been to stand at one of the 'tents, huts or booths' (now forbidden) and watch all these people coming for refreshment after the diverse activities.

Nor must we forget the intellectual side. See, in this clearing, the students brawling in a public discussion over the Categories of Being and sometimes there is a man making a speech all by himself; for practice maybe. For the by-laws evidently consider a speech without a meeting to be a possibility, since they distinguish clearly between making a speech and holding a meeting for the purpose of making a speech.

Alas, it is all gone for ever. No longer the happy shouts of the bowls-players or the lowing of beasts of draught. We are lost and desolate in the pleasure-ground doing our puny crossword puzzles and drinking thermos tea where once their red-blooded laughter echoed under the trees.

And what giants they must have been! I had to stand on a box to read the by-laws, which are in small print eight feet above the ground.

No Business Like Small Business

IN THE COMMERCIAL areas of cities, where big warehouse doors are padlocked across cobbled entrances, and the cold evening wind blows through narrow, deep streets, most people have at some time observed curious shop windows full of second-hand tea urns, or thousands of dusty cards containing 'Fancy Buttons', or the wire skeletons of lampshades. And many, remarking that these businesses are scarcely more prosperous-looking by day, never thronged with customers, will have speculated sadly on their grim struggle for survival. After all, if the great satin-and-chromium film industry is

15

bankrupt, what hope is there for little shops selling china vases five feet high, in which there are doors, complete with china hinges painted with Italian lakeside village scenes? The film people at least *look* prosperous.

But I have just been reading a document which shows, hearteningly, how wrong we have all been; how the small men, the purveyors of Tricycles, and Moss Litter, and Mungo (whatever that may be), are all part of the great social fabric. This is the *BIA Mailway*, a list of classified commercial and other interests to which its compilers, British and International Addressing, Ltd., will undertake to send your advertising literature for you. It is in alphabetical order, and each item is followed by the cost of circularisation; it begins with 543 Abattoirs, for £3.3.0, and ends with 18 Zoological Gardens, which come surprisingly cheap at 8/6.

The great and the obscure rub shoulders in a rich panorama of modern English life. Thus there may be giants like 3,311 Foundries (merged unduplicated) for £15.0.0, and the remarkable figure of 465 Fishing Fleet Owners, for £2.2.0; but there are also 7 Grab Manufacturers, for 10/6, which seems rather expensive when you can have 85 Steeplejacks for only £1.1.0. For £1.12.6 you can have no fewer than 88 Orchestras (*Symphony!* Good work, Arts Council!) – but a mere 11 Spats Manufacturers will cost you 12/-. There are many splendid juxtapositions. This is one of the best:–

```
28 Rat Poison Manufacturers  . . . . . . . . . . . .      13/6
605 Rate Collectors          . . . . . . . . . . . . . . . . .  £3.0.0.
```

Incidentally, what *is* an unduplicated foundry? Any foundry may be said to duplicate any other foundry in being a place where molten metal is poured into sand moulds; it duplicates it, as St. Thomas would say, in essence. The fact that it does not duplicate it in existence seems a pretty thin reason for calling it unduplicated – especially if it is merged. However.

It is rather pleasant to see that there are still 1,721 Cinemas (One-man) as against 168 Cinemas (Odeon). But not all the items are so cheerful. A sad note is struck by 1,265 Gamekeepers (pre-war). One imagines the village postman adding another envelope to the ever-growing heap of gun and gaiter catalogues on the doormat in the deserted, broken-windowed park lodge, and cycling on with sacks of mail for the new teachers' training college up at the Hall. And then there is the frankly gloomy entry:–

131 Aeroplane Factories (going down) . . . £1.5.0.

A curious question is raised by such items as 1 Butterfly Farm (8/6), or 15 Windmill Manufacturers (10/-), or 1 Mousery (7/6). One can understand an advertiser wishing for professional help in getting in touch with 11,056,900 Wireless Set Owners (details on application), or with 10 Triplets (Mothers per year), £4.4.0 – or, even more, with 2,187 Richest Public, although he wouldn't get much change out of the preceding item, 399 Rich (Burgesses of *Aberdeen*, believe it or not). But if he were in a small thing like the windmill or the butterfly trade, he would surely know everybody that mattered already. I find it difficult to imagine a mouse-food maker who does not know where *all* the mouseries, not just one, are; or the young man optimistically re-tooling his factory to make windmill sprockets without already having definite information as to buyers.

But this is, no doubt, a technical advertising problem, with a technical answer. It does not in the least invalidate the claim of this list to be a work of art. Indeed, the compilers preface it with as neat a précis of Aristotle's *Poetics* as you could wish to see, for there is a note at the beginning which says:–

'The Inland Section (Great Britain and Northern Ireland) is on white paper. For technical reasons, the first part is at the beginning and remainder is at the end.'

Household Noises

THE DEATH LAST week of the founder and chairman of Boddery Household Noises recalls one of the most romantic commercial careers of modern times. In 1923 Alfred Boddery, young and unknown, was joke editor in a small matchbox firm, where his inventive mind was bringing him more frustration than advancement. To many men the job would have been satisfying enough; but in between reading the proofs of his jokes, seeing lawyers about copyright, and running down to the printers, Boddery realised that he was in a 'blind alley' occupation. Whenever he had a really progressive idea, such as that of having interminable serial jokes so that the public would buy his firm's matches to see the ending, the management turned it down.

Boddery used to say in later years that he owed the idea which brought him success to his wife. As he was leaving his house with her one night she went back to switch on the hall light, for she shared with many others the conviction that to burglars this would denote occupation and thus keep them away. When Boddery pointed out that all burglars knew that trick, she laughingly retorted: 'Why don't you invent a trick they don't know?'

He accepted the challenge, and the result was Boddery's original Thumping Machine – in principle a large box with a sounding-board; an interior mechanism caused the four thumping arms to beat against this, so that when the machine was left running in an unoccupied house it conveyed the impression of a constant procession up and down the stairs.

The Thumping Machine was an instant success. But Boddery laid the foundations of Household Noises not so much by his salesmanship and advertising, excellent though these were, as by the ingenuity with which he always kept one step ahead of the thinking burglar. The latter soon realised that all the bangs and thumps coming from empty houses were unaccompanied by the sound of any human voice. So Boddery brought out his 'Merry Cries' record. The reverse side of this contained the famous One-sided Telephone Conversation. Another popular early line was the Boddery Meal Simulator, a device in which knives, forks, and spoons, suspended from a pulley system, gave a realistic imitation of a hearty meal in progress.

Household Noises rapidly expanded into a major domestic industry. The 1930 advertisement [reproduced here] gives an idea of the remarkable progress made in seven short years.

No scientific development was overlooked by Boddery. Up to his death he was working on new techniques in invisible ray remote control. Last week I was shown over the Household Noises exhibit for this year's Ideal Home Exhibition, in which Boddery had taken a personal interest. As I approached a model house it was wrapped in a ghostly, dark silence. But when I got to within twenty yards and crossed a hidden ray which activated a selenium cell mechanism, the whole place suddenly burst into amazing life. I could have sworn there were three families there. One was singing glees in a front room, another was having an uproarious party somewhere at the back, a third was playing some mysterious game which involved running up and down the stairs.

A child was doing a bit of fretwork, and someone else was on the telephone. Dogs barked, babies squealed, people played 'The Rustle of Spring' and gargled, and there was someone having a bath. Life was being lived very fully and richly in that house.

It may be long before such luxuries are available to the home market,

18

for, as a Board of Trade spokesman said last week, Boddery's products are in high demand in America and the dollar countries. It is a fitting tribute to this prince of gadgeteers.

～∾～

More Than Ninety-nine

THIS ARTICLE IS about the difficulty of talking to doctors in consulting rooms. For I am one that likes to talk. I do not think I am fanatical about it. I do not prod persons in public carriages and ask them to agree that Summer Time is wicked. It is true that on the rare occasions when I enter a railway compartment not peopled entirely by women with string bags and Jacobean legs, or those *middle-aged-*looking babies, I am sometimes the initiator of a conversation. But when, as is more often the case, I am surrounded by men who produce about a hundred old envelopes and three notebooks from an inside breast pocket and start doing little sums, I leave them alone.

But in a consulting room it is different. I interpret the word 'consult' in its widest sense. One consults *con*, or with. Two persons are required. Yet the doctors never respond. I cannot think why. If *my* only companion in a rather dingy room was lying on a cold horsehair sofa without any clothes on whilst I tapped him with little hammers, and he bravely attempted to talk about our export position, I should back him up. 'Your point about bimetallism in hard currency areas with one-way specie blocking is interesting, Mr. Jennings,' I should say, 'but have you thought of the consequences to sterling redemption of a free silver market? Other leg, please . . .' Every doctor whose interest I have sought to distract from this boring hammer business by asking him intelligent questions has replied with a grunt, or not at all.

I know that many doctors come from a country where the word 'blether' is freely used of any conversation not concerned with things that can be measured with a steel ruler; I know that doctors tend to become so absorbed by the sordid plumbing of the human body that they forget the soul. But even doctors whom I know to be excellent fellows elsewhere assume this cloak of taciturnity in the evidently

19

unilateral consulting room. They make me feel like a neurotic. They make my intelligent opening gambits sound like the nervous chatter of a man about to fight a duel. They make it sound like whistling in the dark. I begin to feel strangely as though I were standing on a cliff, shouting against a high wind, my words being blown back in my face, like pieces of wet black paper (you see what I mean about 'neurotic').

The odd thing is that most of my encounters with doctors in consulting rooms have been purely formal ones, necessitated because various firms or the Army have wished to know my state of health before employing me. The doctors have thus not had the excuse of pre-occupation with diagnosis. And I have always been very careful to say *intelligent* things. The only actual treatment I have had for years was the closing up of a varicose vein. 'Tell me, doctor,' I said, 'when you cause this thrombosis why doesn't the clot rush up to my heart and kill me?' This seemed to me a terribly intelligent thing to ask, but the only reply I got was a grunt from the doctor as he held up his hypodermic against the light. Does the Hippocratic Oath include a vow of silence?

However, this article is not written as a personal complaint. It is a warning. Nature abhors a vacuum, and so does the modern governmental machine. Unless we have a vigorous system of free conversation operating when the burcaucrats really get their hands on medicine, you can bet your boots they will start a kind of National Health version of that old compulsory conversation scheme, the Army Bureau of Current Affairs, or ABCA. Millions of little booklets will be printed, called 'Consulting Room Topic of the Week.' I see it all. At the back there will be a form, on which the patient's replies to the questions must be entered. It will fold up ('Fold your form HERE') showing an address in S.W.1. At the bottom there will be one of those tremendous reference numbers, like G.B. and Co., Ltd./5000/OB/L948/OB/OB/247. Lifts of 200.

Question 1. What do you think of bimetallism in hard currency areas? . . .

So look out.

Quo Vadis

IN THE FIRST half-hour after I have left a theatre I am always convinced that I am going to write a play. It is a curious sensation because I never know what the play is to be about. I just have a general impression, and yet at the same time a very clear one, of dramatic confrontations, of sharp, agonised words cutting into the hearts of a tense audience, without ever knowing what the words actually are.

This doesn't happen at the cinema. There is too much machinery in the way. However moving the film, one will also have seen a newsreel (when I go it always seems to contain a waiters' race in Paris) and a trailer, with little cameos of people being slapped, or surprised in embraces. One remembers all the time that the film is just one more activity of this teeming world.

Yet this week, utterly illogically, I was inspired to write a film too. I wasn't actually inspired by the film, but by the stills and posters on the muffled way out; for these were to advertise M.-G.-M.'s 'Quo Vadis'. They all looked curiously unreal. I thought of the queue in togas at the studio restaurant, of the obvious gap between modern America and ancient Rome. And it was then that I thought of my film, which will bridge this gap by having the dialogue in Latin.

It is called *Balbi Murus*, 'The Wall of Balbus'. It is the story of a young engineer, Balbus, who has been commissioned by a Government agency, known by its initials, SPQR, to build a wall, that the city may be defended against the Carthaginians. It is the story of his love for Julia (*Balbus amat Juliam*), who is the daughter of Marcellus, a prominent member of the SPQR. It also tells of the lone fight of these three against big-time graft in the heart of the world's mightiest empire. But read on.

The film opens with Marcellus making a passionate speech to the wavering SPQR, who have already delayed their decision about the wall for three years. He warns of the danger from the Carthaginians, and ends with a great peroration. This is above politics, he says. *Hoc est aliquid magnum, majus omnibus nobis. Per totam orbem sunt milia milia populorum; parvi populi, solum similes nobis, cum hoc spe in cordibus suis.* ('This is something big, bigger than all of us. All over the world there are millions of people; little people, just like you and me, with this hope in their hearts. . .')

The SPQR applaud warmly. The contract is given to Balbus, and it is

21

while they are crowding round to congratulate him that he first sees Julia. It is love at first sight. *Nonne* aliquis tibi dixit te pulchram esse?* ('Did anyone ever tell you you're beautiful?') he asks. He dates her for the evening. *Ego te feram ad parvum locum quem cognosco, solum nos duo* ('I'll take you to a little place I know, just the two of us'). *Ubi fuistis omnem vitam meam?* asks Julia ('Where have you been all my life?').

But this idyll is shattered by the machinations of a grafter called Caesar Romerus, of whom he has already been warned by Julia, *Iste homo est periculosus* ('That man is dangerous'). Romerus puts the word about that Marcellus, who is a stone merchant, is supplying Balbus with fake stones, made of plaster, for the wall. Balbus, angered by the rumours, goes down to inspect the wall, and finds to his horror that they *are* fake stones.

That night, dining with Julia, he is moody. *Num† est altera mulier?* ('Is there another woman?') she asks. He confesses his doubts about her father's honesty, and there is a quarrel in which he accuses her of making love to him to shield Marcellus. *Nolo talem amorem* ('I don't want that kind of love'). *O mel, da mihi fracturam, et tibi demonstrabo quod non est vere* ('Gee, honey, give me a break, and I'll prove it isn't true'). *Mel, debes audire,* she implores ('Honey, you've got to listen').

But Balbus is unmoved. He rises stiffly. *Hoc est vale* ('This is goodbye'), he grates. Broken-hearted, Julia walks home alone. She hears voices coming from a cellar and listens. It is Romerus and his associates, who are in league with the Carthaginians, plotting to substitute more fake stones. Startled, she cries, *Sic illud est ludus tuus* ('So that's your game').

Romerus hears the intruder, and she is caught. *Tu mane ex hoc, soror* ('You stay out of this, sister'), he snarls, as she is kidnapped. Next day, in a Rome worried by the news that the enemy is throwing forces across the river, a repentant Balbus is frantic at Julia's disappearance . . .

It would spoil the suspense of this mighty drama to reveal how Balbus, on bail awaiting a corruption charge with Marcellus, tracks down Romerus and rescues Julia. *Cape illud* ('Take that'), he grits, as his fist rams home on the grafter's chin; and how the pair, dishevelled but reunited, arrive at a dramatic moment in the trial of Marcellus. But look out for the posters:

Nunc, BALBI MURUS, maximum spectaculum omnis temporis.
(Now, THE WALL OF BALBUS, the greatest spectacle of all time . . .)

---

* Question expecting the answer Yes.　　† Question expecting the answer No.

Miss!

ONE OF THE best examples of man's tendency to hold on to an ideal long after experience has rudely shattered it may be seen in our attitude to the theatre bar in the interval. When we are working, in the practical daytime, and the anticipation of a night at the theatre flits into our minds, we see ourselves like people in an advertisement, in some elegant foyer with palms and flowers and flunkeys; men are clean-cut, in elegant clothes, with that standard, young-lieutenant-colonel kind of face; one hand in trousers pocket, the other holding a cigarette. Girls are in ballet-length dresses, smiling up at escorts. In some way we too are actors, living in a world rather brighter and larger than our own.

If we are among those who have refreshment in the interval this is a much more formal, crisp and studied act than having it anywhere else. In this mental picture we have, there seem to be about twenty-five minutes for relaxed, elegant talk about the play. No rude bells sound in this dream, no one ever has just beer, or coffee. And, most of all, there is no hint of the sordid struggle by which drinks are actually obtained in real life. The mind closes over this aspect of it like a self-sealing petrol tank.

Now I come to think of it, though, nobody else does seem to have this struggle except me, because all the other people in the bar are terrific personalities. It is only I who seem to be a normal humdrum man, unable to attract the servers.

Every time I try to get a drink in a theatre bar I make a resolution to come next time on stilts, making myself nine feet high, to wear a red beard, and to demand drink with Latvian oaths. I stand sideways-on to the bar, and gradually work forward until I have one elbow on it and finally two. But before I can do this the man in front, holding two glasses, steps back from the counter. I politely make way for him, and somebody on the other side of him immediately steps into his place. I adopt a kind of twin personality, turning round with a gay smile to the girl who is waiting for me, just to show her I am not having a round with some boon companion I have discovered in the press, and then return very unsmilingly indeed to the struggle.

When I do get to the front, I am always either faced by a large bowl of flowers or I am at the bend in the bar, or in a kind of no man's land

23

between two servers who, if they ever hear the first syllables of my despairing cry, 'Two light – ', hiss 'Just a minute' crossly at me through teeth which are holding a pound note. Normally they don't say anything at all; they are too busy flying up and down whisking bottles open for people who seem to be ordering enough refreshment for a Watteau country picnic.

Yet the other people have such personality that they can get served simply by speaking in cool, authoritative voices from wherever they happen to be. 'Six champagnes, please,' says a plummy-voiced, well-bathed man in a bird's-eye suit, who is standing *behind* me. I have a strange feeling that I am getting smaller and smaller.

Sometimes, when I get a seat at the end of a row, the moment the curtain has come down on the first act I rush to what is often called the saloon (this is one of those words that are often printed but never spoken, like Passengers Alighting and Aerated Table Waters and Luncheon). Often it is on the other side of the theatre, so that after I have run up and down stone steps so long and untheatrical that I am surprised not to find myself coming out under Blackfriars Bridge, the place is full when I get there. But if it is on my side, there often happens something very eerie indeed. *Nobody else comes.*

There is the bar all right, with brown linoleum and a little geyser affair with low blue flames, making burnt-smelling coffee. There is a shelf with three or four bottles on it. And there is a woman in black, like a *concierge*. But, as I say, nobody comes.

I have an urge to shout, or sing, for I have a lurking fear that my reflection will walk out of the glass at me, or that an eighteenth-century flower-seller will come in, or that the woman in black will suddenly point at me with a horrible wheezing laugh. I begin to have the same feeling about the theatre that Muslims have about artists – that God will look at the paintings they have done and then say: 'All right, now make them talk.'

I drink my beer and wish I had waited in a queue for it; even if the queue is full of pushers, at least they are human beings.

Nichtaus!

IT IS NO accident that, while the English have exported soccer to almost the entire non-American world, including Scotland and Russia, their dreamy, green-and-white summer game has never had so universal an appeal, even at home. It may be only a minority even of Englishmen who do not regard the summer as a boring, dusty time between two football seasons, full of hot, empty Saturday afternoons with children endlessly demanding ice-cream. This is because soccer is more obvious and elemental, a simple formalisation of tribal warfare, of battle cries in the sharp, youthful air. But cricket involves contemplation as well as action.

The fleeting northern summer, though Amaryllis daunce in greene, is subject to the wreckful siege of battering days; it is more real in the evocation of our poets than it is in reality. By all means let soccer be played under the harsh, obvious Mediterranean sun, on sandy grounds in India, in Bolivia; cricket is bounded by great trees and telephone wires, in which the gentlest summer breeze presages autumn gales and winter ruin. At any moment a cold wind may spring up, the wives in deck chairs will put on their coats.

Although in many ways the quintessence of Anglo-Saxonness, cricket is best understood when we remember the old Western tales of sunset lands, of the heavy, doomed Cornish summer of Tristan. It is an aesthetic strength, not a weakness, of cricket that Rain often Stops Play, whereas hardly anything stops soccer. Soccer could never prompt anything like the well-known lines of Francis Thompson:–

> For the field is full of shades as I near the shadowy coast,
> And a ghostly batsman plays to the bowling of a ghost;
> And I look through my tears on a soundless-clapping host
> As the run-stealers flicker to and fro, To and fro:–
> O my Hornby and my Barlow long ago!

Any sincere attempt, therefore, to translate cricket into a foreign context commands our curious and attentive respect. Now, by far the most serious attempt I have ever seen is an article called *Cricket, das Englische Nationalspiel*, which appeared some time ago in a Swiss paper; and attentive respect is what I have been giving it ever since.

25

The article was written by someone who clearly knows England, and is aware that cricket is our *ausgesprochenes Sommerspiel*, out outspoken-about summer game, and that *ein guter Cricketspieler* is as famous as *ein grosser Politiker*. But it is no good. The very title sets us thinking of preposterous games by Tyroleans, under the great Alps, with harsh cries of '*Wie ist das?*' and *Nicht aus!*' mingling with the yodelling and cowbells.

The stern German language gives the gentle terms of the game a brutal, military force. The bat is the *Schlagholz*, or Beating-wood. The game is played on a *Rasenplatz*, a shaved or level place, like the parade ground at Potsdam, between the *Werfermannschaft*, the Throwing-man-company, and the *Schlägerpartei*, or Beating-party. The latter leaves *nur zwei Leute*, only two people, in the *Feld*, the other nine remaining outside the *Spielplatz, gewissermassen in Picketstellung*. I should like to think that this means playing guessing games behind the picket fence, but I doubt it.

As might be expected, the German is at its best when describing sharp, climacteric moments in the game. One can be out *wenn ein richtig geworfener Ball das 'wicket' berührt*, when a rightly thrown Ball '*berührt*' the wicket. What an admirable word this is for the fatal crash the batsman hears behind him. All is over, his wicket is beruined.

There are many other details of the way in which one can be out, as when one brings *seinen Körper zwischen den weggeworfenen Ball und das Tor*, one's Body between the way-thrown Ball and, most curiously, the Gate, or Arch. Above all, one can be out *wenn er sich 'unfair' benimmt*. 'Unfair' is evidently untranslatable.

The author is perhaps more generous in describing the thoroughness with which cricket is taught in England than correspondents to 'The Times' would admit. *In der Schule*, he writes, man learns *Geschicklich-keit, Genauigkeit, Schnelligkeit und Reaktionsfähigkeit*. Well, I can remember being taught, not very successfully, the last two – speed and quickness of reaction. I don't think one could be *taught* a native quality like *Genauigkeit*, which I take to be a kind of cunning Knowingness. And as for *Geschicklichkeit*, I find it very consoling to learn that we are acquiring *that*.

Sometimes, on the green grass, under the heavy July cumulus lazily troubled by rumbling aeroplanes, surrounded by cottages and ladies making tea, we feel uneasily that we are fiddling while Rome burns. It is somehow reassuring to learn that all the time we are becoming *schick*.

Bursting the Barber's Balloon

IN A BARBER'S shop I always have a slight feeling of guilt, or at least of unease, at having lived so long without properly exploring this curious world of theirs, where the business of life is suddenly stopped among the calm smell of unguents. What is a vibro-massage, and why do I not have the courage to find out? Why cannot I talk easily to the barber, like the man in the next chair?

He is always the same kind of man, with a ruddy face and an air of effortless but somehow dubious wealth. He is always fed by the barber with the right questions, such as: 'You been to America, sir?', and of course he has. He 'flew in last week', in fact. Or he has 'just picked up a Jaguar'. Or he knows all about boxing.

I restrict my demand to a brusque 'Trim, please', although secretly I long to try this vibro-massage, from which I am sure I should emerge equally ruddy, with gong-like Holst chords humming in my clear, tingling head – *vibrant*, in fact; but this man, still talking about Ezzard Charles, has mysterious, effeminate-looking operations that even involve the use of a *hairnet*.

Gloomily I reflect on the barber's shop as a weak social survival of those great Roman baths where elegant and relaxed conversation went on in clouds of steam. By the time the barber gets to the razor bit round my ears I am adrift in a lonely sea of ideas which would be impossibly *outré* in conversation, compared with the Jaguar man's – ideas like Petronius or Quintilian languidly asking '*Aliquid habes pro tres triginta?*' (Have you anything for the three-thirty?') . . .

At my last haircut I decided to try the Wilfred Pickles approach; I asked the barber if it was difficult to get apprentices these days. The response was gratifying, for he had just seen on his television set a film about the training of barbers in Germany. It was not, however, the pity and terror of this tragic subject that moved him.

Before I had mentally filled in the details – a mad Emil Jannings in some terrible Expressionist shaving saloon, with the walls closing in and corpses waiting on the benches reading frayed copies of 'Simplicissimus' – the barber went on indignantly: 'It showed the trainees shaving balloons, and they said this was a new idea. Why, I did that when I was an apprentice twenty-five years ago.'

Shaving balloons! Even the old Ufa people couldn't have thought up

27

anything as macabre as that. I saw Emil Jannings more clearly now, barking orders to the row of young boys, grimly lathering balloons which, in a happy non-capitalist society, they would have been childishly chasing outside in the Tiergarten. '*Ein, zwei, drei,*' he rasps. '*Beginnen sie die Ballonen zu rasen,*' and no sound is heard but the squeaky noise of razor on rubber until a horrid pop; Jannings advances on the hapless apprentice, and is about to twist his ear when the doorbell tinkles and in comes a figure which sits down in the vacant chair.

Jannings approaches it obsequiously. A muffled, rubbery voice asks for a shave. Jannings now sees that the figure is merely an awful, stuffed simulacrum of a human body, but instead of a head it has a – , no, it's too horrible.

After all, I thought, this happened in our own England, twenty-five years ago. There would be a Cockney humour about it. '*This perishin' balloon's going down.*' '*That's the advanced course, mate – old man with wrinkles.*' I wondered how the apprentices got on with their first real faces, confronted with noses and lips after the simple curves of a balloon. Or was there, perhaps, a special barber's balloon, with proper features – with *hair*, even? And if so, whatever would it look like when deflated? What kind of expressions would this balloon be made with?

One always thinks of balloons at fairs, having large moony smiles, floating with a balmy, withdrawn joy above the people earnestly seeking mechanical amusement. These balloons would require special faces, with the down-drawn mouth of all men when shaving.

Did they give the balloons vibro-massage, too? And did some earnest but not very intelligent apprentice ever attempt a singe? Did the trainees ever get nightmares in which they nicked a man's chin and he *burst*? Above all, what of the man who first had this extraordinary idea? Do older barbers feel sorry for him, in his retirement, as he watches this inspiration taken up, like another British one, the tank, by more enterprising countries? . . .

But I couldn't ask any of these questions – not with the Jaguar man there.

The Loss Force

ONE OF THE mysterious ways in which the material world reminds us that we do not control it is by abstracting personal possessions from us. In our brash human way we then say that *we* have lost them; but in fact we have not done anything, we have been acted on by Loss Force. This is analogous to, and much more mysterious than, Shaw's Life Force.

Who has not known that feeling, almost of terror, when one searches a room for a book that one saw five minutes ago? Yes it was on that table, in the cosy, intellectually ordered world in which we were living before we missed it. But after this awful, this magical disappearance, we resort to methods of discovery which mere intellect tells us are mad.

We look under large articles of furniture that have not been moved for months. We telephone our friends and ask if they've borrowed it. We look in the bathroom, under the bed, more and more wildly. These are not rational acts; they are a kind of possessed ritual, to propitiate the Loss Force.

On a select band of us the Loss Force acts in a special manner, just as a kind of racial wisdom and innocence operates through the type of Dostoievsky's Idiot. People like me are dedicated to it. I lose pens and matches and glasses and handkerchiefs all the time; and every four months or so there is a Grand Loss – a spare wheel, an overcoat, a typewriter (if that was only burglars, why didn't they take anything *else*?).

I have been able to organise my life on a rather beautiful, resigned acceptance of these facts. But it is a resignation that has only recently healed the scars made, three or four years ago, by the dreadful fear that I had been selected by the Loss Force *to lose other people's things as well*.

My friend Harblow, who has stayed on in the Army, was passing through London, and I put him up on the Friday night. He had business in South London on Saturday morning. I was working in Baker-street. We arranged to meet for lunch; and to save him carting his bag around I was to take it to the office and hand it over at the restaurant.

I got on the bus with his bag. Near Marble Arch I saw the bus I wanted for Baker-street coming down Park-lane. I leapt lightly off the first bus and on to the second. We had gone about 300 yards, to

Portman-square, when I remembered Harblow's bag. For once this wasn't a crawler bus, but I got off it somehow. I hailed the first taxi that came – an incredibly old one, driven by a man like a walrus. Indeed, he seemed to be some sort of manifestation of the Loss Force. I could feel it in the air throughout that ghastly day, informing the cold grey buildings, making London hostile, brooding and unhelpful.

It seemed ludicrous to be chasing anything, even a bus, in this high, pram-like machine. Nevertheless, I breathlessly instructed the dotard to drive furiously down Wigmore-street, which is parallel to Oxford-street, and try to intercept the bus at Oxford-circus. We lumbered off. All the lights were against us. We got stuck in an appalling jam. No bus.

I telephoned London Transport and asked them what was the earliest hour at which a 12, a 17, or an 88 (for it could have been any of these) could be coming back again. They didn't seem at all taken aback by this appalling poser. I heard a rustle of pages, then a voice said 11.31. So at 11.30 I stood outside the C. and A. For two hours I stood at the head of the queue, looking in every bus, in the little place under the stairs, but never getting in. It must have looked mad. No bag.

I had a sad lunch with Harblow. The bag, he said, contained his service dress, his squash racket and clothes, his camera, pyjamas and shaving tackle, £15, all the papers for a court-martial in which he was the prosecuting officer on the following Monday. I saw the headlines, OFFICER GAVE FRIEND SECRET PAPERS, COURT TOLD. OFFICER HELD ON BUS BAG LOSS. MR. X TELLS COURT PSYCHIATRIST OF 'LOSS FORCE'. . .

That afternoon I found out enough about London Transport's layout and running schedules to write the script for a training film. I made calls to countless garages. 'Just a minute,' a voice would say; and for a quarter of an hour I would hear hollow echoing bangs, and whistling, and engines, and cinema organ music; then the voice would say, 'No I'm sorry'. . . And all the time the crooks were photostatting the court-martial papers, sharing out the £15, taking the camera to a 'fence'. Or were they? Had the bag, in fact, just *disappeared*?

But at six o'clock the Loss Force realised it had got the wrong man. The bag was in a garage at Merton. Now if it had been *mine* . . .

Bucyrus

ONE OF THE biggest errors made by the simple-minded towns-man, as he jovially enters country pubs, imagining that the unseen villages behind the folded hills are just the same as this one, is his assumption that the countryside is catching up with *him*. He looks at the pylons and the wires on wooden poles, and smiles at the self-consciousness of rural electricity compared with his own, which comes smoothly underground. If he had eyes to see, he would realise that these pylons are just one more manifestation of a strange Force, half human and half a modern reappearance of forgotten natural gods, that is *up to something* in the country.

The more I travel in southern England, the more I am aware of extraordinary machines; big grey things, with hoppers and spindly arms. They are not simple combines. They have useless-looking wheels up in the air. Sometimes they are in fields, sometimes they are being towed purposefully, with that air of thinking quietly to themselves that snails have.

Almost I have the feeling that they are taking up positions, that one night, one fateful night, something will be set in motion. The country air will be filled with clanking; these things will walk with a terrible tread over the fields, like awful iron insects. They will form rings round the ports. Motorists will find an unwinking barricade across the Great West Road at Slough. In some way at which we can only guess, the dark country gods will wake from their sleep; the forces in the whispering woods and brooding hills will be abroad, in twentieth-century forms.

Now, what is so enigmatic about all this is the attitude of the country people. Whose side are *they* on? The townsman, in their pubs, hearing them talk of the television, may think to recognise fellow souls. But is he right? Let him look again. Let him recall that initial feeling of interrupting a private joke, between these scarf-headed women, dissolving into hoarse laughter at which he smiles uneasily, and these men in rubber boots. Where do they all go, disappearing off the main road in station wagons? How much do they know? Is there not something more than an uncomfortable feeling that they know how to deliver calves and he doesn't? Let him question the safe feeling that television makes us all one.

Let him recall the name on many of these queer machines –

Ruston-Bucyrus. Let him ask, out loud, about Bucyrus. *That* will cause a silence, glasses half way to lips.

What is this rustic god, this Bucyrus? What is this sly half-joke about rust, rustic, this suggestion of something like a furnace of Moloch found half-buried, rusting in the pastoral graveyard of some old civilisation – and yet not dead at all, only *waiting*?

May we not guess that the root of our unease in the country lies in this, that the people know about Bucyrus and will not tell us? True, they see 'What's My Line?' and have the vote. But ever and anon we stumble behind the screen, we get hints of a sinister fellowship. Near a bustling, matter-of-fact city – Coventry – I saw a month or two ago, in a field, a notice-board outlined against the watery Midland sunset. It said:–

TRESPASSERS WILL BE PROSECUTED. By Order, Combe, Binley and Warwickshire Association for the Prosecution of Felons.

It is a fairly safe bet that these felons are not prosecuted in any *ordinary* court. What are these hooded figures with lanterns? What is this slamming of station-wagon doors in a dark lane at dead of night, this converging on a copse in a damp field? What tribunal is this, where obeisances are made to an effigy of the dread Bucyrus, before the shivering felons are dealt with by a society compared with which the Ku-Klux-Klan or the Mau Mau seem like naive, artificial college initiations?

Impossible to tell. Perhaps this is just a ritual developed to express that feeling we have all had, under the summer trees, that to look at the landscape is not enough; we must commune with it, eat it, *be* it. We must make it care about us.

Or perhaps Bucyrus is on the move. Just to be safe, let us watch those machines.

Buying Fever

IN THIS CENTURY man is observed more than ever before. Every university bulletin gives further evidence that we are under the microscope as well as the evanescent atoms. Here is someone at Oxford investigating 'the effect of emotion on intellectual performance'. A London graduate is granted expenses for 'an inquiry into neuroticism of emotional instability among apprentices in the printing industry'.

We may have the feeling that these investigations of human beings never really get very far away from the great laboratories. The picture we have is of the scientists arriving in tweed jackets in the morning, changing into white coats by the institutional radiators, looking briefly out at the misty sun and sighing, before putting on their glasses to look at their bubbling spirals. We do not see them comforting neurotic printing apprentices, faces stained with ink and tears, screaming or twitching among the giant presses. And every researcher must, at times, feel dismayed by the contrast between the thin, formal voice of his questions and the unfathomable *being* of the people who answer them – like the dry unreality of Alexandrian commentators after the thundering ocean of classical literature.

Nevertheless, we are all ready to give some credence to university researchers. If they aren't right, who is? We are vaguely comforted that they have issued forth from the tabernacle, from their quiet geranium gardens and cool libraries, to make some sort of intellectual sense of the roaring modern world, to tell us what we are.

No, the people we really doubt are the commercial investigators, announcing proudly that this product, that method, is proved the best by tests on 4,327 women. The fact is that commerce, particularly the act of buying, involves the subconscious. No doubt sellers are rational and know what they are doing, and can be described by mere statistics. But buyers are infinitely mysterious, and provide just as fit material for the cunning, inductive minds of scholars as those apprentices do.

I keep waiting hopefully for a real, scholarly investigation of Buying Fever (or *Ementia*, from *emo*, I buy). Instead of the advertisers telling us how logical we are, let us have a proper academic explanation of this terrible, irrational, indeed *mad* urge to buy that can assail the sanest of us.

I am sure everyone has, every now and then, the kind of experience I had last week. I was walking down a sober, office-lined London street, in the dreamy urban mood always induced by these unreal buildings, where people may be glimpsed through windows, endlessly frozen in the act of handing each other pieces of paper, when, quite suddenly, with no sort of preparation, I thought how nice it would be to have a piano. With the lunatic's impatience of awkward facts I convinced myself that I could afford it. I felt about this piano the way Toad of Toad Hall felt about his motor-car. I saw it arriving, the men wiping their brows; the lovely shiny wood underneath the corrugated cardboard, the rearrangement of the furniture. I could *smell* this piano. I would practise from eight to nine every morning . . .

In a mindless piano-dream, I found myself walking into the nearest shop that could *possibly* sell pianos, although its windows were full of sheets and chairs. 'I'm thinking of buying a piano,' I heard myself saying. I seemed to be the only customer. The sheet and chair salesmen all looked at me as I was conducted over deep carpets to the Music Dept. I had the feeling this hadn't happened since 1928.

There were about a hundred television sets and two pianos. 'Overstrung . . . very good maker . . . lovely tone . . . care to try it?' the man was murmuring. I played a few ecclesiastical-sounding chords. Fortunately it was horribly out of tune. Through the mists of Buying Fever, like a man dimly recognising flowers in the ward after delirium, I commented on this. Ah, said the man, it doesn't pay us to keep them tuned all the time; but the tuner's coming on Thursday. Would I like to try the action in a running passage? I played a formal little piece by Bach, with many mistakes, aware of the sheet and chair men listening.

Then, quite suddenly, I began to hate this piano. It was too big, too old-fashioned, not at all like the compact, modern-looking, dulcet-toned one of my Fever. I said, 'I think it's too big.' the man wrote down its measurements, for me to check at home. He said he would ring me on Thursday.

But, when he did, his voice was from another world, like that of someone met in the street who, in the bustling common day, tries to renew the false intimacy of a hospital friendship. I was cured, for the time being, of Buying Fever. . .

The Law of Natural Gentlemen Selection

ALTHOUGH DEMOCRACY IS in itself a wonderfully poetic idea, it is very difficult to *experience* it as poetic or even meaningful. The mere mechanics of its diffusion among 40,000,000 people – splendid, diverse human beings getting married, needing orange juice or wigs, even using explosives in their work (see para. 1 of Income Tax leaflet) – make most of its members insensitive to the Shelleyan effulgence of it all.

Even a poet such as Walt Whitman, when he comes to write of 'Democratic Vistas', does so in prose. It is an unlikely title for poetry, suggesting as it does a wooded avenue in a kind of heavenly Richmond Park, with men in overalls doing a limitless solemn dance away into the infinite; accompanied, however, not by twangling harps and ravishing flutes, but by a gigantic silver band.

It is perhaps just because of this that the most democratic of us, seeing a great English country house staring with blind windows over the terrace and the summer lake, are aware of a vanished, but not quite vanished, concentration of *poetic* living in England:–

> Footfalls echo in the memory
> Down the passage which we did not take
> Towards the door we never opened
> Into the rose garden.

Irresistibly the pictures form of the house bright with music under the roaring winter elms, of the dreamlike childhoods, of the great eighteenth-century drinkings. We are aware that this is, or was (or is?) a nerve-centre of racial poetry, of the business of creating formal human life with, rather than against, the inscrutable landscape. But presently a prim notice informs us that we have been looking at the regional offices of British Electricity, or a lunatic asylum, and we return vaguely dissatisfied, to the arterial road.

Now space and luxury are as necessary for poetic living today as they ever were. We should all rejoice, therefore, at the news that Britain looks like evolving a typically ingenious compromise for combining all that is best in the aristocratic heritage of a full, meaningful life with modern democracy. I have just been reading the draft Report of the Natural Gentlemen Selection Board. This body, set up three years ago on an all-party recommendation, has made a close study of the benefits conveyed to our national life by the country-house aristocracy of the past, with a view to seeing how the system can be modernised. Its proposals, although bound to be debated in some quarters, should go a long way to calm the disquiet of those who had feared the complete disappearance of a major English glory.

Basically, the Board's plan involves the evacuation of all historic country houses by boards and institutions, and their domestic occupation by 'natural gentlemen' (and ladies, of course). These will have to pass stringent tests *every ten years; and the tests will be open to all*. Successful aristocrats will have State assistance to enable them to live up to the standards demanded by their houses.

The Report emphasises that we are in a transitional stage, and forestalls the criticism that many of the qualities looked for in the tests (which will be organised somewhat similarly to War Office Selection Boards) may be found preponderantly in the existing aristocracy. These qualities are based under four main heads: Unbourgeois Gayness, Eccentricity, Continuity and Leadership. Several examples are given of the opportunities thus offered to new blood. Unbourgeois Gayness, for instance, includes artistic enterprise; and people who could give wonderful entertainments, with poignant madrigals, sung at dusk on lakes reflecting Chinese lanterns, will stand a much better chance than gentlewomen who can only do chaste water-colours.

Service members of the Board pointed out that the emergence in the last war of a Royal Air Force pilot class drawn from all ranks of the community has proved that the eighteenth-century concept of the officer-aristocrat can be widened; many future squires, clearly, will have handlebar moustaches. A Trade Union member emphasised the value of financially independent 'crackpot inventors'; he envisaged a sort of pyramid; at the apex are a few mad but workable ideas, like Mulberry Harbour, and at the base are millions of mad and *unworkable* ideas dreamed up in eccentric private laboratories in east wings.

Most ingenious of all, perhaps, is the differential marking system, whereby the yeoman virtue of continuity, of keeping beautiful estates in good heart, is made able to compete with the more spectacular qualities, while *all* aristocrats are nevertheless kept on their mettle by fear of the next test. All in all, the scheme should do much to restore poetry and myth to British life.

Note. – The Report also embodies recommendations received from the Scottish Lairds' Advisory Council.

The Urban Idyll

THERE ARE MOMENTS in even the busiest urban life when our relationship with the city is suddenly changed. A meeting ends early, we have time off to see a doctor or solicitor – whatever it is, for a couple of hours we stroll, we are relaxed, we possess the city, instead of being held ourselves in the grip of its routine. In summer, light winds move through the warm streets, reminding us of our trade with the hot lands, the bales of calico, the boxes of spice. In winter, the afternoon sky goes a heavy pink, the lights come on, we are wrapped in a northern dream of gaiety under the chandeliers. The city has the irrationality of a flower, the power of a volcano.

But such a mood cannot be deliberately invoked. It must come by accident, although we do at least know that we must be on foot, for only thus can we emulate the casual, sideways motion of butterflies, or of bees, drinking the city's nectar. Wheeled things go in a straight line, to infinity; you cannot *cover* a city, or have any part of it, on wheels . . .

I was on foot. I was in Grosvenor-square, just after lunch, and my next date was in Lower Regent-street, at three-fifteen, when this delicious mood suddenly arrived. I walked past the great bulbous cars outside the American Embassy – cars with windscreen wipers at the *back*, cars which, if the wrong person opens the door, blow their horns and make lights come on, cars with strange peaks over the windscreen, for all the world like rather awful golfers' caps. Somehow the thought of America made me feel more autumnal and mellow than ever, and I had the absurd feeling that it was I personally, who had invited them to park their cars, in my Grosvenor-square. I felt so expansive, I would have liked to ask one of them large general questions about how they liked London, or to have an amiable discussion about the beautiful, complementary balance between the Englishman's distrust of machinery and the American's faith in it. However, I didn't know anyone in the Embassy, and just then I found I was outside an advertising agency where I used to work; I went in and demanded, like an emperor, to see one of my friends there do his famous Joke.

How satisfactory it was, to see them all working, and to interrupt them! It was five years since I had seen my friend's Joke, and it was well worth waiting for. Briefly, what he does is to *act* his contention that the banquet scene in *Macbeth*, where Macbeth sees the ghost of the murdered Banquo, is the silliest scene ever written.

My friend, who is a deceptively solemn-looking character from North Wales, imitates all the people mouthing and smiling at each other over the banqueting table, quaffing cold tea from stage goblets, talking politely about Arsenal's chances, and then suddenly Macbeth goes absolutely mad, clawing at the air, seeing this ghost. Lady Macbeth kicks him under the table, hissing 'Shut up, you fool!' under her breath, while she turns to the guests with a frozen smile and says sweetly, 'My lord is often thus, and hath been from his youth' – and they always just shrug their shoulders, as if to say mildly, 'H'm, what's up with *him?*' and get on with the stage eating. As I say, I had seen my friend do this before, but it had never seemed so funny as this time.

After that, I tried stranger, more exotic blooms of the city. I went into odd little art galleries, where I was the only visitor, a piece of the Public blown like a leaf into these places where artists, with their alarming integrity and their veiled, secret way of looking at you when you use *words*, shout out quietly that the world is not at all what it seems. The city also played up by presenting me with a beautiful street drama, a splendid row between the crossest kind of taxi-driver and a man who had merely done something that taxis themselves are always doing – making a U-turn in the street.

But, best of all, the city arranged that I should meet one after the other, three more friends. It was like being in eighteenth-century London, with the illusion that we were all walking about gracefully saluting one another, like people in the early part of a ballet. And it was then that I thought what a good idea to apply the Famagusta plan to London.

For what they do, in this admirable town, every Sunday night from six to eight, is to prohibit all traffic from certain main streets, for the sole purpose of allowing people to walk up and down, meet their friends, and have Turkish coffee in the middle of the road. Why should we not do this in central London – not only on Sunday nights, but all the time? Think of it, a wonderful quiet area from Park Lane to Charing Cross-road, from the Mall to Oxford-street, full of beautiful people relaxed, shining, talking animatedly or gravely to one another. We had a hint of what it would be like on the nights preceding the Coronation, when the Mall was simply a great promenade, a susurrus of strollers, a murmuration of mortals. Is not this what cities are for?

And do not think it would slow up business. A week later I had to do the same journey by car, and it took longer.

The Art of Megalomania

UNTIL RECENTLY MY favourite world's biggest thing was the organ in the Municipal Auditorium, Atlantic City. It has seven manuals and 33,000 pipes; and either I read, or dreamt I read, that there is a caretaker's flat inside it. Anyway, for years I have had pleasant fantasies about this caretaker's unique life. I would imagine him striking up a casual friendship in a bar, and inviting his friend home.

The latter would not, of course, know he was inside an organ, and they would be chatting quietly when, suddenly, the room would begin to shake with sound. Vases and plates would dance and clatter, pieces of plaster would fall from the ceiling. As the fugue came to the heroic *stretto*, things would get worse; paint would blister, water would seethe in the bath, nay, mirrors would melt, fried with the hellish roaring of tubas; whole suites of furniture would dance about, the visitor would fall down senseless, while the caretaker and his wife unconcernedly chatted . . .

If you are going to have the world's biggest anything, one might think, that is the way to do it: let there be *panache*. All *our* records, in England, seem to be of the kind one learns about from quizzes in unsensational magazines. 'Where is the world's longest tunnel?' they ask: immediately one conjures up a vasty scene of mountains, tourists photographing their wives against a grandiose concrete entrance, the emergence, after hours underground, into a new country – new soldiers, new money showing new solemn girls in helmets – but no; the answer, upside-down on Page 93, is 'the Morden-Edgware line'.

'What weekly magazine has the world's largest circulation?' Once again we imagine one of those deadpan American international affairs, with letters in correspondence column for Tiflis, Big Neck and Bexhill-on-Sea, until Page 93 informs us that it is our own comfortable timetable, the 'Radio Times'.

There can, however, be art in megalomania, and there is a certain civic elegance in these British records, an attempt to fuse the trivialities of everyday life with technological triumph, the great with the small. Indeed, I used to think we had taken the initiative in this new, subtle megalomicromania, as it were, with the music hall poster I saw announcing

THE SMALLEST AND MIGHTIEST ORGAN IN THE WORLD.

What could this be? Some sort of terrible mouth-organ that would make cities crumble? Alas, one has to admit that this is simply a wild claim, not a description of any possible organ. And anyway, the championship has now gone to America again, as far as I can see for ever, with this announcement from a recent evening paper:–

New York, Wednesday. – A giant paper bag fourteen feet long has been perfected here. It is claimed to be the largest paper container in the world. – Exchange.

This is the real thing. This bag, with its monster serrations, undoubtedly exists. It has been *perfected*, after years of effort in which lesser bags, say ten feet long, have failed miserably. Quite light objects, such as nine-foot meringues, when placed in them have caused immediate collapse; but the technicians, undaunted, have worked on. As the workmen began to shovel the cream into wheelbarrows off the floor of the Bag Testing Shed, we imagine the chief designer murmuring, 'Yet it *should* be all right, we double-checked the seam alignment' – and, eventually, this fourteen-foot bag was produced, capable of holding not only giant meringues, but giant tomatoes, giant caramels, six tons of sugar, *anything*.

And who ordered it? There are reasonable explanations, such as that some hotel wanted one big bag for its bagwash instead of a lot of little ones, or that someone wished to get cheap freight rates by registering as 'One Paper Bag and Contents' a consignment of 2,000 alarm clocks. But inevitably, as with all world's biggest things, the man-scaled mind drifts off into fantasy again.

This bag is for some burly millionaire, who plans to burst it, with hydraulic rams, at a monster party. Or can it be that up in the unimaginable hills there is a noise as of thunder, and presently the skies are darkened and a great shadow leans up over the street of little shops; here, terrible as an army, is the largest housewife in the world. Or at any rate someone quite different from the people on the Morden-Edgware line.

The Dwarfs of Birmingham

AS A NATIVE of Coventry, I have always felt that there is something mysterious, unknown, and perhaps a little frightening about Birmingham. It has a lot of things that Coventry and other Midland towns have not, such as a University, a musical life, a B.B.C. diocesan headquarters; it has big shops, visited on windy Saturday afternoons by vast shuffling crowds.

But there is something else, something that eludes the visitor to Birmingham, something that makes him wonder what holds it together. To one brought up in an ancient walled city Birmingham has a quality of agoraphobia. It is *open*. Its windy, brick hills are an outpost of the pitted escarpments that go on through Wolverhampton and Shropshire into Wales. Those strange-sounding suburbs – Lozells, Deritend, Digbeth, Fazeley – lie open to wandering airs, as though they were tinmen's *camps*, rather than solid streets. Since the eighteenth century, these tinmen have subjected themselves to the rational, mechanical discipline of engineers like Boulton and Watt, whose great works at Soho were the forcing house of the Industrial Revolution.

But in addition to actual machinery, Birmingham produces a huge stream of basic items of metal – bolts, nuts, needles, brass rings, grommets, screws, tubes, rods, metal pots and cups – small, elemental things; tinmen's, tinkers' wares. Some hidden part of Birmingham's consciousness is in tune with the ancient nomadic life of tinkers, on the windy road to Wales, with the primitive passion of that legendary Flaming Tinman who fought in Mumper's Dingle; with the ancient magic smiths, with *dwarfs*, labouring under Welsh mountains.

Here is a paragraph that appeared on September 21 at the bottom of page seven of the 'Liverpool Echo' (of all things):–

'Birmingham Corporation is to provide midget factories for use by very small industrial concerns.'

Is there not something evasive about this, do we not feel that the full story is being withheld? Somehow these very small industrial concerns do not sound small simply in their turnover – producing, say, a mere two gross screws a week. The diminutive of 'factory' in this sense is not 'midget factory' but 'workshop' – a small building but containing

41

normal-sized men. No, the *least* extraordinary interpretation of this story is that the midget factories are for very small, albeit ordinary, men – a whole tiny low estate situated, naturally enough, at Small Heath.

Everything would be scaled down, like the tiny desks in a Montessori School. The ordinary-sized visitor, stooping to get through the little low doors, would see rows of happy little men tinkering away, making midget radios, or tiny screws for watches, or armchairs for mice. It would be pleasant, also, to think that special programmes of 'Music While You Work' were dispensed by that ensemble which often appears in the 'Radio Times', Frank Walker's Miniature Orchestra . . .

But are they even ordinary, these small men? The mind boggles at the thought of their intercourse with the outside world of six-footers. Take sales, for instance. Either a large customer comes to them sitting awkwardly with these little men at a conference table that only comes up to his knees; or their sales manager goes out for orders – and how will he impress buyers if he has to be lifted up on to a chair so that he can bang on the table with his tiny fist? What true commerce can they possibly have with the roaring, red-blooded industry of Birmingham?

No, inevitably we begin to see these little men as far from ordinary. In spite of ourselves we begin to think of them as wearing pointed red hats. But they are not making some beautifully contrived present out of beaten fairy gold for an enchanted child.

There is something about the wording of the paragraph which suggests that Birmingham Corporation is 'providing' these midget factories against its will. There is something threatening about these dwarfs, who have materialised out of Birmingham's past, out of old tinkers' legends. If they hadn't got their midget factories they would have plagued Birmingham with elvish troubles, pinching workmen black and blue, squeaking and grumbling under the stage during quiet passages of concerts played by the City of Birmingham Orchestra, altering the points at New Street Station so that the Manchester train goes to Coventry. Birmingham was wise to recognise them.

Puss in Space-boots

AS I MOVED with the crowd shuffling out from the crystalline splendours of the ice pantomime, out into the formless technical horizons of North London with its silent-humming factories brooding on low rises, its jumble of lace-curtained houses and long industrial fences and misty railway yards, I heard behind me a curious voice. It was at once clear and muffled, childish and reverberating. It sounded for all the world like a boy with his head in a goldfish bowl. I couldn't resist turning round to have a look; and it *was* a boy with his head in a goldfish bowl. I had seen my first space-suit.

The boy's words, though indistinct, were comfortingly terrestrial, for what he said was, 'Mum, can I have another chocolate?' I wondered how on earth this would be accomplished. How do you eat, or blow your nose, or kiss, when you are dressed like a cross between a diver and a lamp-post? Even if you got the food – chocolate or Space Vitamins or whatever – inside this silly bowl, on a little tray below your chin perhaps, you would still have to get it to your mouth. You would have to jerk it upwards and catch it like a seal. Then it would *all* come loose; you would have chocolates wedged behind your neck, capsules of Space Drink would melt in your midget radio. You would shake your head to get all the stuff round to the front again, performing, in your lead boots, a lugubrious dance like some mad heavy old bird . . .

Nevertheless, I couldn't help feeling that this was a very appropriate place to see my first space-suit. The ice pantomime has, after all brought a sort of embryonic cold Space into the theatre for the first time in its history. For centuries audiences, cheerfully warm and human within the formal limitations of the range of the unaided human voice and of cosy theatre architecture, have been spellbound by the infinite range of feeling as expressed by actors. Now, suddenly, the 'infinite' element has been transferred from human characterisation to the endless geometrical possibility of skating patterns. In an insignificant part of the vast hangar the mere singers and speakers have become limited, isolated. Looking, often, like a small choral society that has got in by mistake, they are buzzing and mumming silently into the microphones (for the sound must not seem to come from *them*); cut off, like dusty bees inside a jar.

Meanwhile, ever greater parabolas are described by the skaters. Once the formal unity has been thus broken, we should not really be surprised if the breach became wider and wider, so that the skaters sailed effortlessly up and out of the building, amazing the night sky over Hendon and Watford with their twinkling convolutions.

The next development might be a vast pantomime on skis, covering most of Switzerland (to which, after all, mass flight becomes cheaper every year). Huge tumbling echoes of electronic fairy music would issue from the Alpine peaks, whole valleys would be merrily filled with expert clowns and brokers' men pretending not to be able to ski (the one intrinsic joke possible in this medium). But there is an interim air about this. What the children of that boy in the space-suit may well see is the Space Pantomime.

While the vocalists are humming and bumming away in an enormous fusty studio, Jack, one of the Space heroes in a galaxy of plots, will be whooshing up the space-stalk for a date with Cinderella, moping in the icy tundras of the moon. Elsewhere, Dick Whittington rests on a rocket station and is comforted by his Space-cat, miaowing and purring into its goldfish bowl. 'Oh, Puss, Ai am so weary (Miaow). But hark (*kling klong klang; ah-aaah, ah ah AAAH*), Ai hear bells – or is it the music of the spheres? (Rising) Ai'll be Lord of Space yet (Slaps thigh). Yes, for we'll face the light-years, you and Ai – with – a – (cue) – A SONG AND A SMILE . . .'

And of course there will be plenty of scope for speciality turns; knockabout juggling by Castor and Pollux, Cassiopeia and her performing Dog Stars, a contortionist adagio dance by the Gemini Twins, while Thoroughgood's Twenty Thousand Space Babes clatter and chant on the Milky Way. To say nothing of the dramatic bits when the Demon Thing, leading an army of those foul little green men with one hair, appears in a burst of radioactivity:–

> I have you now, you foolish mortals,
> For now you've crossed my dreadful portals, etc.

At this point the Queen of Space, or someone, will enter, waving not a wand but one of those idiotic finned Space pistols:–

> You nasty Thing, begone from here!
> You're cluttering up the stratosphere;
> If you don't mend your horrid ways,
> I'll blast you with my gamma rays.

And so on, leading to an enormous finale with millions of people in spangled space-suits coming down a celestial staircase, pausing at the bottom to smile into the cameras – for of course the whole thing will be televised. After all, nobody need know it is *all* done in the studio.

NUR + ASLEF = FUNERALS

IN THE VERY nature of things a strike on British Railways is utterly different either from a strike in any other British industry or from a strike on foreign railways. However complicated the quarrels of dockers in Liverpool we know that in some obscure pub there are actual men, quite often Communists, who make definite plans, who know what they want; given time, and a sort of godlike eye, an inquirer could find the whole truth. The thing is real, prosaic, even boring. So is a strike on, say, French railways. They want more money. British Holidaymakers Are Stranded, Reach Ports in Lorries, and that's that.

But with British Railways we are on a quite different plane. This is not just another industry. This is the mysterious, Delphic origin of *all* industry. From the strong hills and black towns of the north of England, British Railways sprang forth fully armed, the magical genius of Motion which changed the world for ever. They carry the residual splendour of that first visitation, just as the actual place where Prometheus lit the first fire is for ever set apart.

But they also body forth the tragic grandeur of a basic conflict, of the two equally valid interpretations of the world open to time-bound but immortal man. Long ago the Greeks wrestled with it. Motion is all, said Heracleitus, everything changes, reality is an illusion. But change is an illusion, said Parmenides; if existence means existence in space and time, you cannot have more of it in one place than in another; what is, is. And so on. Now British Railways, the *first* railways, are the supreme expression of this classical doom. From London they trundle across the unchanging fields to the sea; the blank seaside stations bring all to a stop. We get out, we look over the wooden railings at the lapping waves. But in the little town below there are lamp-posts and asphalt, we have not changed. There is something about British Railways that induces the question 'What is man?'

This has always been implicitly recognised and is doubtless one reason why the strike was accepted with a sort of reverence. There was an air of dreamy, philosophical doom about the whole thing. A *Times* correspondent referred to the family and spiritual life of the railwaymen in his old constituency. If the Emperor's marvellous astronomers predict that on a certain day the sun will be darkened and no birds fly, it will be so: if British Railways, after weeks of grave meetings, say there will be no trains, who are we to argue? NUR is RUN spelt backwards. ASLEF is an anagram of FALSE. These are all portents.

But this time there has been a hint of something even deeper than all this, a suggestion that the Transport Commission and the Government have been working together, merely behind the façade of a strike, on some deeper problem, a social problem intimately connected with this special *vagueness* of British Railways. I have a feeling that what they were really doing was rounding up the railway Wanderers, that increasing lost population of amnesiacs who simply live on our trains.

I first became aware of these people not on a main line, but on the Tube. I go home on the Northern Line, which splits at Camden Town into two branches, the Barnet and the Edgware. Often I have leapt on to a train at, say, Tottenham Court-road without having time to look at the destination board. Breathlessly I have asked the passengers 'Is this Barnet or Edgware?' and have then seen that they are not ordinary passengers but zombies, who stare at me glassy-eyed and make no reply at all, or at best, say dreamily 'I don't know.' This wouldn't matter if they were getting out before Camden Town. But having checked at the next station that I was on the right train, I have watched them specially. They have stayed on. There must be thousands of them wandering vaguely in the woods at Barnet, sleeping in doorways and stealing chickens at Edgware.

After this I began to look at the passengers on national trains more carefully; and I saw at once that some of them were in a class by themselves, quite different from the alert, talkative people who were obviously going to get out at some definite place, where they would make commercial calls, or be met by a fiancé, or have a holiday. These Wanderers had lost all contact with the outside, the non-railway world. Some sat blank, others indulged in activities at once dreamy and compulsive. In a hopeless attempt to look as though they were travelling on business some would fish scores of old letters from bulging inside pockets and feverishly make notes on the envelopes. They would tot up rows of figures in dog-eared, patently obsolete account books. Others were Eternal Students, staring for hours at unlikely fat books but never turning the page.

Others would bring down tremendous bags of food and start nervously gobbling great piles of thick bready sandwiches, going on to flasks of tea and a perfect cornucopia of fruit, and thence to a melting sort of chocolate. But none of it looked like proper food bought in shops, on land, so to speak. The chocolate was the chocolate from those glass wagons at stations, the bread was a rearrangement of buffet sandwiches. As tramps live off the land, so these Wanderers obviously lived off the railway, evading inspectors in lavatories, sleeping in sidings. They were not exactly dirty, but they were not clean either. And all of them had this vague look, as though bemused by change and the rattling of trains and longing for a static reality.

Only a thing like the sudden stopping of nearly all our trains could have enabled the railway police to catch them unawares; and I should like to think that even while Mr. Baty and the rest were having their 'talks', great crowds of these Wanderers were being given hot, sweet tea and blankets in vast sheds at Bletchley, Crewe and Swindon, while the W.V.S. operated a relative-tracing service and doctors sorted out the more serious cases. It would be much nicer to think this than to think that British Railways had a mere vulgar strike.

The Tropical Suit

PERHAPS TO-DAY TOURISM has replaced tribal migration, *Völkerwanderungen*, the restless, instinctive movements of population that were the ground-swell of history.

Seen from the airport bus humming through fainting airs, over a parched landscape, to some white southern city, the ancient symbolic horizons take on a fearful novelty (shall we get out, now, and walk straight over them, with our overnight brief-cases?). For a moment we feel again the *otherness* of the world, its invitation and bright promise; a huge thirst clamours within us, we shall know the unknowable. The earth will speak to us.

But just because we *are* individuals, weighed down by the strange bathos of human clay – or perhaps because we are only tourists – we keep returning from these vast, nameless thoughts to trivial personal worries. In the heavy afternoon, when the locals retire behind white walls, and we hear their distant radio music, we vaguely want tea. We worry about postcards, we buy useless foreign ball-point pens. We count our money. We fill the interstices of the day with needless trips to our hotel rooms.

My own particular worry, as a tourist, and as one occasionally sent or invited on exotic journalistic jobs, is clothes. Recently, for instance,

47

I was invited on what amounted to a day-trip to Tangier. Naturally, I wanted to go. But I didn't want to be worried, under the palm trees, by itchy, hot flannel trousers; for my lightest suit is of grey flannel. Nor did I want to buy a tropical suit for one day in Tangier.

In the end I compromised with a second-hand one. It was in cream linen, and it cost only four guineas. I felt rather pleased as I looked at the sixteen me's in the little fitting cubicle. I looked like the Manila City Council, or a group photograph of Lieut. Pinkerton's brother officers in *Madam Butterfly*. True, it seemed a bit loose-fitting. But then, it was a tropical suit.

I began to have my first doubts when I tried it on again at home. It *was* loose-fitting. I noticed now, also, that the lapels were old-fashioned and short, in the style of the early thirties, instead of long and meeting over a single button. This coat had three buttons. A laundry label said *Hammond*, tersely. I began to feel a pygmy in the clothes of this Hammond – a tough, red-faced man with short-cropped grey hair; heavily-built, running a little to fat after a muscular, pig-sticking youth; Hammond, retired after a lifetime building railways and bridges in the tropics; Hammond, reading *Blackwood's* in a wicker chair. . .

I didn't dare appear at Waterloo Air Terminal as a pseudo-Hammond. I wrapped the suit in brown paper. I thought I would change at Gibraltar. By Gibraltar I had discovered that all the other journalists had suits which, while lighter than my grey flannel, were unmistakably *them*, part of their ordinary wardrobes. However, it was too late now. It was hot, and the flannel was itchy.

My emergence from the B.E.A. manager's office where I had changed caused a mild sensation. I reminded one journalist of some rajah he had known. I said shamelessly, 'I've had this old thing for years, and it is so comfortable.' (It was, except that the trousers kept slipping down.)

We took off on the twenty-minute last lap to Tangier. We sailed over the white city, we stepped out at the quiet little country airport. There were Berbers with enormous hats, and thin brown horses; bright green patches of cultivation, and far stony hills. Africa, *Africa*. I wanted to start straight off and walk down to Kano, the walled city of Nigeria. But we were all driven off in an enormous Chrysler, to marvellous meals and swimming and cocktails and polo and bazaars and cool Moorish courtyards. Occasionally (at the polo, for instance) I thought about my suit, and noticed that it was getting more and more rumpled, like a pair of pyjamas.

All the same, I didn't want to start the homeward journey in my grey flannel. At 2.30 a.m. of the morning we were due to leave I remembered

I had lost the original brown paper, and I had planned to change back again in the aeroplane. I lifted the bedside telephone.

'*Allo*,' said a thick Arab voice.

'*Est-ce que vous avez un morceau de papier brun?*' I said. The voice was silent. '*Non*,' I went on wildly, '*pas un morceau, avez-vous BEAUCOUP de papier brun? C'est pour mon taille*' (was that the word for suit? It was 2.30 a.m. and it had been quite a party). '*Je veux changer dans l'avion, et il faut faire un package*' (that didn't sound right either).

'*Pardon?*' said the voice.

I tried Spanish '*Yo quiero papel bruno.*' (Heavens, had I said 'I love brown paper,' not 'I want it'?). '*Papel bruno. PAPEL.*'

'*Ah, si*,' said a voice, '*café*. You want coffee?'

I felt sure this kind of thing never happened to Hammond. But then he was not a tourist.

Disorient Express

THE VERY CROWN and flower of railway magic is surely to be found in the Continental *wagon-lits*. Pregnant, aboriginal, they stand at Calais, labelled MILANO OR WIEN. They open up an *infinite* potentiality of passionate cities, of cathedrals articulate in the sunlight; of unknown night streets, of doors opening into bright mysterious rooms and a marvellous hubbub of voices. They are scientifically designed for the good life on wheels, they satisfy the Baudelairean canon of *luxe, calme et volupté*.

Nothing could be *calmer*, more conducive to womb-like thought and meditation, than the little cell of polished brown wood, full of buttons and switches and folding ledges. In the midst of the most bustling station, while foreign cries are heard outside in the windy night, while mysterious bumps and complex whistlings denote that the very composition of the train is being altered, so that one imagines wagonloads of snoring Finns from Helsinki or Turks from Istanbul joining up or being cast off – in the midst of all this one is marvellously alone. It is like being in a high-class mobile monastery; almost one could wish one was better at copying out beautiful capital letters on vellum, with birds and bright angels, or at meditating on Immanence and Transcendence. But one also has *volupté* and *luxe*. At any moment one can saunter forth into a dining car and, surrounded by elegant and exotic people, consume artfully prepared meats and wines.

At least, this is what I imagined until I returned from Switzerland recently. There, waiting at the junction under the great mountains, was the *wagon-lit* train, labelled PARIS: LONDRES. How satisfactory to *belong* to a train like this, to get on at the terminus! I found my compartment, tested all the little switches and lights and taps, and washed and changed. No hurry, just a gentlemanly, leisurely preparation while I savoured my growing appetite. Then I sauntered out to the dining car.

I discovered that there wasn't one. It was to join the train two stops further on, in half an hour. I went back to my cell. It did not seem quite so luxurious. The bed had been made, and it is somehow awkward to sit on a train bed; one can only really lie on it, and I didn't want to do this in my best suit. At the end of the half-hour I was really hungry.

At last the welcome bumps and whistles were heard. Again I went down the long train. Trying not to notice the cross, disappointed-looking people squeezing past me on the way back, I went right to the door of the dining car. Through the glass I could see it was full of hateful people who had been on all the way from Vienna, they were stuffing themselves with food and drink, talking animatedly and laughing. A waiter shook his head and said, '*Une heure.*' I had the feeling these people were laughing at me, although I was much better dressed than they were.

I went back to my cell. Crossly, I got out a little bottle of brandy (a parting gift from the hotel; it was that kind of hotel) and undid the paper from an enormous china bowl containing a *pâté* (I had commented on the excellence of the *pâté* in the *hors d'oeuvres* one night, and now I was in dreamlike possession of this – this *basinful*, costing nearly five pounds; we have since been having *pâté* for breakfast). Naturally, I had no eating implements, so I cut the *pâté* with the little yellow *carte de contrôle* that one fills up endlessly on journeys through France, all about *nom, prénom, nom de jeune fille* (on the way out, for this latter I had put 'Lulubelle', and no one had said anything).

In between sips of the brandy and the impossibly rich mouthfuls I read the notes on the back. They seemed more and more fascinating. 'Write to the *Service de la Police de l'Air et des Frontières, 60, Boulevard Gouvion Saint Cyr, Paris 17.*' After this, having no other reading matter, I read my hotel laundry bill, in three languages. Also fascinating. Who ever sent 'washing-clouts' (*Waschlappen*) to the laundry? Except possibly some early-nineteenth-century milord with 'trowsers' and his lady with a 'hair-dressing-mantle' and the mysterious 'layers' (*couches, Unterlagen*).

In *wagons-lits* they give you little sort of hassock things to use as foot-rests when sitting on the high bed. Climbing up to get one of these off the luggage rack, I seized a kind of stirrup-pump handle as a hold. To my horror it yielded to my grasp. It was the communication cord. ANY ABUSE WILL BE PUNISHED – and, even more alarming, JEDER MISBRAUCH WIRD BESTRAFT. I imagined these terrible *police de l'air* hovering over the frontiers in balloons or helicopters, called down by radio to bestraf me. Very well, I would be the haughty Englishman. What is the meaning of this? Can you not see my trowsers are bestained with *pâté?* Bring me a washing-clout . . .

I pressed the button for the attendant. Perhaps he had some wonderful valve for cancelling the alarm before it worked on the engine. By the time he arrived it was clear the train wasn't stopping anyway. I hadn't pulled hard enough. So I said, '*Il y a du pâté sur ma carte de contrôle. Une autre, s'il vous plaît.*'

I got into the dining car in the end. It was worth waiting for.

Forty Green Bottles

FOUR YEARS AGO I became a householder (strictly speaking, a mortgagee). By signing incomprehensible documents about curtilage and messuage I crossed the last great gulf between golden, unfettered youth and Responsibility; and within the first three months I thought I knew all there was to know about a man's preoccupation with his house. I learnt that high winds and torrential rain always come at week-ends, when builders have dispersed. Sunday evening is the time for panicky excursions with candles (can't find the torch) into the loft; for agonising contortions as I try to locate the cracked slate that must surely be causing that spreading patch on the bedroom ceiling.

But of course if one has a light inside the loft one can't expect to see light coming from outside, through a cracked slate, especially as it's dark anyway. I withdraw backwards on my stomach over the dusty beams, my wife guides my descending foot on to the back of the chair she is fearfully holding. Something gives ominously, up there, money falls out of my pockets, I have a crick in my neck. After a night of relentless monsoon and furious wind (what would happen if the house *blew* down, would I still have to go on paying the building society for a non-existent house?). I return at first light on Monday. But no light shows through the roof – and anyway, what could I do if I did find the place? The whole thing is a mad anxious dream, creeping about in the roof while London sleeps.

I have an ear permanently cocked for the pistol-like crack of beams suddenly subsiding with dry rot. I turn off the water at the mere suggestion of a frost; and if there *is* a frost the little grating over the main tap, outside, becomes frozen over in the night; I go into the shed, in my dressing gown, to find the chisel to lever it open, I grope in the grey light, and hundreds of tins fall down with what the Elizabethans described as *heyho rumbelo*.

But there is something more than this. After these four years I have discovered that this preoccupation with the mere fabric of the house is only the beginning. The householder is concerned not only with this death force, with the huge, hydra-headed forces of seediness and decay, but also, for much more of his time, with a strange, perverted life-force as well. For the fact is that a house actually *generates small heavy objects*. The householder must conceive of his house as though it were a jar containing a colourless, impalpable liquid, the ground of life, in which are suspended many non-soluble objects which tend to *sink to the bottom*. The higher the specific gravity of the things, naturally the quicker they sink. It is not a matter of size. It is quite natural for a bed – big, soft, fairly light – to stay upstairs. It is the small, dense objects which form a sediment at the bottom of the house unless one keeps everything in constant agitation.

In the bottoms of cupboards, in the lower part of the house, a heavy, concentrated sediment is constantly forming; of dense piles of damp magazines, old vacuum flasks with mouldy corks, heavy little gramophone motors, ice skates, gas rings, headlamps, a secondhand-looking pile of about *thirty* dinner plates with those gold edges. And, of course, bottles. We put as many in the dustbin as we dare, and heaven knows what orgies the dustmen think go on in our house. But the bottom of our house is inexorably filling up with bottles.

We possess an extremely heavy little Oriental table, a charming wedding present which, nevertheless, doesn't belong, somehow, in our small drawing-room. We keep it in the spare bedroom. *But it keeps coming downstairs*. Periodically we find ourselves panting and grunting round narrow angles of the stairs, taking it up again. It is made of some dense Oriental wood, full of sharp corners that tear the wallpaper. I don't remember ever bringing it downstairs (which would be just as awkward, and therefore just as memorable). But we have carried it up at least four times.

We bought our shed, as we innocently thought, to house the pram and garden tools. But now the pram will hardly go in; to get at the shears I must remove vast bundles of heavy carpet, things keep sliding down – a strange bath made of papier mâché, big old attaché cases that seem to be full of tinsel and curtains, a tremendous spindly easel inextricably locked with a bucket, miles of rope – and of course *more* bottles.

And then there are the boots and shoes. The other day, on a long car journey, we turned off the main road, deep into the silent country, for a picnic lunch. We stopped in a tiny lane. Cows lowed, birds sang, leaves rustled. There was a gentle, earthy smell; no houses were in sight. I walked ten yards from the car, and there, in a ditch lay at least two hundred old shoes. There were bits of charred paper; someone had made a half-hearted attempt to burn them. Some householder had driven out all this way, the back of his small car crammed with shoes, shoes spilling forward over the front seats whenever he braked . . .

Before I became a householder I should have dismissed this strange, ugly pile as mere urban vandalism. But now it's given me an idea.

You and Non-You

WHEN A SCHOOLBOY begins Latin, the second thing he learns is how to say 'O Table!' It so happens that the word for this, *mensa*, is exactly the same as that for the first thing he learns – simply 'a table'. Doubtless this causes many, at the very outset of their education, to dismiss the ancients as crazy people who went about talking to tables.

But it can also be a reminder, never quite forgotten, that this 'dead' tongue had a special case, the Vocative, for that living mystery of speech as addressed *to* someone (or even just to a table). Language is not just a resonant flow of empty syllables, a gigantic notice-board suspended in the mind, but communication, the Word.

Even in this flat and busy age the Vocative still has an elusive and mysterious being. Some newspapers make mechanical attempts to restore it, simply by writing often in the second person. UP GOES YOUR H.P., say their headlines, or YOU ASKED FOR IT. The Government, too, is compelled to try. YOUR RATION BOOK, it used to say. DO NOTHING WITH THIS PART. WHAT YOU MUST DO. DO NOT FILL IN (F) UNLESS YOU ARE A MERCHANT SEAMAN.

All this is the Bogus Vocative; it is more unreal even than saying 'O Table!' The B.B.C., adult, disenchanted, lean over backwards to avoid it. They try to be anonymous, to look as though they were not talking to us. But radio, and even more, television, is the apotheosis of the Vocative; and if it cannot confront us with absolute Truth, if we can't have Outside Broadcasts from Heaven, if we can't see weeping or smiling Graces walking in immortal fields, neither can the B.B.C. make it impersonal, and we get something in between; the Sub-Vocative, the speech used to strangers.

I think I have discovered where the Sub-Vocative, the essential speech of our time, finds its purest expression. This is not on television. It is on little cards and notices. What could be more modestly communicative than these bashful little messages, these low blue lights generated by the million chance encounters of complex civilisation? In a secondhand shop I saw a violin with a card by it saying, SUITABLE FOR VIRTUOSO. One felt that they didn't really *expect* a virtuoso; they would have been disturbed if a man with long hair flowing over his astrakhan collar had come in, picked up the violin and bewitched them all with the Devil's Trill. But they wanted to say *something* to us. So, too, with the overcoat which I once saw marked OF LORDLY APPEARANCE; or the card, on one of fifty perfectly ordinary pairs of men's shoes in a shop window, saying suddenly YOUNG IN SPIRIT, in a tiny solo.

These cards give the impression of all being printed by the same firm, usually in thick capitals on shiny white celluloid. Now I suggest that this firm could expand enormously, that these cards could fill a long-felt want in our daily lives, when we need the Sub-Vocative. There are hundreds of occasions when we would like to say something, but less emphatically than in live speech, the True Vocative that is used only to friends or enemies. The Sub-Vocative is for addressing *strangers*.

Take motoring, for instance. When one's engine stalls in traffic and the idiot behind starts hooting, one does not want a stand-up row; but how nice it would be to have a properly printed card that one could stick

54

out of the window, saying SORRY, IT OFTEN DOES THIS, or HAVE STOPPED FOR A PICNIC, or, perhaps, DO NOT DISTURB. There could be about two hundred standard phrases for motoring, like those for overseas telegrams. Obvious ones would be YOU'RE IN THE WRONG LANE, MATE, and, of course, SHUT UP . . .

Think of the number of situations in life when it would be useful to be able silently to hold up a card saying ALL RIGHT, I KNOW. I myself would like one to put on the baby's pram for all those passers-by who clearly think I am pinching him, saying IT'S HIS TEETH. When I hold open the large door of some hotel foyer for a laughing party some yards behind and they make no effort to hurry, I should love to be able to flip out a card saying I AM NOT A DOORMAN. When I am trying to keep near the door in a rush-hour tube-train, I would like to be able to show the guard that I am not wilfully, anti-socially resisting his despairing appeal to 'pass *right* down the car, please'. He, and the other passengers, would see my card saying GETTING OUT NEXT STOP. As it is, I can't bring myself to *say* this out loud, and we all hate each other.

Once these cards became generally accepted, I am sure they would ease many tensions. And of course I have given only a few examples. YOU WILL BE ABLE – I'm sorry, the reader will be able to think of many more for himself.

Mice Will Play

OF COURSE, ONE reason why the whole idea of Japanese waltzing mice is so fascinating is that we are faintly surprised and pleased to detect, however fancifully, a human note so far down in the scheme of creation. There is a vast dark penumbra of idiot or hostile things that we can never know – amoebae, crabs, newts – and flies, forever buzzing about, alighting, and neurotically rubbing their hands like Lady Macbeth. But the moment we get into the mammal class here are these little creatures, with their beady, knowing eyes, capering away down there in tiny mirth, and 'Good gracious,' we say, 'it's just like a waltz.' We are in our own part of the spectrum. We do not have to wait until we get to the intelligent primates, to the Chimpanzees' Tea Party, before we see something we think we recognise.

Mice are the point at which the Hegelian Idea, the world becoming self-conscious, really gets going. It is significant that in Beatrix Potter the smallest characters, beneath which life is obviously not intelligible, are Mr. John Dormouse and Timmie Willie. There is no smaller (or more basic) cartoon figure than Mickey Mouse. Indeed, if we imagine a sort of reverse process of creation, analogous to that of running tape backwards through a tape recorder, so that human beings came out all garbled, small, jerky, madly nimble and high-pitched, but still vestigially recognisable, we can see *ourselves* as mice.

I once played the harmonium at a wedding, and on one of the bellows there was affixed a stamped metal plate saying MOUSE PROOF PEDAL.

This seems to express perfectly our curious, ambivalent relationship with mice. It somehow seems both natural and extraordinary at the same time. It is natural because *all* types of mouse would seem at home in a harmonium. We can picture church mice living there quietly, in dim light filtering through the green cloth at the back. But we can also imagine the gayer and more theatrical type of mouse, perhaps even the Japanese waltzer, taking naturally to it. For despite its ecclesiastical veneer, there is something showy about a harmonium. To play it requires the same sort of skill as that of a music-hall juggler; it is a kind of holy one-man band.

In playing the harmonium no part of the body is unoccupied. One pedals with one's feet, and sometimes there is a knob called *Prolongement*, operated with one's heel, as well. With the knees one moves wooden flaps that control the volume. With the hands, of course, one both plays and works the stops. If one pulls the wrong one, everything below middle C suddenly drops about four octaves; the church is filled with a gruff, reedy bumbling, well described by the stop-name *Bourdon*.

There is a wanton nineteenth-century air about the whole thing. The harmonium was preceded by exotic inventions with names such as Organo-Violine, Aerophone, Aeolophone, Seraphine. All kinds of sensual and voluptuous effects were devised by bearded Frenchmen. Stops are called *Voix Celeste*, or simply *Expression*, and there is a tremendous roaring one called *Grand Jeu*. It is easy to imagine not only Japanese Waltzing Mice, but French Can-Can Mice, scandalising their church brethren with tiny bacchanalian squeaks as the *Grand Jeu* brings some wild dance to its climax.

And yet it *is* extraordinary too. Doubtless a harmonium, with its rods and pallets, its wires and struts, its tubes and passages, its little doors opening and shutting, might at first seem like an exciting playground specially made for mice, a delicious three-dimensional maze, with comfortable leather bellows to sleep on after the merry games were over; but surely the first experience of the thing being played would be so traumatic as to scare them off for ever. It would suddenly go all dark, there would be a monstrous gale of wind, terrible clankings and creakings would strike terror into the heart of the stoutest mouse; trap-doors would open, floors would tilt, and then an unbelievable, an unbearable intensity of sound would compass them about. Surely any mice that escaped would tell their fellows that this enormous palace was in reality just a new and diabolical form of mouse-trap, designed to *kill with sound* . . .

But there it is. Obviously mice have got into harmonia in sufficient numbers to make this special pedal necessary. How were they discovered? Can it really be that someone, playing *Evening Meditation* or *Simple Voluntary*, noticed another, a shriller note, a tiny squeaking above the throbbing *Voix Celeste*? Or, finding the bellows lacking in power for the *Grand Jeu*, discovered the tell-tale teeth marks in the leather? And how do they *test* the Mouse-Proof Pedal? 'O.K., Mr. Bates, the action's fine, Let's just try it for mice.'. . .

I should like to think they have a special test piece called *Three Deaf Mice*.

Load of Hoggin

IT WAS ONLY just light (and it gets light an hour earlier in the country) when the front-door bell rang and there was a man saying tersely, 'Load of hoggin.' For the moment I couldn't think who he was, or what hoggin was – indeed, I'm never quite sure who *I* am at that hour in the morning.

Hoggin, now what could it be? A kind of rude cider? A fertiliser made from pigs' ears and washed leaves? Some sort of intermediate product in brewing or tanning ('the sparge-arms scrape off the hoggin, which is then pressed into these giant kieves')?

A huge, square, high-sided lorry stood outside in the mist; the kind of lorry you follow for miles, it bears some name like FRANK COGGS, sandy mud dribbles out of it at the corners – and then I remembered, hoggin is a sort of gravel. I had ordered it for my front path.

I had planned to smarten up the front, at least; I had to choose between making a large, diffuse impression at the back, creating a tiny vestigial human spoor in the wilderness – a little bit of lawn, a cultivated plot of maize won from the jungle – and making a real garden at the front.

In fact the front became an obsession, one thing led to another. I planted hundreds of bulbs, I attacked it with the misplaced frenzy of the urban gardener, although in my heart I know you can't win like this, you have to attack the country when it isn't looking. You must be born in it, you crouch slyly over your handlebars, you have sacks containing moles or voles, *bang* goes your mysterious gun in the foggy twilight; you know what the owls are saying.

I didn't even know that bulbs have a top and a bottom until one of these bicycle men pointed it out; half my tulips will come up in Australia. I made some marvellous lawn edges; I painted the railings white. For two pins I'd have had a flagstaff and some whitewashed bricks. Then I saw that the front path, just old pebbles and mud, wouldn't live up to the surrounding splendour; and the man with the bicycle said:'Ah, you want to get a load of hoggin.'

It was a huge load, filling the lorry right up to the top. It was four cubic yards. The builder whom I first asked for this hoggin said he wasn't allowed to deliver it at all, and the actual hoggin people weren't allowed to deliver *less* than four cubic yards. There was some confused reason for this, all about A and B licences. Indeed, the hoggin, binding shingle and washed sand world is more complicated, in fact exciting, than I had imagined. On the back of the note I had to sign for my load it said:–

FOR THE USE OF INSPECTORS ONLY

This Conveyance Note having been produced to me at (place) . . . . at (time) . . . . on the . . . . . . day of . . . . . . , 19 . . . , I found the same to contain materially incorrect statements, particulars of which are as follows . . .

– followed by a lot of Notes, all fatalistically expecting trouble. So *that's* why those lorries are forever lurching suddenly down side roads; they have spied the Hoggin Inspector in his car, the chase is on. It is like smugglers and revenue men in the eighteenth century, although heaven

58

knows who would want to smoggle hugg – to smuggle hoggin. Perhaps it all belongs to the Crown, like swans, and since half England seems to be shakily founded on the Bunter Pebble Beds these Inspectors are constantly tracking down illegal operators.

It was such a big load that I couldn't decide where to have it dumped. After fruitless, panting attempts by the driver and me to pull up the railings I saw it would have to be outside the garage. I had the foresight to get my car out first. Immediately it began to rain, the weather began its ceaseless attack on my hood. The driver tipped his lorry. A vast mound of soggy sand, with a pebble here and there, cascaded across the entrance.

After a hurried breakfast I got busy. I wheeled barrowful after barrowful. At midday, after twenty-nine barrows, the vast heap seemed hardly diminished at all. The path was littered with awful giant molehills. Plodding with my barrow, I felt like a Chinese coolie making an airstrip in some sodden rice-field. As a rest from the exhausting wheel-barrow I raked this dreary hoggin and tried to roll it. The roller simply sank in, it was like rolling mud. It *was* rolling mud, that's what hoggin is; it's mud.

I telephoned my builder, he sent me two men with bicycles to help me, we just managed to clear the way through the hoggin for my car as darkness fell. Now, the stuff on the path gets wetter and wetter, there are parts that simply suck one down. The laundry man, who, surprisingly, materialises out of the dark fields at about eight in the evening, was white and shaken.

'I thought I'd stepped into wet concrete,' he said. I didn't tell him it was a quicksand. But I shouldn't be surprised if there are cries for help one night, and I have to go out with ropes and ladders to rescue some unfortunate victim, like Carver Doone in the bog. I don't think I like hoggin.

Alfa Bravo Over

SOMETHING HAS HAPPENED to toys, you no longer get the feeling that they are made by little old men with glasses on the ends of their noses, in some place like Nuremberg. Toys have gone industrial, they use plastics; chemists who know all about di-chlorotricyclbicyclpolyputaketlon are involved in their manufacture. They have gone serious – or industry has gone frivolous. Somewhere, in some serious-looking factory, draughtsmen, fitters, shop stewards, storemen, have been concerned in making, for instance, an insane-looking marsupial, dressed in blue bathing trunks and a Cambridge scarf with red tassels, which sits on a wheeled platform. In front of him is a xylophone containing three tuneless notes; and when this contraption is pulled along, the animal, staring madly out of its four eyes (for it is painted on both sides) beats dementedly at this instrument with its spring arms. It sounds like a Balinese orchestra being pulled on a porter's trolley at Euston.

Someone must have taken a drawing of this creature into a superior's office. He would look at it in silence, then say 'I think you've got something there, Carter' – adding, with the irresistible urge of all executives to make 'creative' amendments, 'I think you'd better give him a little red skull cap like *this*.' Then, briskly, flipping an intercom switch, 'Alastair, get on to Jobson and Tukes, ask them to quote for 10,000 xylophone notes, urgentest. And send Hawkins up, we'll have to re-jig No. 3 . . .'

Actually this thing is made of wood, a traditional material much closer to Nuremberg than most of the toys which appeared in my house this Christmas. Consider, for instance, the Bubble Boy Bandsman. This is a plastic homunculus obviously turned out as mechanically as a carburettor (more mechanically, when you think of all those fiddling little screws and washers and springs in a carburettor, I bet *they're* put in by little old men, probably watchmakers). Indeed the Bubble Boy has some resemblance to a carburettor, for inside the pink saxophone he is holding is a complicated plastic mechanism of pipes and rings, and what you are supposed to do is to *pour small amount of bubble mixture into open end of saxophone and then press Bubble Boy's hat* (he is wearing a rubber bowler) *& watch bubbles appear*. But however hard we pressed nothing happened except a lot of clicking and gurgling, and presently bubble mixture began to ooze out through his boots.

Then there was the Dan Dare Interplanetary Walkie-Talkie. This should really have been called a Sittie-Talkie, for it is just two plastic telephones connected by wire. Like all the industrial toys, it was a bit advanced for our children, since the eldest is four. But my friend Harblow and I had a wonderful time. He went into the kitchen with one telephone, I stayed in the drawing-room with the other:–

Me: It says here you have to say 'Over', otherwise your friend won't know when to move it from his mouth to his ear. Can you hear me, friend? Over.

Harblow (*very faint*): Table cake arresting, table cake arresting, table cake arresting . . .

Me: We'll never get anywhere if you don't say 'Over'. Remember Signals Procedure. Over.

Harblow (*complete silence. Then a far-away blowing, then a sound like a tin mouse whistling. Suddenly Harblow appears at the door*): I say, I can't hear a thing.

Me: You were listening while I was waiting for you to talk. I heard *you*. What was all that about table cake arresting?

Harblow: I said Able Baker Testing, Able Baker Testing.

Me: They've changed it since our day, it's Alfa Bravo now.

Harblow: What, again?

Me: But you still have to say 'Over'. Now you go back, and I'll speak first (*Exit Harblow. I read from box.*) Rotate planet 59 deg. E on 'N' axis and attack with full force of Disintegrators. Over.

Harblow (*still very faint*): Hah, ha, ha (*shrieks of laughter*). Over.

Me: You're very faint. Over.

Harblow (*roaring*): Alfa Bravo, Alfa Bravo, Alfa Bravo, what do they mean, Alfa, not Bravo at all. Over.

Me: I can hear your real voice above the telephone now. Hold it very close and whisper.

Harblow: You forgot to say 'Over'. Over.

Me: Sorry over. Over.

Harblow: I say, what did the umpire say when he lost count. He said, Is the over over? Over. Hahaha, over over, over. Over.

Me: That wasn't whispering. Over.

Harblow (*surprisingly*): I say, can you bring a hairpin over? Over.

Me: Did you say a *hairpin*? Over.

Harblow (*complete silence*).

The silence went on for so long that I borrowed a hairpin from my wife and went into the kitchen. It was full of bubbles. Harblow was pressing the Bubble Boy's hat, his saxophone was belching bubbles. 'You had the jet clogged,' said Harblow. 'I've cleared it with this paper clip.'

Wool-Gathering

MORE AND MORE psychologists seem to be devising tests, with ink-blots, or barbed questions, or interlocking bits of wood, or whatever, which already determine whether a recruit is to go into the Royal Corps of Signals or the band of the Irish Guards, and seem well on the way to determining men's careers, perhaps even choosing their wives. But why bother to *devise* tests, why create hypothetical problems and invent ambivalent phrases, when life itself offers us so many omens and oracles? The ordinary man walks along an ordinary road through an amazing, an unknown country; sulphurous flashes light up caverns and plains peopled by men he knows to be his brothers, he *must* understand them – but what are they saying? In one single day last week I saw a headline saying JAM IN TUNNEL, a large envelope on which was printed URGENT – DATED PERIODICALS, a huge van saying ABBESS (in Gothic type) OFFICE FURNITURE, and a small office plate, in Bedford-square, saying FAILING SUPPLY LIMITED

Listen, psychologists, there are only two kinds of men; the ones to whom these things mean no more than the croaking of frogs or the silence of rocks – dead, cold, inscrutable, nothing-to-do-with-me; and the ones who see a marvellous St. Elmo's Fire round them all, a sort of deep, luminous ether of human reality, much *more* real than the mere cold economic or other facts which they presumably connote. To this latter class the very first thought aroused by JAM IN TUNNEL is, well, jam, in a tunnel; about a foot deep, oozing from the walls; *blackwall* jam in Blackberry Tunnel.

Men of this class see an ageing figure in a dressing-gown, smoking cigarettes through a long holder, waiting impatiently for his Dated Periodicals – yellowing copies of *Vogue* from which, sighing, he cuts out pictures of women in cloche hats. They see these nuns in their office, the desks with brass eagles' heads, the carved Gothic filing cabinets, the seven-branched candlesticks lit after the tea break. They see this huge, sad warehouse, the dying rays of a Spenglerian sunset filtering into dusty corners once clangorous with buyers, before Supplies began to fail . . .

There are only two kinds of men – Yogi and Commissar, Schlegel and Wilcox, Poet and Peasant, Sense and Sensibility, Realist and Nominalist – nay, Plato and Aristotle. Here is your test, psychologists; show your subject that real, that actual volume of statistics labelled, I swear, ADULT POPULATION OF THE UNITED KINGDOM BROKEN DOWN BY AGE AND SEX.

We who belong to this second class are by turns proud of our sacramental conception of reality and guilty because we seem to be cut off from the great bustling commercial world. Every now and then we resolve to abandon this airy-fairy business, to study economics, politics, reality – to see the world as no more than a kind of vast clock.

Thus, I thought I would look at the advertisements in the *Radio Times*. There can surely be no poetic nonsense here. A page in the *Radio Times* costs £4,000. Hard-headed men sit in leather chairs round grim tables, they have intense, practical discussions on the best way of spending their advertising appropriations. 'Well, gentlemen, let's kick this around a bit,' says the Sales Manager. 'We've got to blanket the country with this. I suggest a page in the *Radio Times*.' 'Nay, lad, tha'lt not waste our brass like that,' says Sir Luke Ramsbotham, the Chairman . . .

Well, what do they advertise in the *Radio Times*? Why, far more than anything else, week after week, *sheds*. There seems to be a full page ad. for sheds at least once a month. That's £48,000 a year. Let us assume that these shed people spend even five per cent of their turnover on advertising; that means their turnover is £960,000 a year. And suppose the average cost of the sheds is £50 (and some of them are enormous), that's 19,200 sheds, for just one firm. There are at least ten firms. That's 192,000 sheds a year. It's fantastic. Who buys them? What do they *do* in these sheds?

Another glance at the *Radio Times* suggests what they do. They are forever making rugs, and knitting – not with needles, but with knitting *machines*. As any husband knows, a woman clicking absently away with two ordinary needles, in odd moments of comparative relaxation, can effortlessly pour out a stream of sweaters, gloves, socks, blankets, helmets, breechettes and what not to keep a family of six warm, and still have time left over to be always making things for *friends'* babies. But the ads. for these machines say 'eighteen times as fast as hand knitting!'

63

A machine eighteen times as fast as the average wife would make two cardigans, ten pairs of socks, half a dozen scarves and a strange heavy-duty thing for lifeboatmen, in one evening.

That's what those sheds are for; they are warehouses, feverishly bought to cope with the ever-increasing flood of knitting. All over England there are these sheds, crammed to bursting with jumpers, helmets, rugs and druggets. Why, wool must be creating a vast new prosperity, as it did in the fourteenth century. It would be nice if these wool mercers were to repeat history by building lovely churches, endowing comfortable almshouses, creating beautiful new towns of warm grey stone. But no; all they do is buy more and more sheds.

Poets on Tap

ANY FOREIGNER DRIVING about this country must surely be struck by the extraordinary number of waterworks. It is not necessarily that England has more waterworks than any other country, it is simply that they are so immediately recognisable. Just as Greek architecture achieved a classical immutable perfection in the age of Pericles, so did British waterworks reach their final form in the nineteenth century (who ever saw a *modern* waterworks?). They are all the same, made of dark red brick, covered with ivy. They have windows rounded at the top. They are set among coldly perfect lawns and poplars, or other municipal trees with metallic leaves that rustle in the cold spring wind.

Formal paths cut across these lawns, leading to lonely, detached waterworks houses in the same style. But no men can ever be seen, nor is there any sign of waterworks women and children in these houses. There is just a big quiet emptiness, with a hint of something numinous – almost, one might say, ecclesiastical. Just as old churches, quiet, filled with a green light, just off the humming roads, are forever apart, troubling the most casual passer-by with the fact that the multitudinous dead are real, cannot be written off, and may even have been right – so do these waterworks, withdrawn, silent, stir in us drowned memories of primordial ocean. As W. P. Witcutt remarks, 'water, according to Jung, is the commonest symbol for the Unconscious. Whoever is about to be invaded by the Unconscious dreams about water. He descends, by night, to a lake and looks in fear at its unknown depths. De Quincey first had "dreams of lakes and silvery expanses of water" which, "from translucent shining lakes became seas and oceans."'

So numerous, and so big, are these waterworks that I cannot help feeling they are not all concerned with sordid pumping and filtering. I should like to think that if we *did* stop the car and walk across the trim grass, and actually go in, we should find ourselves in a high cool hall. At one end of this hall, it is true, there would be dials and levers, shiny copper pipes, thick green glass bubble gauges, powerful motors humming under gratings. But the men working there would be poets – *Georgian* poets. Waterworks are an ideal place in which to make real the link between officialdom and this great British Unconscious, the universal water-dream, of which poets are the oracles.

The tradition that began, perhaps, with Charles Lamb in the East India Company, of giving poets and dreamers some sort of vague, easy employment in the public service flowered magnificently in the nineteenth century; it inspired that wonderful Max Beerbohm cartoon of Mr. Jos. Chamberlain surprising Mr. Austin Dobson and Mr. Edmund Gosse composing a ballade during office hours at the Board of Trade; and it reached its height in the period that ended with the Georgians, with men like Humbert Wolfe, or Maurice Baring in the Diplomatic Service. But poetry got hard when life got hard, in 1914. The great Government departments were reorganised, soulless efficiency experts came in . . .

Except for the waterworks. Here, far from the ugly industrial bustle of today, a place is reserved for Georgian poets, with thoughts of beauty quietly a-dancing till all the world grow young again. What could be more appropriate, or convenient? There cannot be much to *do* in a waterworks: just a routine check of meters twice a day.

A telephone rings. Footsteps across a shiny parquet floor. 'No 3. Pumping, Wiltshire, here,' says a voice. 'Back head flow 500. Close auxiliaries.' (Pause); 'I say, is that you, Herbert? What about this? –

> I met a roving tinker man
> A-roving in the wild
> And O, he was more merry than
> A merry laughing child . . .'

and so on. An animated discussion develops, other poets on the line cut in, there is talk of rondels and sestinas. Unnoticed, gauge needles creep past red lines. Sand and tadpoles come out of taps in Reading, torrents of water shoot up from gratings, policemen are photographed rescuing people from the upper windows of cottages by means of those punts that the police always seem to have ready in times of flood, even in places miles away from any river (can it be that there are police boathouses, with these punts kept always at readiness?). Buzzers and alarm bells go off in some regional headquarters; a real water engineer, crackling with fury, yells 'Get those damn poets off the line. Open the main cocks'. . . .

All this, recollected in tranquillity, would be useful material for verses on the grand, symbolic, ancient human memory of the Flood; and if that isn't the stuff of poetry, what is?

The Goons

THE SUBURB OF Shepherd's Bush, an amorphous area of dull houses entirely surrounded by trolleybuses and hidden sidings, is the unlikely home of many strange fantasies intimately affecting the life of Britain in the mid-fifties.

Not only does it contain the high concrete barns of Lime Grove, where television developed from a tiny, private side-line of the B.B.C. to its present ubiquity; over a fruit shop in Shepherd's Bush, up three flights of narrow brown stairs, there is an office containing teapots, typewriters, electronic devices, encyclopaedias, and books ranging from *The Dialogues of Plato* (translated by Jowett, in four volumes) and *The Tragedy of the Caesars*, to *Birds of Our Country*, and it is here that the extraordinary hallucinations of the Goon Show are hammered into script form every week by Spike Milligan and Larry Stephens. The result is the purest form of surrealist humour yet reached on steam radio (in Goon parlance, 'talking-type wireless') – or anywhere else, for that matter.

Milligan is the key figure, both as scriptwriter and as one of the three protean performers who dodge, giggling from one microphone to another, in some sad hall or ex-theatre where the show is recorded on Sunday nights. They populate the air with a dozen or so weirdly compulsive characters who are now familiar to most people under forty (and many over). Milligan is The Famous Eccles, a lovable, toothless dimwit who owes something, but not all, to Disney's cartoon figure Goofy. He is Abdul the twittering bearer or dragoman; he is the vague, hen-like Minnie Bannister; he is Count Jim Moriarty, that impoverished cosmopolitan of the twenties.

The last-named acts as a sort of seedy Leporello for the larger, smoother villainies of Gryptype Thynne, played by Peter Sellers in his George Sanders voice. Other Sellers roles are the shameless, ex-Indian Army Major Bloodnok, Henry Crun (also vague and poultry-like, living in a dubious Victorian relationship with Minnie Bannister), Willium, a croaking, despairing Cockney ('I bin 'ere all night, mate'), Bluebottle, a ludicrous personification of schoolboy dreams of glory – and, in the Goons' not infrequent representations of the House of Commons, Sir Winston Churchill.

These and other remarkable figures revolve round the central figure of the plot, Neddy Seagoon, played by Harry Secombe, who looks but does not sound like an owl that has take Benzedrine. There are certain basic, unchanging elements. Seagoon is usually involved in a quest – an empire-building mission, laying a telephone line to '17a, Africa', a drum race from John o'Groats to Land's End, or he is after some prize or treasure of which the villains easily defraud him.

The essential thing, however, is the combination of a quite special, ultra-modern humorous idiom with a nostalgia for our Victorian, imperial past. It is as though Britannia were having not a nightmare but a sort of comic dream; it is as though Dali, Kipling and Dickens had co-operated. The character Henry Crun, for instance (in full, Henry Albert Sebastopol Queen Victoria Crun), was originally conceived as one of a firm of lawyers called Wacklow, Futtell and Crun, who might well have been in *Bleak House*.

The dialogue contains lines not unworthy of Groucho Marx. 'Minnie, I'm taking you away from the squalor that you live in – to the squalor that *I* live in'; or, in a brisk Service voice on the intercom of a criminal airship which has stolen a bank by lifting it with hooks, 'What course are you on?' – 'Prunes and Custard.' These shade off into a post Marxist surrealism. Thus, Seagoon (King Morte d'Arthur Seagoon) is trying to get into a Cornish castle ('Excuse the mess, but we've got the sea in') and demands the key. He is told 'There are no keys to this ladder, it's always open.'

This, with an equally surrealist use of sound effects (an important figure in the control room at the Goon Show is a small bearded man who speeds up records of bugles, trotting feet, railway trains, etc., by whizzing them round with his finger), is part of what Mr. Milligan calls, with undoubted seriousness, 'Dimensionalism'. The radio listener, he maintains, is in a dream world, where the rigid dimensions of time-space unity need not confine him, ('Open the door and let's get this room in.')

Milligan is a much more aggressive and uninhibited man than the other Goons. The big, mobile mouth in the long face, the sudden relapses from laughter into genuine, bitter sadness ('The human race has failed. We ought to be *fighting* for *Hungary*') remind one of his Irish ancestry. But he is also a born eccentric, almost a professional misfit ('the people who like the Goons are Outsiders'), and a sworn enemy of bureaucracy and greyness.

A lot of the 'imperial' background to the show is a reflection of Milligan's personal life. He was born in India, where his father was a regimental sergeant-major. He came to England to train as a pilot, failed the examination disastrously, and ended up in the Royal Artillery. In Italy he met Lance-Bombardier Harry Secombe, when both were working in the Central Pool of Artists.

After the war, while Secombe was making his name as a comic, at the Windmill and elsewhere, and Sellers establishing himself as a wonderful mimic, Milligan was playing the guitar in 'The Bill Hall Trio'; he also plays the trumpet, and one of the best things in the Goon Show is never broadcast – it is the riotous jam session during the audience warm-up. He found efforts to break into the conventional music-hall dispiriting, and later he simply signed on at Deptford Labour Exchange.

But the old friendship with Secombe, and a newer one with Sellers, was kept alive, and the Goon Show was born in 1952 when the B.B.C. had finally showed interest in a privately made recording. Although Milligan admits a debt to no one, the organisation which had known 'Itma' was adventurous enough to take a chance, which has been amply repaid. The listening figures in this country are six million, and the Goon Show is increasingly popular on American, Canadian and Australian networks.

Milligan is the centripetal element. In him goonery is actual. In Secombe and Sellers it is potential, sparked into brilliant reality when they are together. These two naturally contribute ideas; there is a strong sympathy of temperament with Milligan. But they have other pursuits.

Secombe, who comes from Swansea, is a kind of Ideal South Walian. Like Michael Bentine, a founder member of the Goons who left them to tour Australia, he is fundamentally a visual comic, and he creates his own material almost spontaneously. The act with which he convulsed Windmill audiences, a glum lot who do not really go to be *amused*, depicted shaving as practised by a boy for the first time, by a man using ice-cold water, and by a nervous case. But he also possesses a heroic tenor voice of real promise. He studies singing seriously and has made records of *Vesti la giubba* and other arias which have been respectfully received by the critics. Off-stage he is exuberant, kindly – and a well-informed, voracious reader. He lives in Sutton, and like all the Goons is a husband and father.

He has no theatrical antecedents. But Peter Sellers, the youngest of the trio (he is thirty-one), appeared in films at the age of five. His uncle was manager of the Victoria Pavilion at Ilfracombe, and here he learnt the repertory business from the bottom, beginning as assistant stage-manager. Gradually his impressions of the famous superseded his other work, and formed the basis of the act in which he, too, appeared at the Windmill. His private manner is quiet. He looks like a scholarly well-dressed young house agent. He is in demand as a character actor, supplies U.P.A. with cartoon film voices – and, like Secombe, can sustain a top billing in variety.

So much talent makes for a centrifugal tendency and a strong need for discipline and forceful direction, if the Goons are ever to do something less ephemeral than their weekly broadcast: a film, for instance. And that means a very strong director indeed. Milligan himself is not very hopeful. A certain British director of comedies was once pointed out to him on a small rock off a fashionable *plage*. Milligan put on his mask and flippers, swam under water, and popped up to greet the great man with 'Do you come here often?' The raised eyebrow he got was typical of the reaction so far of the British film industry to the scenario for a Goon film which he has up his sleeve.

Doubtless there would be great clashes of personality, just as there were over the promising venture of the Goons into television, *A Show Called Fred*. But those who love pure, quicksilver, and above all *new* comedy must continue to hope that films will one day be made. In the meantime they are grateful that the Goon Show, as is obvious to anyone physically present at the broadcast, is performed by these brilliant and talented young men at least as much for love and high enjoyment as for money.

To Chiswick in Error

ONE REASON WHY London no longer contains Dickensian characters (apart from the fact that it never did, there never where people quite so much larger than life as Mr. Jingle or Dick Swiveller) is that nowadays so few people work in the small, localised world that is the fruitful soil of character. It was all right for an hostler, in the atmosphere of a coaching inn; but he wouldn't be able to hostle to-day. He would probably work for London Transport, with 87,000 others, all of whose character seems to have been drawn off, as it were, to feed the giant, diffuse, half-felt personality of modern London itself (we started talking about the 'spirit of London' only after the blitz. London, for Dr. Johnson, was a smallish collection of knowable people, not a monster with a 'spirit'). The red buses are the red corpuscles in London's bloodstream (and taxis, I am sure, are the anti-bodies – cross little black things, turning round sharply against the general flow).

London Transport itself seems aware of this; it is a function of a function, not a collection of human characters. It advertises for 'stationmen and stationwomen'; they sound like German wooden toys with round faces, black dots for eyes, red dots on their cheeks. You couldn't sing, *Oh Mr. Stationman, what shall I do, I want to go to Birmingham and they took me on to Crewe.*

Even the Irish and the Jamaicans give up their natural exuberance when they become conductors, or ticketmen. You never hear the Irish sing out, ' 'Tis the great proud hall of Euston Station we do be passin' now, with the trains roarin' inside it, and the clouds of steam billowin' up to the fretted roof of it, and wisha, the trains do be startin' off to the western sea, me soul is afther them like a bird, flyin' back to the lonely hills of Kerry,' and so on. Nor does one of those lovely mellow Jamaican voices sing:–

> *National Gallery, in Trafalgar-square,*
> *See all de pigeons wheelin' in de air,*
> *Ole Nelson standin' up dere so high,*
> *He got one arm and he got one eye . . .*

When London transportmen do emerge occasionally as individuals; it is still very much as members of the organisation. At some empty hour of the evening, like seventeen minutes past nine, three huge, booted, mackintoshed figures, inexplicably carrying lanterns, as though they had come in from some wild storm, will get into the tube at some station like Belsize Park. They wink and talk among themselves. Once, when the train stopped, I heard one such say, 'Ah, it was different in the old days, Mr. Armitage used to come and talk to us.' They have their own history, their own withdrawn communal life, their own green memories of Mr. Armitage talking, gently talking, under the institutional lampshade. We shall never know them, as we knew Sam Weller.

How can we ever know, for instance, what had happened on the day when I saw an abandoned bus in Baker-street, with a board propped up behind it on which were the words beautifully printed in chalk:–

> WENT
> ~~GONE~~ TO CHISWICK IN ERROR

How could they possibly get to Chiswick in error? It's quite hard to get to Chiswick on purpose. I have never yet discovered the middle of Chiswick, if it has one. It is all residential culs-de-sac. When you are in, say, Kew, you know that Chiswick is vaguely over *there*, with Sir A. P. Herbert mysteriously somewhere around; but you never see it, or him.

At first one imagines a whole busload of passengers, getting increasingly uneasy as they catch glimpses of the river, thinking to themselves, 'H'm, this doesn't look like St. John's Wood,' but afraid to question the conductor staring moodily from the platform (perhaps it is just a monster diversion). But then one recalls that the bus wasn't *in* Chiswick, it was in the middle of London.

Perhaps the driver and the conductor were a notorious pair, known at some depot as The Dreamers; they simply took an empty bus to Chiswick to start their shift, remembered the schedules had been changed, went back to Baker-street, and then, finding that a very nasty inspector of whom they were afraid had called in another bus in their place, dared not go back and so left this notice ('We can't say *Gone To Chiswick*, it's back here now. Let's say *Went*').

Perhaps, thinking they might as well be hanged for a sheep as a lamb, they then went *back* to Chiswick by tube, boldly flourishing free passes, and spent the day on the river (perhaps it was a lady conductress, or ticketwoman; they drifted idly under the summer willow, savouring a stolen rapture). Perhaps it wasn't the busmen who went to Chiswick in error, but the breakdownmen, perhaps they got a call for help from Baker-street and thought it was from Chiswick. But why?

And who taught them that lovely printing? Mr Armitage, perhaps.

The Boy's Got Talent

GENTLEMAN (31), wide knowledge ancient history, especially ancient Egypt, comparative religion, rationalism, very experienced public orator and lecturer, author of daring thesis on the origin of world civilisation, artist, fluent Spanish, many years commercial experience, seeks position where this unusual combination of talents could be used.

The Times personal column, Feb. 3.

WELL, IT'S PURE imagination of course, but the picture I have is this: When Lucas Pickering's young wife bore him their only child in 1927 there was plenty of head-shaking among their neighbours in the little grey weaving town of Bragdyke. Some of them resented the slight fair-haired girl whom this tall, solitary, deep-eyed man, apparently a confirmed bachelor at fifty-one, had unexpectedly brought back as his bride from a rationalist congress in London. Others, discovering that Elsie Pickering was not a London hussy but a quiet, shy girl ('Aye, a gradely lass to be wed to thon old atheist'), pitied her.

Most of the townspeople were used to the sight of Pickering on his stand outside the Corn Exchange every Saturday night, rain or fine, declaiming passionately from Herbert Spencer, Bradlaugh or Ingersoll to a few curious bystanders or giggling adolescents. He was respected as a solid craftsman (after many years as a ring-doubler and two-end winder he was now overlooker in the cheese-winding department), and Lucas Pickering's credit was as good as the next man's. But undoubtedly he did not fit into the cheerful Bragdyke life of pub and club and the annual performance of *The Messiah*, 'Happen it'll be a lonely life for the child' was the verdict.

In some ways this was true. But Herbert Renan Pickering, who grew up a slight though healthy boy, was adored by his father. Together the two would go for long walks on the moors. Gazing down at the town, from which the sound of church bells floated up, Lucas would exclaim 'Eh, the daft fools, there they go worshipping their gaseous vertebrate. That's what Haeckel called their God, lad, the gaseous vertebrate – but thou aren't listening.'

'Oh yes, dad, I am,' said Herbert, looking up with a start from his sketch-book. For it was clear the boy was an artist. A rich local lady (and church worker), Miss Thwaitethwaite of the Manor House, swallowing her dislike of Pickering, told him 'that boy's got talent'. With her generous help Herbert became an art student.

The exciting turmoil of post-war London was a fertilising influence on the dreamy eighteen-year-old from Bragdyke. He was particularly influenced by the History of Art classes given by kindly old Professor Tonkins, and spent many hours in the Egyptian Room at the British Museum, in a trance before the glories of this hieratic art. On holidays in Bragdyke he would try to explain to his father. 'Well, dad, it depends what you mean by religion. Now when Amenhotep IV founded his religion of the sun . . . ' But he loyally accompanied Lucas to rationalist meetings in the dales, himself becoming a very experienced public orator.

Suddenly there was tragedy. Lucas caught a chill at an open-air meeting and was dead within a week. Herbert abandoned his art studies and went into commerce to help his mother. He got a job with Jarkins, Clanger and Pobjoy, Importers and Exporters, hoping to be sent to their Cairo branch. But because of Middle Eastern politics he found himself a trainee in the Buenos Aires office of J.C.P. He tried hard, learning fluent Spanish, studying Company Law. But his heart was not in it, and one day his boss, Mr McCluskey, a tough old South America hand who spent all his leisure drinking whisky in the English Club and had no time for artists, came unexpectedly into the office and found Herbert writing in a large exercise book. 'Well, Mr. McCluskey, it's a kind of thesis on the origins of world civilisation. I . . .' The result was a blistering letter to Head Office, and, eventually, this advertisement.

Meanwhile, in the dark, rich, oak-panelled City offices of Wilbye, Morley and Bateson, Sherry Importers, Travers Morley, Old Etonian head of the firm, is saying angrily: 'Can't we keep a manager on our *fonda* for six months? Here's a letter from that young puppy Henderson. He's resigned and goin' to be a *Jesuit*, if you please. Carter, before him, went off to learn bullfightin'. Can't understand why these young fellers get bowled over by Spain nowadays. I was there meself, turn of the century – enjoyed it, larked with the gels after the fiesta an' all that – but none of this rot about *hispanidad* and dignity. We want a chap immune to all that, philosophy of his own, able to talk to the Marquis – he's a dotty old scholar, mummies an' that in his castle, but our vineyards *are* on his land; a chap able to harangue the *obreros* in their own lingo if there's any trouble – but, above all, immune to all this Spanish-civilisation stuff – yes, Simpson, what is it?'

Well, you know what Simpson, the head clerk, is excitedly bringing in.

Glossary Jiggery-Pokery (1)

IT IS EASY to say that nowadays we are deafened by literature, that every basic human emotion has already been dealt with in a past when people could still say 'bright is the ring of words'. Newness is no longer where it ought to be, in the forging of marvellously intimate and accurate language that is not merely about, but mysteriously *is*, the human heart and mind: it is where it ought not to be, externalised in cold space, or in a spectral, somehow irrelevant dance of particles in a cloud-chamber.

And yet, and yet – these splendid human things, words, never quite die. In a curious and subtle way we can see them throbbing with a strange potential life, not so much in literature as in arbitrary collections – dictionaries, glossaries, even mere lists. Two thousand years after Aristotle said that style consisted in the judicious admixture of common and unusual words came the surrealists; and now we can see that common words are unusual, too, if they are in a list.

Let us take a list at random. Here is a list of plastic engraved plates, 6 in. x 1½ in., which may be had from stock from Abbey Craftsmen Ltd.:–

BATHROOM	PLEASE WALK IN
CLOAKROOM	PRIVATE
CONSULTING ROOM	RESERVED
ENQUIRIES	SMOKE ROOM
DINING ROOM	STAFF ONLY
GENTLEMEN	SURGERY
PLEASE SHUT THE GATE	TELEPHONE
KEEP LOCKED	TOILET
Mr. A. N. OTHER, etc.	BREAKFAST
LADIES	PUSH
LOUNGE	PULL
MANAGER	NO EXIT
NO ADMITTANCE	TRADESMEN
OFFICE	BUYER
WAY OUT	ACCOUNTS
WRITING ROOM	ENTRANCE
BED	EXIT
ENGAGED	VACANCIES

Who, reading this, does not immediately have a vague picture of some kind of serious intellectual farce, a combination of Ben Travers with Beckett or Ionescu, with Mr. A. N. Other mysteriously behind locked doors or entering bedrooms, terrible surgeons operating in a smoke-filled room, deaths and entrances?

It follows that in a glossary or thesaurus, where words are assembled in a definite, semi-literary order, this effect of new life in old language is heightened. Now, I have just come across a supreme example. It is called simply *English Glossary*, by E. C. Broeckhoven and O. Praem, and is published in Brussels and Paris. And what it does is to invent an entire new language, as heady and exciting as was English in Shakespeare's time.

Several things contribute to this. The printers, for instance, have invented inspired new words on every page. *Birth-prangs, to blow a heave gale, a squab of men, I feel fiddy, a face long as a friddle, quacksalver, polferer, frisly, frabbergasted, outmeal, naststrong, bossom friend, flappancy;* and, under 'SLEEP – to yawn, to gape, breathing deep and regular, long-drawn. *Retching* and *reaming.*'

It is, however, not only our language that goes through these birth-prangs, shodding skins like a snoke. Our very consciousness of ourselves, as a race, is transfirmed and renowed. We read much about the impact of the East, or of Renaissance Italy, on writers in our Elizabethan prime; but what about this, under 'HATS – A hat, a felt hat, a top hat . . . a velvet hat, a veil, a wimple, a helmet, sallet, kepi, sombrero, derby, bonnet, calash, toque, cap, mobcap, turban, tiara, beretta, mitre, calotte, zucchetto, the brim of a hat, to feel quite at home in it, it is too young, frivelish.' Or, under 'LEARNED – sharp as a needle, a bally intellectual, he has inborn knowledge, all there, he's a twister.' Or this, under 'SCHOOLMASTER – teacher, instructor, schoolmistress, leader, regent, professor, preceptor, pedagogue, abecedarian, academician, a frail, pregnant school-teacher.' (I hope no one suspects that bally intellectual.)

These extraordinary things are fused with normal expressions which really *would* help the foreigner learning our idioms. Thus, under 'ATHLET [sic] – To turn somersaults (culbutes), spring, sprong, sprung . . . *little left winger.*'

In my next piece I shall try to show how this new language, which is the kind of thing that Joyce was looking for, only much more fun, is fitted to be the instrument of a new literature. All I have room for here is an 'accidental poem' which appears word for word, printed exactly as follows, under STAIRS. All I have added is the title

THE BARISTER ON THE LANDING.

Flight of stairs, staircase, the stairs, step, barister, the landing, on
   the landing
A moving staircase, a spiral staircase
Downstairs, upstairs
Lift. The lift well.

Do you not see this barister, rather like J. Alfred Prufrock, indecisive
on the landing, startled by the ironic voice of the poet? Then the sharp
warning cry, *Lift!* in italics – and the awful, final last phrase, the barister
hudled lofeless at the foop of the–
   Watch this space.

Glossary Jiggery-Pokery (2)

I WROTE LAST time about an *English Glossary* published in
Brussels and Paris by E. C. Broeckhoven and O. Praem. Let me
summarise again the means by which this surrealist thesaurus provides
the modern English writer with a whole new language.

   1. *Daring, poetical or Freudian associations of ideas.*
     Here are two typical entries:–
     LIP. – Upper lip, the gums. Lip-stick, ripe lips.
       To bite one's lips, to set one's kips, to osculate, kiss, smack,
       beslobber.
     GREY. – Pink, purple, beige.
     The word *kips*, above, is a good example also of

   2. *Creative misprints.*
     For instance:–
     DESEASES (sic). – To catch cold . . . Fever, feverish, a slite
     fever, to be taken ill, to send for a doctor, to want a tonic, scarlet
     fever, rheumatism, flew. Indigestion . . . I have a pain under my
     pinafore . . . derangement of bile, gale, gall-bladder, secretion of

the liver, bile, gallgall-sickness; gall-bladder (again!). Messles, kidney trouble, epidemics are raging, cancer.

Who has not suffered from the Messles – a vaguely psychosomatic illness involving bad focusing of the eyes, a tired feeling at the back of the neck, a tendency to cut oneself when shaving, a subtle change of the shape of one's body so that clothes suddenly look messy?

3. *New images of ourselves –*
   – both as Englishmen seen by foreigners and simply as human beings viewed from the surrealist consciousness. Thus:–
CRICKET. – Cricket match, a team, a pitch (*le terrain*), the wicket, the stumps (*les guichets*), the wicket keeper, a bat, batting, a batsman, fieldsman, the bowler, to bowl, twister, hole, croquet, he scores no marks, to share the hole, to swing the ball, an over; eight balls, to hit the ball, the ball is being retrieved, the batsman is out, outfield, fine leg, a duck's egg, off, over, out.

This passage should be read aloud, with a shout at *twister*.
SAILOR. – Seaman, mariner, navigator, a son of Neptune, crew, a boatswain, cockswain, steersman, admiral, captain, mate, first mate, squire, to dive, master, cook . . . to go to sea, to bind for . . . to upset a boat, to overtune . . . to immerse in a cliff.

The net result is a new language, wonderfully apt to express the subtle, nervous twentieth-century consciousness; a language for men who see, not exactly a theological order in the world, but a unity which somehow escapes them *but is there;* a language like the paintings of Klee.

Sometimes the taut golden wires jangle with terror (*What is that squire doing on the poop/I dare not look/He has set his kips/O farewell, now shall we be/immersed in the frisly cliff*). Sometimes the style is pure lyricism. The following, exactly as it appears in the *Glossary*, seems to me to combine the joyful cataloguing zest of Whitman with the delicate fixing of the elusive moment that we associate with Chinese poetry:–

INSTRUMENT. – Viol, violin, violoncello, lute, bassoon, banjo, flute (the finger Holes), clarinet, trumpet, saxophone, trombone, tuba, french horn, basset horn, oboe, cor anglais, harp, accordion, guitar, organ, piano. Bagpipe, cornemuse.
The piper.
To play upon an instrument, the dazzling sheen of the instruments, the glittering.
Gong, to bump on a gong.

I should like to make up some more to this:–

> Come, gong-bumpers, bump your gongs
> Flutenists and lautists, set your kips,
> Bong the dram, and boom the bagpips –

– but here, instead, is a poem which I hope justifies the claim that we have in the *Glossary* a new language. Every word is taken from it.

A COUNTRY CHILDHOOD REMEMBERED FROM A BED-SITTING ROOM.

> O once the wind blew southingly
> Gay as a friddle leapt I in the hisky sun,
> Frisly among the dolphins was my fozy love;
> Alas my swang-song! Now I poind away,
> Wretched momentity, among the slotful streets,
> Retching and reaming after outmeals harsch,
> Pocky and boody, overtuned and slite,
> A polferer lost and snar.

But of course this is only the beginning. *We* can invent words, too.

Knight Driving

HOW VERY ODD it must feel to be a peer. Most people are concerned only with being people, but a peer must surely also feel that he is a watershed, a contradiction, a meeting of real and unreal.

The most obvious contradiction is, of course, a socialist peer, a phenomenon of which the British are not sufficiently proud – for here, walking among us on two legs, is a sublime triumph, the Realisation of a Hegelian Idea; muted and far off are the clashing of billhooks and partisans and the revolutionary shouting, forgotten and transcended the irreconcilable European hatreds between cottage and castle, the blood on the barricades; here, in quiet England, is this literally noble fusion. The *socialist* peer. The socialist *peer*. (And, after all, 'peer' means 'equal'.)

But there is a paradox much deeper and subtler than this. Many peers have an air of unreality; they are real, undeniable end-products of ghostly history; the ancient heraldic battlefields somehow seem more real than the actual men, often wearing spectacles, who sit in the House of Lords. They don't represent even a class, they represent History. Modern industrial democracy doesn't quite know what attitude to adopt towards them, it feels embarrassed when it comes to classifying them.

In the *Classification of Occupations*, 1950 (H.M. Stationery Office, 13s.6d.), which gives a list of all the occupations in Britain, peers come right at the end. They come after Code 979 (*All Other and Undefined Occupations*), which includes Articulator of Bones and Skeletons, Cadman (who *he?*), Clock Winder, Jack of All Trades, Maggot Breeder, Marquee Erector, Pavement Artist, Rifle Shooter (what, profession-al?), Synagogue Collector. They come in Code X, right at the end, scornfully called *Other Persons* (*no Gainful Occupation Stated*), and including B. A., Bedesman, Capitalist, Doctor of Philosophy, Gipsy, Lunatic (Trade Not Stated), Page of the Backstairs and Tramp.

Peers are with us and not with us. Never mind what Lloyd George did to them, or what Mr. Bevan intends to do. They are not to be thought of in terms of crude power; yet neither are they really as irrelevant to the nation as all these Lunatics, Bedesmen and Maggot Breeders. There is something *distilled* about peers, a thin concentration of England, an essence almost elfin. House of Lords debates are like a thin, high music, mysterious, never quite unheard, and finally ignored at our peril.

This is what makes peers so fascinating, this is why people queue up to go round peers' houses, almost as though they expected the residents to give off a faint light (as indeed many of them do on television). We can never quite believe that peers are the same as ourselves, despite all the evidence.

The other day I saw, stuck in the windscreen of a 1937-looking beige car, a sort of heraldic badge with the words HOUSE OF LORDS CAR CLUB. Now, we know very well what *ordinary* car clubs do. They have rallies and treasure hunts. They arrange artificial hardships, and later there is laughter in convivial rooms as they recall how old Roy's wife muffed the map-reading, how Geoffrey skidded on the icy road near the check-point in Montgomeryshire and along came this feller who spoke only Welsh . . .

But not the members of *this* club. Inevitably one sees them in a frieze against an opalescent dawn as they set off, a panoply of cars; a kind of medieval London-to-Brighton race. From far off we hear the sound of their horns, like the far call of Roland. Unseen by us, unknown to the A.A. and the R.A.C., they pass through Arthurian woods, they park on a mystical heath, spread with bright flowers and fringed with feathery trees as in a tapestry. Splendid striped pavilions are erected, tables are spread with subtler meats than ever came from Fortnum and Mason.

The fairest débutante of all takes her place as Queen of the Lists, the herald sounds his klaxon, and the Black Knight enters the arena, helmeted, impregnable-seeming in his powerful black Bugatti. There is a roar of applause; then silence, a moment when the crowd catches its breath as the young, unknown challenger appears on his frail Vespa. There is a clicking noise in the loudspeakers, then a stentorian voice echoes over the field:–

> *In God's name, and the king's, say who thou art,*
> *And why thou com'st thus knightly clad on wheels,*
> *Against what man thou com'st, and what thy quarrel . . .*

There is no place for Bedesmen or Capitalists *here*.

Timber in Tension

IN ONE OF Malraux's books (what am I saying? I've only read one, *The Walnut Trees of Altenburg*, so it must be in that) there is a fascinating discussion of the qualities possessed by a *shāman*:–

'A Siberian medicine man, isn't it?'

'Something else besides: Lenin was a great man, but he was not a *shāman*: Trotsky is less great, but he is a *shāman*. Pushkin, Robespierre, Goethe? – not at all *shāmans*. But Dostoievsky, Mirabeau, Hölderlin, Poe; great *shāmans*! There are little *shāmans*: Heine. Napoleon was not a real *shāman*: he believed too much in things. *Shāmans* are to be found among geniuses, and also, of course, among idiots. . .'

A *shāman* is a kind of informal priest. Half the time he doesn't seem to be listening to you, he hears other voices. He has a wandering, unpredictable kinship with clouds and stars. He knows when the crops are going to fail, but doesn't seem to care much.

There are things about a *shāman* that cannot be written down. If you are explicit you are not a *shāman*. Yeats was a *shāman*, Shaw wasn't. Beckett is, Osborne is not (goodness, what a lovely game); the B.B.C. is, I.T.A. is not (although, of course, the B.B.C. has a stated social and philosophical theory, it is *more* explicit than I.T.A. It's not as easy as all that).

Now, I am sure this game of classification could be extended; to cover professions, for instance. A doctor is a *shāman*, a dentist is not. A barrister is, a solicitor is not. And even more mysterious, a carpenter is, a plumber is not.

This is because a carpenter has to do with wood, which is a *shāman* material. All people who have to do with wood are faintly *shāman*. Not for nothing did Chekhov write a play called *The Wood Demon*. There is in Britain this society called The Men of the Trees, calling softly to one another from behind great beeches, disappearing with elvish nods. There are tree *surgeons* ('Tell me, did you ever fall out of one of your patients?' said Groucho to one of them on his TV show. But Groucho is not a *shāman*. Harpo is). I have even seen little vans going about saying simply TREE FELLERS. I always want to hail one and say 'Him feller oak-um belong me topside, him big feller branch you lop-um, savvy?'

The most un-*shāman* thing in the world is an insurance company; and look at the way they go on about wood. My insurance company, who in some way I do not understand, persuaded some *other* company to put up the mortgage on my house, nearly dropped the whole thing when they heard the house was old and full of wood. *Their* ideal house is made entirely of aluminium; they distrust sly, shifting, *shāman* wood, lowest form of organic life, the uneasy base of that pyramid of which the apex is man.

If all this about wood being *shāman* sounds far-fetched, consider this, from the *Carpenter and Joiner*:–

DEFECTS IN TIMBER

1. Deals with wide annual rings should be rejected for good work, also those with *waney* edges.
2. *Knots* are a source of weakness for timber in tension.
3. *Foxiness*, dull red stains, the forerunners of decay (and denoting growth in a marshy soil) generally found in the heart of a tree.
4. *Quagginess*, having the centre full of shakes and clefts.
5. *Cup-* or *ring-shakes* occur between two (consecutive) annual layers.
6. *Rindgall*, surface wounds caused when a tree has been damaged.

81

7. *Doatiness* or *Dotteness*, a disease of a spotted or speckled appearance.

8. *Heart Shake* is a flaw produced by the separation of the fibres.

9. *Upsets*, defects of the grain.

10. *Dry Rot* is the decomposition of the substance of felled timber by the action of certain fungi.

All this simply confirms what any *shāman* could have told us about wood. Shifting about and creaking in the middle of the night, wood is *alive*, it gets the same diseases as men. Go into any saloon bar and you will see, sitting on his regular stool a man suffering from *Foxiness*, complete with dull red stains on his cheeks. Who does not recognise *Quagginess* as the occupational disease of politicians? Who has not known the flat, mid-afternoon state of being *waney*? And it is only necessary to walk down Oxford-street to observe the incidence of *Doatiness* or *Dotteness* among the population.

Some of these wood-illnesses are beneath our human scale (*Rindgall* is probably something that makes sheep feel pretty low, too). Some are communal human ills, like *Doatiness*, a kind of mild mass hallucination. Others, increasingly desperate and tragic like *Heart Shake* or *Upsets*, are private things, at the heart of our sensibility. Wood *knows* about these things.

Let There Be a Fountain

*I*DEA. – Now (1956) that we live in the country, let us clear this overgrown garden and realise the dream of every urban Englishman. Let there be, screened from the Viking winds by rustling trees, this secret plot where thoughts and flowers grow; a *garden*, that marvellous form of man imposed on wild nature; a bright formality of blossom and shrub, a *hortus conclusus* walled in by yew. Let the arithmetic of seasons and the geometry of growth flower into the poetry of petals.

Perhaps, sitting in this tiny classical Mediterranean park, set in the windy flats of East Anglia, I might read and at last understand that other East Anglian, Sir Thomas Browne, and all that stuff about quincunxes ('and contemplating the calicular shafts, and uncous disposure of their extremities, so accommodable unto the office of abstersion, not condemne as wholly improbable the conceit of those who accept it, for the herbe *Borith*.' Wouldn't dreame of condemning it as improbable, but what does it *mean*?). Above all, in the middle of *my* quincunx or lozenge, let there be a fountain.

Fountains no longer an aristocratic luxury. No need for slaves or mules to work bumping creaking machinery, oak beams, huge sodden leather bags, in underground rock tank behind noble villa. Just a fractional h.p. motor, some of that polythene piping. Pick up fountain for a song at some old yard. From sale at Big House up yonder.

REALITY. – Where *are* these old yards? Never seem to pass any. Buy fountain at shop in Euston Road. £25. Little lead boy poised gracefully on one foot. Salesman says model of Verrocchio in Vatican Gardens. (How they got it? Workmen from Euston Road dress up as *monsignori*, get into gardens, Roman summer day, hasty measurements with calipers, pretend to be reading breviary when real *monsignori* come round corner, how explain cassock all wet?) Jolly little green motor, £12, Gamages, heavens, £37 already. Boy holds serpent (Hercules?) round upraised right arm, copper pipe comes out. Fountain attachment, bright brass thing, looks funny till weathered, lead boy holding snake holding brass candlestick. Lawn sown and growing now. Dig it up again to put polythene pipes. Dig huge pit, line with concrete.

IDEA. – Classical lead boy lightly poised, bringing permanent kiss of south to Suffolk garden. Should be on light, inconspicuous pedestal, pillar would be too heavy (anyway, where *get* pillar?). Will make simple concave pedestal; diminishing squares of marble, cemented, then increasing in size again up to base of statue.

REALITY. – Get marble (old washstand). Waste half of it; just when any piece roughly right size, slight hammer tap to remove remaining jagged point breaks it in two. Cement won't stick to marble. Pedestal slowly rises, festooned with drips of cement. Upper part of pedestal top-heavy. Put huge dollop of cement, if press next square of marble too hard, whole thing snaps at thinnest point; if not press, come back next morning and find top square not stuck. Pedestal finally ready April, 1957. Breathlessly put lead boy on. Pedestal snaps again. Ready again June 1957.

Men putting damp course in house cut polythene pipe with spade. Dig lawn up again. Fountain operating September, 1957.

IDEA. – Sit in garden. Dream by tinkling fountain. Find bit of T. Browne I can understand. '. . . of Flying, of Limpid Fountains, smooth

Waters, white Vestments and fruitful green Trees, which are the visions of healthful sleep, and at good distance from the Grave . . .'

REALITY. – Fine when no jet planes like mad blowlamps whanging about Constable sky. And when not raining.

IDEA. – Wonderful for children, remember dreamy garden with fountain when grown up.

REALITY. – Forced to make hideous trap for youngest child, wire-netting over complicated framework leaving hole for lead boy. Idea is to remove it in evening when children in bed, enjoy uncluttered line of pool and fountain again. Child breaks framework. Mend. Child breaks again. Mend. September, 1958, framework catches lead boy when being lifted off. Christmas Eve, 1958, lead boy back again.

IDEA. – Well, older children will remember it.

REALITY. – May, 1959, older child swinging baulk of timber knocks lead boy off and breaks pedestal. Lead boy now has dented head, neck seems shortened, seems to be clutching stomach with non-fountain-holding hand. Pull arm back. Split lead at armpit. Boy looks like mad gargoyle with appendicitis. I have only fountain in world where water comes out of armpit.

The Saucy Black Maria

SURELY ONE OF the most inscrutable groups of men in London is the river police. Of course, *all* police have this odd, shut-away side, this private life of rank and hierarchy. They hold brief inspections, officers with black moustaches, (there is a police moustache, different from both the Army and the R.A.F. varieties), carrying gloves, inspect rows of men at attention. There is no shouting or marking time, it is all done quickly, casually behind some building, in some semi-private field, when they think the public isn't looking.

Their uniforms indicate only the Shakespearean ranks – captain, sergeant, constable; you never hear of a police-major or a police-corporal, these suggest some Latin republic in the nineteenth century. There is something elusive about police rank. Is a police captain a *real* captain, with those chromium-looking stars?* It seems halfway between the real and the metaphorical, the Army and the Salvation Army.

But it is tremendously real to the police themselves, in that inward-looking side of their life (they do not hate us or love us, they are just different. They have marvellously confraternal meetings with foreign policemen; they don't feel different from *them* at all, even if they wear swords or pick their teeth or take bribes. They have the same moustaches. You couldn't have Interarm or Internay – look at the Nato squabbles – but Interpol has been working harmoniously for years). And it would be nice to think that the river police are only a kind of internal function, that they don't actually arrest pirates or smugglers, or even look out for them, but simply bring this rank business to a secret and perfect conclusion, with police-commodores gravely, silently saluting a police-admiral, in a mysterious marine dance, on some hidden stretch of the river, Policeman's Reach.

Yet of course real action is instantly suggested by their boats, which embody an odd contrast between rakish lines, hinted-at powerful engines – and a lot of varnish and glass, a superstructure that seems to be made of office partitions; enclosed, impersonal, a tiny police station on water. More often than not these boats seem to be moored, empty, locked-looking, near some jolly trippers' pier at some such place as Charing Cross.

Where have the occupants gone? One imagines impossible dialogues. *Head her a point to starb'd. Aye aye, sir. Steady as she goes. We'll make a landfall at Charing Cross and head those scoundrels off*. Or one sees them, sunburnt, lean, carrying reports into Bow Street or Savile Row stations with a rolling gait, slightly envied by the pale land-policemen at their humdrum desks. Perhaps there are even river police shanties —

> I'll tell you the tale of Inspector Brown
> *Haul, haul away O!*
>
> He sailed the canal to Camden Town
> *Way, haul away O! etc.*

But the fact is, one can't imagine the sort of crime that police deal with (as opposed to Customs men or Board of Trade officials) happening actually *on* the river. Surely it is all in mysterious buildings bordering it. The furtive figure in the fog, the shadows in the warehouse, the creaking steps, the hoarse whisper, *Here come liver policey-men. Open tlap door* (kersplash). *Good evening, Inspector. It's all*

No. I've checked. He's a Chief Inspector.

up, *Fan Tan, we've got your master Van Klompers. So, Inspector?* LOOK OUT, SIR! . . . all this seems to require ordinary land-policemen, in glittering capes, waiting under piers, softly blowing whistles at Wapping Stairs.

If, on the other hand, we are in Hammond Innes country, spies escaping abroad in fast launches, surely there would be signals to the Nore, slim grey shapes would nose out from Chatham, it would be a job for the Navy. Unless, of course, these river police managed to head them *up river. I'll open her up when we get past Tilbury. Flat calm forecast. Get me to K5 in Antwerp in six hours, there's 50,000 Swiss francs for you. Ahoy there, I have a warrant for your arrest. Curses. Hard about. We'll give them the slip at Henley Lock, there's an Auster in the meadow . . . Dash it, Henderson, what are all those Chinese fellers doin' in the club boathouse?* . . .

But I had regretfully to dismiss all these fantasies and to think of the river police as just roaring up and down and looking inscrutable, when I saw with my own eyes the following message scrawled on a Martini advertisement at the Monument Tube Station:–

SCOTT TO THE RIVER
RED-HEAD SEMI-COMA

I wish I'd been at Charing Cross when the river policemen, called from their bunks in some shed hidden under the bridge by a terse radio message *Scott B4*, dashed down the steps, whipped off tarpaulins and roared away. I hope they got to Red-head in time.

Freddo Ma Non Troppo

THERE IS SOMETHING about any hotel, even when you are paying your own money to stay in it, that reminds you of man's condition as but a stranger and a sojourner here. The far-off laughing of maids at the ends of corridors; the strange lonely emptiness of the bedroom; the travesty of domestic slippered ease in the lounge (everyone relaxed but wakeful, afraid of snoring); the young fattish bespectacled men in dark suits whispering behind glass, looking up briefly at you – all this makes you want to go out, into the unknown city.

You share more life with the anonymous crowds on its pavements than you ever do with your withdrawn hotel 'hosts', mysterious behind green baize, lattice bars, doors marked PRIVATE.

This feeling, I discovered recently, is even stronger when you are merely *lent* a room in an hotel, 'to freshen up'. I was one of a party – a planeload from London, a busload in Italy, of journalists, M.P.s, specialists in this and that, a few wives. We had been trundling through the marvellous Alps all day; in twenty minutes there would be this official dinner.

Twenty minutes. I opened the shutters. We were still quite high up. A wide valley sloped away, filled with a sound of water falling, in a coldish spring dusk. What on earth was I doing in Italy, in this beautiful hotel? How quiet it seemed. Where were the rest of the party? Suppose they were all dead, suppose I went down to Reception and they said '*What* party?', suppose London disappeared, suppose England fell into the sea, suppose all the aeroplanes in the world suddenly wouldn't fly, suppose a voice spoke from the clouds (yet somewhere, in this sky, in these mountains, in this hotel, in a cupboard, in a little box, was the Meaning of Life, that's the effect hotels have on me) . . .

Well, presumably I must have a bath, although this always seems silly when one is going to put on exactly the same clothes again; a mad solitary ritual, in an hotel. Besides, when I examined the elegant little room adjoining the bedroom (spotless, warm, towels, blue terrazzo floor, a room in a room in an hotel) I saw there wasn't a bath; only a shower.

I had an odd feeling the real guest would come into the bedroom, saying how dare I undress in here and rumple his bed. He would be smarter than me, too, more efficient with this idiotic shower. It was the kind that squirtles sideways as well as down; most of the water spattered furiously at the plastic curtain I hastily pulled round it.

Then I had to open the curtain again to get at the taps in the wall. F and C, Freddo and Caldo. I always think of them as two Italian young men, terrific friends; Freddo rather boyish, freckled, Caldo smooth, saturnine, withdrawn. This is to avoid the confusion of thinking of them as Coldo and Hotto, because of course *Caldo* is Hotto. (Also, lurking in the background, Bishop Hatto.) The trouble was that both taps were coldo (or freddo) for a long time; when the hotto (or caldo) at last came through there was already a lot of water on the blue terrazzo floor, having squirtled out through the gap in the curtain; but the moment I turned back the freddo (or coldo) to reduce volume the shower became scaldingo; then I turned the caldo down, and I was back where I started, with freezingo.

Another maddening thing about a shower is that you have to do all this adjusting twice. First I got this damned freddo and caldo right,

87

then I got in to get wet, then I got out to apply the soap, and had to turn it off while I did so because there was now an alarming lot of water on the floor. Then I adjusted the caldo and freddo all over again. I drew the curtain round as quickly and as closely as I could, I was practically wearing it. I desoaped absolutely as quickly as possible, soap went in my eyes; but when I came out there was an appalling flood; half an inch of water, lapping at the walls.

Surely it wasn't meant to do this? Or was one *supposed* to wet the floor, could this shut-looking little brass affair let into the terrazzo be some subtle modern sort of plug, styled by Farina? Perhaps I could lever it open with a 100-lire piece. No, stay, this might let the water into some room below, down the electric fittings on to a sumptuous bed perhaps. And anyway, there, indubitably, was the drain right under the shower. I tried swooshing the water back but it wouldn't go over the little three-inch wall (ah, I saw it all now, you had to keep the bottom of the curtain inside this little wall. But how? You couldn't get in and draw the curtain until you had got Caldo and Freddo right).

Heavens, the twenty minutes must be up by now. But I must do something, perhaps the terrazzo wasn't even meant to be waterproof, perhaps it was all seeping, horrors, through the ceiling, like indoor rain, on to this sumptuous bed where some *marchesa* was taking a rest, wearing dark glasses. She would scream, ring bells, point volubly to the ceiling, managers in dark glasses would come thundering on my door. . .

At this point my underwear, which had been on the little cork-topped stool, fell off into the water. It was the kind of solution which occurs to problems in hotels, if mopping up five gallons of water with some underwear, squeezing it out into a basin, taking some paper from a chest of drawers and making a damp parcel with it, leaving it at Reception, and eating an official dinner without any underwear on can be called a solution.

Label by Appointment

THERE IS SOMETHING very mysterious about those cast-iron notice boards with lettering in relief which are found, sometimes round, sometimes diamond-shaped, sometimes oblong, at the ends of decaying lanes, by hump-backed canal bridges and obscure level crossings, on tarred fences in abandoned docks, on weedy disused embankments. They belong to an earlier technology than ours, which has now become a subtle, baffling, *indoor* thing, with many little secret grey boxes, transistorised, resisting the amateur screwdriver. They belong to a masculine Victorian spring morning of mechanics; puffs of white steam in a blue sky, the ring of shovels, men in oilskins on windy nights, creaking signals, new cast-iron piers in high tides, tarred planking – the immense solid brand-new Railway itself. Dusty, unread, obscured by tall grass and purple flowers, these notices remember Brunel, even Brindley.

In an age of curious streamlined scrimping – plastic instead of leather, driving-licence holders buff cardboard instead of the good old red cloth (still got mine, boast boast), those new £ notes – they have a lordliness, a lavishness. The people who made them had plenty of time and money to spare, on funny little fusty compartments for Ladies in trains, on complicated park railings, on huge chairs and sideboards with claw feet, on the immense diversification of pubs into many bars separated by scrolled wood and glass, made once only.

The cast-iron notice is the supreme example of this, pushed to the point of paradox; for really it is the *opposite* of printing. Instead of an expensive printing plate containing the letters in reverse, which is then inked and produces many cheap copies (for such was Gutenberg's revolutionary idea), this thing has the letters the right way round; there is only one of it. If you used it for printing everything would come out backwards (except in the case of the word CHIDEOCK. If you print CHIDEOCK on a piece of thin paper which is then held against the light upside-down, it comes out the same, CHIDEOCK. It is a village in Dorset with a population of 800. However.).

Even in its first career, industrialism has never been quite so cavalier about economic realities as this, and I have always suspected that these notices came from an older, *pre*-industrial source. I now claim to have discovered this.

The other evening, walking among the loud silence of reeds where a Suffolk river melts into the sea, I came to a climactic point, a human statement of concrete and sluices, iron rails and rusty cog-wheels, a reminder on the calm summer evening of the roaring winter floods. Behind me England; lamp-posts, policemen, electric kettles, news-agents, maternity wards, factories. In front of me, vague flats, mud, the sea, Nothing. And there was one of these things. It said, in part, BYE-LAWS . . . PROVIDE, INTER ALIA, THAT ANY PERSON INTERFERING WITH OR DAMAGING ANY LAND DRAIN-AGE WORK, INCLUDING SEA OR RIVER WALLS, SLUICES OR WATERCOURSES . . . IS LIABLE . . . TO A FINE NOT EXCEEDING £20 AND A FURTHER FINE OF £5 FOR EVERY DAY ON WHICH THE OFFENCE IS COMMITTED OR CON-TINUED.

And ah, in the bottom left-hand corner it said, I swear, ROYAL LABEL FACTORY.

This explains everything – the marvellously unpractical, out-of-date wording, the assumption that the kind of people who damage watercourses know what *inter alia* means. At first I saw cloaked figures at night with crowbars (spades? Ferrets? Gunpowder? How *do* you damage a watercourse?), holding dim lanterns up to read the notice.

'That don't say noathen about *night*, Jem. Lookit, five pun for every *day*. Hur hur. What be thisyer *inter alia* then? Har, that be Squire's Latin, us can't read un, hur hur.'

But perhaps they *do* know Latin; perhaps damaging sluices is a weird compulsion neurosis that affects overworked scientists. *It's no good, Phoebe, I've struggled against it, but I can't break the sequence, I MUST go down and damage another sluice, this will be the seventh consecutive day* . . .

But these magic words, ROYAL LABEL FACTORY, I now see, must surely refer to some forgotten sinecure, some aristocratic privilege, some survival like the Pipe of Green Wax or the Elizabethan printing monopolies, that has escaped reform. The Master of the Labels was a job created by Charles II to reward some loyal Royalist; or perhaps it was a job in even earlier times for some royal bastard.

In the Royal Label Factory, hidden away behind Woolwich Arsenal, perhaps, full of antique Caxton presses, there was, as technology advanced, an increasing gap between the actual printing staff and the Master, who would either be a decadent foppish dandy or a red-faced hunting man.

'Cast iron! Damme, what'll you fellers think of next?' such a one might say, on one of his grudging visits to the factory, to the Royal Label Foreman-Sergeant; he would sign the indent without reading it

90

properly, and go back to the Pytcheley. But his son, a weedy scholar, would take an eccentric and embarrassing interest in the proceedings, writing the notices himself, insisting that the letters were not reversed. 'I think they're *b-b-beautiful* things, we m-must p-p-put them up *just* as th-they are . . .'

It is a pleasant picture. I was quite disappointed, on the only occasion when I have actually telephoned Buckingham Palace and spoken to a Spokesman, to find that it's simply not true.

⚬⚭⚬

The Unthinkable Carrier

John o'Groats, South Atlantic, November 13, 2000.

STRANGE TO THINK, as one sits under the palm trees gazing at the dolphins in the calm blue waters, how nonsensical that dateline would have seemed in 1960. Strange, also, to realise, amid the happy laughter of our children as the world looks forward eagerly to this most wonderful of all centuries, that less than forty years ago the world was racked by the fear of war. Although the British still knew in their hearts that they were the only people in the world with any common sense (except for that curious aberration at Suez), not many of us said so out loud, feeling that we had lost our nineteenth century power of imposing this common sense on the world through the Pax Britannica.

Economically, Britain stood hesitating between a Commonwealth with dwindling Imperial Preference and a Common Market run by foreigners with peculiar ideas on the Congo, Algeria, the Polish frontier. An election was fought on the issue of 'a telly in every garage', while America and Russia made bigger and bigger missiles. There seemed to be no leadership, and . . .

. . . and all the time we were working secretly on this superb plan which has brought the world its ardently-desired peace.

The scientific committee set up in the last days of the Churchill Government to investigate the possibilities of making Britain float began with three great advantages.

91

1. *So much of the work had been done already.* The task of cutting Britain loose from the solid earth was a logical follow-up of our advantage in a long history of mining from the Phoenicians in Cornwall to all that modern coal-and-iron-getting at which we, as pioneers of the Industrial Revolution, had worked longer than any other country. Mining, as Lewis Mumford points out, is, in German, *Abbau* or unbuilding: and the committee found that what with the Cheddar caves, the Yorkshire and Derbyshire potholes, and all these mines, there were already enough 'unbuilt' parts of Britain for it to be feasible to join them all up and fit them with buoyancy tanks.

2. *Britain's early lead in atomic know-how.* It was widely thought at the time that this, dating from Rutherford's Cambridge experiments, had been lost to Russia and America. But the world learnt otherwise on that extraordinary day in June, 1966, when Britain, propelled by the giant atomic engines strategically mounted round her coastline, moved majestically towards the South Atlantic. The essential secrecy was greatly helped by

3. *The absence of a 'middle-class' in scientific knowledge.* Science in Britain has always been sharply divided into geniuses and an uncaring general public. The former were all 'in the know'. The latter were easily lulled by all kinds of explanations of such preparations as could not be hidden. They were perfectly ready to believe that the engines were 'atomic power stations', even though there was plenty of power already and the huge gaunt buildings were all on marshy desolate coasts far from any possible *demand* for power.

The vast establishment at Harwell was explained away by ingenious stories of 'peaceful application of H-power', complete with handouts about temperatures much hotter than the sun obtained for *millionths of a second* (!) in little glass things. There were even photographs of a circular wooden fantasy (made by a Harwell carpenter) mysteriously called *Zeta*.

The increasingly frequent window-rattling explosions as the un-building was hurried forward with atomic blasting were explained as 'aircraft breaking the sound barrier'; the public were easily convinced that sound travels at over 700 miles an hour, whereas anyone who has observed, say, the time between flash and report of a gun on a quite small sports field might have guessed that in fact it travels very slowly (15.27 miles an hour, in fact). Even the littering of the country with huge machines plainly marked EARTH MOVER only suggested road making.

Now Britain enjoys this scientific extension of her traditional balance-of-power policy, and the world's peace is no longer at the mercy of a few cross-looking American admirals or Russian generals. The world knows that any missile, instantly detected by British radar, would automatically set off the Ultimate Weapon – a 'full speed ahead' order to our mighty atomic engines, causing the country to leap forward at 800 knots and make a tidal wave that only we should survive. Much more than in the nineteenth century, Britain now *is* the British Fleet.

The fears of the Isle of Wight that the tow-chain might break, or the island be used simply to carry the luggage, have long since disappeared (and how happy Ireland, in this Jubilee Year of her President, Dame Siobhan McKenna, now feels as the only island off Europe!). By careful course-plotting we are able to have three crop-growing seasons a year, and we have become a net exporter of food.

The off-shore coal and iron mining rights we have maintained in the old sea area we occupied for so long bring in huge revenues. Our own output, now that the industrial strife of the past, attributed by psychologists to the 'Old Climate', is just a memory, flourishes in the clean air of our healthy sub-tropical climate, which has also made the wonderful sandy beaches of the Northumberland Riviera one of the world's great tourist centres. Our currency is the hardest in the world . . .

But we should not be too complacent. Our agreement with Japan, whereby she, under licence keeps the Pacific peace as we keep the Atlantic, has worked splendidly. But we may not always keep this technical lead. There are rumours of an imminent German-inspired break-off of Spain from Europe, and China is known to be experimenting with Korea. A world in which every country was a giant marine nuclear dodgem would be a horrifying thought, reviving the worst fears of the sixties. No doubt, however, Britain would come up with a solution. She usually does.

The Cheesechase Chore

ACCORDING TO THE Resistentialist philosophy of Pierre-Marie Ventre (*'les choses sont contre nous'*) the 'total' logical course for man is to accept the hostility of the physical world; not to diffuse his energies in open combat in activity in areas where the World-Thing (*dernière chose*, the Ultimate Thing) is explicitly against him, but to search, as unobtrusively as possible, for areas where the World-Thing-Process (Ventre's term) has not yet evolved to 'total thingness' – i.e., where some illusory freedom for man is still possible.

Yet such is man's dual nature that he sometimes fights on in these hopeless 'Thing-areas' – indeed some Resistentialists see in this a kind of perverse and irrational glory.

Blackcurrants are in the Thing-area for me. The World-Thing-Process has evolved to consciousness of any desire to grow blackcurrants. It employs special birds with steel beaks that can bite wire. Like commandos, they make breaches in my fruit cage, through which the infantry then pour. I say infantry because they do indeed come on foot; in fact they waddle, they climb heavily up the bushes. They can't fly, they're too full of blackcurrants.

Or the World-Thing, with its infinite resources in chaos and destruction of form, may take the currants away even before the birds can eat them. One year it invented a joke disease called Big Bud. *Big Bud is watching you, Jennings*, it said, and presently brussels sprouts, or so they seemed, began to appear on the bushes, in March.

Nevertheless (O, the glory of man!) this year I got *two pounds* of blackcurrants (there are 537,590 blackcurrants in two pounds. They go down). I mended the wire, I made an awful semi-man of cushions, called Little Bud, and put him in the fruit cage. I walked in it carrying a bored cat (called William Byrd; he couldn't care less, he only eats partridges and toast). There would be strange confrontations in the cage; myself, Little Bud, these birds flapping heavily against the wire (I couldn't even throw anything at them because of all the foliage). They were too drunk to find the holes where they had come in. I stared at them, they stared at me, Little Bud stared at all of us, he seemed to be on their side. In the end I simply held the door open like an attendant, and they lurched out

All the same, on a hot day I picked these two pounds. There is something about currants, in summer; a madness, they're halfway to grapes. I have always remembered that old man in the film 'The Grapes of Wrath' who wanted to rub the grapes over his face, to squash the juice out, in the sun, to *be* the grapes. Somewhere there are dusky dances, cymbals, sweat, thirst-madness, bloody juice, communion in a blazing noonday . . .

. . . and the next day, getting this great bowl of two pounds of blackcurrants out of the refrigerator, I knocked a saucer of grated cheese off a higher shelf, or rather the cheese *dived* on to the blackcurrants. I had a bowl of blackcurrants and cheese.

I had come too far by now to give up these blackcurrants, MY blackcurrants, to the World-Thing-Process. I had a confused idea that science would help (according to Ventre science is a supreme Resistentialist irony; man deludes himself into thinking he controls Things, whereas Things – the motor-car, the aeroplane, and now the Bomb – more and more control him).

I remembered those experiments where you rubbed glass rods with – heavens, what was it, some special stuff, fur, leather, cottonwool? – and they acquired an electrostatic charge, they attracted bits of paper (or were they *amber* rods; 'electricity' comes from the Greek *electron*, amber, how odd. Where do you get amber rods?). Perhaps I could make a sort of cheese-magnet. I experimented with a glass rod (thermometer), a plastic rod (perch from toy birdcage), a steel rod (knitting needle), a wooden rod (spoon), rubbed furiously with every kind of textile. I can state categorically that *nothing* attracts cheese.

Then I thought, surely cheese and blackcurrants would have different specific gravities, or differential mass, or whatever the fool thing is called. I added water to the bowl, somehow expecting the blackcurrants to float and the cheese to sink (then I would do something crafty with muslin). Actually the cheese rose, it whirled about in a kind of cheese snowstorm until the tap stopped, then it all settled down and got right in among the lower blackcurrants as well, instead of just lying on the top; and now it was *bonded* to the currants with water.

Also there now seemed to be more cheese, and less blackcurrants, (Cheese does do this. You can *create* cheese in a grater, more comes out than you put in; once thus encouraged, it begins to grow.) And suppose some of the cheese dissolved in the water, encapsulating each currant in a film of cheese? There would be no hope then.

In the end, of course, I had to wash each blackcurrant separately (although they now occupied less space the two pounds now contained 637,948 blackcurrants); an operation best performed by a three-handed man – one hand dipping palmsful of cheesy blackcurrants into a bowl of water, the second picking out individual blackcurrants, the thumb and

95

finger of the third taking off the cheese. But surely, it might be asked, it would be easier simply to hold each palmful under the tap.

Not with us it wouldn't. If you run the tap like that for long you have to start *rodding out drains*. I'm afraid Ventre is right.

Red-blooded $\frac{3}{4}$ rose

THERE WAS ONCE an article on this very page by Dr. Bronowski in which he said that mathematics ought to be taught as a language. At the time I had fantasies of passages like this:-

'It is time (the Government)^2 up to the situation. On >1 issue $\frac{\text{the country}}{2}$, and unless they treat the Opposition as $=$ in hammering out a bipartisan policy they will not get to $\sqrt{\text{our troubles}}$. All the omens .2 trouble in the Middle East . . .'*

But of course that wasn't the idea at all. Years ago I got off the mathematics train at Quadratic Equations – a neat, airy little station with trellis, ivy, roses, a sunlit platform. There was just a hint of weirdness now and then – the stationmaster made clicking noises in his throat, there was an occasional far-off harmonious humming in the sky, strange bells rang; one knew the frontier was not far away, where the line crosses into the vast country of Incomprehensibility, the jagged peaks of the Calculus Mountains standing up, a day's journey over its illimitable plains.

The train thundered off into those no doubt, exhilarating spaces, but without me. I sniffed the mountainy air a little, then I crossed the line

---

* Crib for art students, beatniks, peasants:
(The Government)^2: the Government squared.
>1: more than one.
$=$: equals.
$\sqrt{\text{our troubles}}$: the root of our troubles.
.2: point two recurring.

96

by the footbridge and went back in a fusty suburban train to my home town, Contemptible Ignorance. This train had no engine; it was simply a train of carriages, rolling gently down through the warm orchards of Amnesia Hill.

The only language we speak in that town is, well, language (we're not *mad* about it like those people at Oxford; we know the world is infinite and real, language is about it, it isn't *it*). But we have got typewriters, and they introduce mathematics into language in their own way. Even without those figures on the top row, 1 to 9 (all you need) there is something *statistical* about the typewriter as it sits there. It contains instantaneously the entire alphabet, the awful pregnant potentiality of everything. I am certain most readers of this article will have read somewhere or other a reference to the odds against a monkey's sitting at a typewriter and writing 'Hamlet'.

For some reason philosophical writers about chance, design and purpose are led irresistibly to this analogy. Nobody ever suggests the monkey's writing 'Hamlet' with a pen, as Shakespeare did. With a pen the monkey would get distracted, draw funny faces, found a school of poetry of its own. There's something about having the whole alphabet in front of it, on a machine, that goads the monkey to go on, for *millions* of years (but surely evolution would be quicker?), persevering after heartbreaking setbacks; think of getting the whole of 'King Lear' right until it came to the lines over the dead body of Cordelia, which would come out:–

> *Thou'lt come no more*
> *Never, never, never, never, ever,*

– or, on *my* typewriter –

> *Necer, neved, lever, nexelm vrevney.*

The typewriter knows very well how to mix language and mathematics, the resources between A and Z and 1 and 9, in its own sly way. Mine likes to put $\frac{3}{4}$ instead of the letter p. How brilliantly this introduces a nuance, a *frisson* of chance and doubt into many words that begin so well with this confident, explosive consonant! How often is one disappointed by a watery $\frac{3}{4}$ale ale! How often does some much-publicised meeting of statesmen result in the signing of something that the typists of both sides know is just a $\frac{3}{4}$act! How many $\frac{3}{4}$apists one knows! How many people praised for their courage are not so much plucky as just $\frac{3}{4}$lucky.

Most of all, is not the most common form of social occasion to-day the cocktail $\frac{3}{4}$arty? One always goes expecting a real party, but nine times out of ten it turns out to be a $\frac{3}{4}$arty; all the people there have some sort of connection with the '$\frac{3}{4}$' arts such as advertising, films, news$\frac{3}{4}$apers – although there is often a real $\frac{3}{4}$ainter or two. After a few $\frac{3}{4}$ink gins one of the $\frac{3}{4}$ainters makes a $\frac{3}{4}$ass at one of those strange silent girls, with long hair and sullen $\frac{3}{4}$outing lips, that one always sees at $\frac{3}{4}$arties (doubtless he thinks she will be $\frac{3}{4}$liable). There may be some V.I.$\frac{1}{4}$. (on my typewriter the capital $\frac{3}{4}$ is a $\frac{1}{4}$)* as the chief guest – an M.$\frac{1}{4}$., or a fashionable $\frac{3}{4}$reacher (nothing so grand as the $\frac{1}{4}$rime Minister, of course. Guests like that are only at real parties, given by Top $\frac{1}{4}$eople); but at a $\frac{3}{4}$arty it is always difficult to get the interesting guest to himself, to $\frac{3}{4}$in him down in an argument, because of the $\frac{3}{4}$rattle going on all round.

Of course this isn't mathematical language in Dr. Bronowski's sense. But you've got to admit it's figurative.

* *That's mathematics for you, I have an obscure feeling it should be either $\frac{9}{16}$ or $1\frac{1}{2}$.*

They laughed when . . .

THE ELEGANT MODERN concert hall was packed. A rather insignificant-looking little man came on, bowing happily and nervously as the audience roared its applause. When it had died down he said, 'I should like – *goodness*, how I should like – to play you Chopin's *Première Ballade*.' He sat down at the beautiful Steinway, and then began the most fantastic public performance I have ever heard.

Technically the music was wildly beyond him; yet there was an extraordinary *rapport* between him and the audience, to whom he spoke in confidential asides, in the manner of Pachmann. At the very third bar of the quite simple opening statement in octaves, *largo*, his left hand began playing at an interval of a ninth instead of an octave. 'Damn, I always make that mistake,' he said. When the great A major melody arrived, he first played the left hand alone, then the right, saying, 'Then you get this glorious melody on top.' Cadenzas and chromatic runs he played *adagio* ('it goes like this, only faster'). The whole thing was a curious outline of this famous piece, like a giant's skeleton seen through bottle glass. He ended on a very loud (and for once correct) G minor chord.

The audience gave him a standing ovation. Afterwards, at a reception in his honour, I heard a lovely girl say, 'It wasn't only your playing, it was the insight of your remarks that gave me a new view of the music.'

My companion, a close-cropped, handsome woman in her early fifties, nodded approval. 'One of our easier successes,' she said. 'This man's report showed he had a strain of brutal sarcasm, exercised increasingly on his wife and two children, threatening to break up the family. We found he was a frustrated pianist. A couple of weeks at this Admiration Centre will put him right. "They laughed when I sat down to play," as your English proverb has it; but here they *admire* him, as you've seen. He'll leave here all sweetness and light.'

The speaker was Dr. Anna List, whose work as founder of the Admiration Centre movement is drawing social workers and penologists from all over the world. It has, of course, long been known that a great deal of crime and neurosis (to Dr. List practically interchangeable terms, as they were in *Erewhon*) stems from the frustration of the universal desire to be admired. But until Dr. List's pioneering work the attitude of society was a hopeless acceptance of the iron laws of heredity, environment and pure chance which make some people admirable and others not.

'There used to be a lot of truth,' she told me, 'in that joke about the psychiatrist who said to his patient, "My dear sir, I'm afraid I can't cure you. You haven't got a complex, you really *are* inferior." But we hope we are altering all that. Basically the secret lies in two things. The admiration must, of course, be genuine; and there must be specialisation.

'Let me tell you about the specialisation first. This particular Admiration Centre is, of course, for music – all kinds, instrumental and vocal. It has a permanent staff of 300 Admirers. There's a similar one for the plastic arts about a dozen miles from here; not such a large staff there, just enough to fill a biggish studio-cum-gallery.

'But most of the other thirty-seven are General Admiration Centres. Not everyone wants to be admired for anything so specific as playing the piano. Nevertheless there are three rough subdivisions: Moral, Witty and Physical. These are the basic desires: to be admired because you are more generous, brave or honest than the Admirer; because you are more amusing, a gayer companion; or (for men) simply a better fighter with better muscles or (for women) more beautiful.'

'Naturally these categories usually overlap. To be admired for being brave often involves both the Moral and the Physical. Certain types of Witty admirees (as we call them) are proud of being *not* brave; and so on. Each case is different, but by now we have built up such a varied staff of Admirers that we can fit any individual, from the complex personality who wishes to be admired simultaneously as Moral, Witty and Physical to the simple, well-set-up lad (I think we can claim to have saved hundreds of them from turning into petty thugs) who merely wants to show off his muscles. In his case our staff often have to let themselves be beaten up.'

'It sounds miraculous,' I said, 'But where do you *get* your staff?'

'Ah, that's the beauty of it – and they're all genuine Admirers,' said Dr. List, the light of the pioneer enthusiast in her eyes. 'The staff of Admirers are people who couldn't get a pass at any of our Centres. No matter how much they were praised, they still know that they were so cowardly, unwitty, weedy, and so on, that they would never be any good. This makes their admiration genuine, but it does not sap their own self-respect because in our country it is a great honour to be an official Admirer. Of course they get certain material privileges – they receive high salaries and pay no income tax – but most of all they, too, are admired as devoted public servants of a system that has emptied our prisons and is fast emptying our hospitals.'

I learned much more from Dr. List; of the highly organised follow-up system – letters to admirees telling how their prowess is still remembered, the placing of laudatory reviews and news items; the special Travelling Admirers (our returned pianist, struggling with his Chopin again at home, might hear a knock on his door, a man with dark glasses on the doorstep would say, in a foreign accent, 'Blease to podden me, I am walking down ze street and I am hearing zis *so* beautifool masterplaying . . .'). I learnt of the ambitious plans to operate the scheme not only for individuals but for nations. 'Some whole countries,' said Dr. List with a twinkle, 'have dangerous inferiority complexes.' And I came away utterly convinced that this great woman has an idea which could save the world.

Waiting for Ulysses

SAMUEL BECKETT WAS once James Joyce's secretary. Is this how it went?

Joyce: Take a letter *a latere dextro*, righthand shorthand lefthand. O calloo callay calligraphy, concatenate with curlicues and peripatetic pothooks, adorable mandoodling on the virgin page, blotting her nymphant shamus. To the Editor, *Transitions*; dear sir or madam, *re* Joyce in the lord, our reference your reverence (Father of) our latterletter. Pencilpoised, or tappingly trip, trippingly tap the tripewriter. *In principio erat verbum –*

Beckett: There's no paper.

Joyce: Ah, then it must be Sunday: we are de-pressed, but newyorksunday is in his western high, or the heraldtribulation sings. See his glinting mirrormail farfreeglancing on the Horizon, see Cyril con a lea in the gardens of the west, later chronicletimes till the evening Star decline in the west, untergangler spengles his spangled miss under Standard rose by yonder burbling beaverbrook to follow her swansong liederwriter.

Beckett: There's no paper. Fogg said he would bring some. Many years ago. *There's no paper, Fogg, I said*. He may have gone to get some.

Joyce: Which fog was that, witch? On a brumestick she strides the murky mistery of man, meaning awhirl in the blackdown blacknight freefall, her voicebells booming in the brumy air. O seasick omnes in that Void, wanton the fog to clearabell meaning!

Beckett: Fogg went away. He may have gone to get paper. I don't know.

Joyce: Then we'll skip the scratchpen scribbling, scratch our scribing. We'll use the obiter-dictaphone, grave the word in a waxen image with our tapewriter electroloquacity. Marvellous mouthpiece into the vulvular valves and filigree filaments of it, the ambient lamps and lambent amps dancing a *coranto*, the English current jargoning into waxwords. Or tape, is it? Or wax *disce puer*? Er, h'rrrm, h'rrrm. Testing testing. To the Editor, *Transitions; re* Joyce in the lord, a greeting and message as it flies by my crow phone –

Beckett: Some say that's a wax machine, some say it wanes. Or it may be tape, which is neither. But there's no tape, of course. Krapp took the last one. Ah, you can talk to that machine. I've talked to it for hours, for years. But it never says a thing back. Krapp, he knew how it worked.

But he's gone. He knew where Fogg went, he went after him. Sometimes I think he left a message for me in that machine. Sometimes I look for paper myself (you remember, we wanted paper), sometimes I juggle the dials every which way on that machine, hoping for the voice of Krapp. Or Fogg.

(*as he twiddles the knobs on the machine there is a sudden burst of marvellous music from it*)

Joyce: O sole mio tesoro, andante an Beatrice! O fatale Don Jove-annie Lauritz Melchoir! Moomy minims, maximum cluster-crotchets quavering in music's steepclouds! There's an errant clearabell voice clear and goldivox populi, arialleluias lovely in larynx of bassopranoperalto, heldentenor in a score of wunderbars riposting to a sweetish nightingale, with Orpheus O'Grady at the panharmonium and royalty in his red-plush stalls. Swooning sighstrings to his reedplaint till suddenly all's clear in a brassburst thunderclap on the lightning conductor of the bee bee sea seem funny orchestra.

Beckett: That wasn't Fogg. Or Krapp. They weren't musicians.

Joyce: Pigeonpost it then, a loftletter fluttering through chancy airs, highflown pigeonenglish by birdleg wing high o'er the western wave. To the Editor, *Transitions* –

Beckett: You'd still want paper. There isn't enough here to go round a pigeon's leg. Fogg went to get paper, years ago. Every day since then I have wanted to write letters, marvellous letters. But there was no paper to write them on. Every day I sharpened my pencil some more, till now it's only a little bit of a thing.

(*shouting fiercely at sky*)

D'ye hear me? I'm here, waiting to write with me little bit of a pencil, before the stars go out.

Joyce: We must wait till Fogg comes back.

(*Beckett stares at him*)

No Fogg, no paper. It's a pity, though, that they weren't musicians. Fogg on the flute, Krapp on the violin. We'd hear their music, drawing nearer, as they came back, perhaps with paper . . .

(*pause*)

Beckett: Ah, and then what a stirring stringsong tirralee triumphonium, the fillfluter's divine windrush afflatus! Ah the fillharmonious ball of musicperforming writes of Springsong on the printemps page, tomtom the paper's sun went to bed with meaning's very self in a musicflash songburst –

Joyce: Here's some paper. You write with your stylo, I'll write with mine.

Common Garden Time

ONE OF THE great things about gardening is that when the huge wave of summer does finally break, and its leaping curve of green flings into every garden a marvellous iridescent spray of petals, in colours our language hasn't caught up with yet, this joyful and indiscriminate tide lifts *everyone* off his feet – both proper gardeners and people like me.

Expert and amateur, in summer we all have enough to do just treading water – mowing the lawn, weeding, shouting at birds, disbudding, watering, weeding, furiously eating a lot of peas that have come all at once, squirting useless liquids at insects, weeding – without trying to swim, to impose our tiny personal motion on the flood.

In those rattling packets of dead-looking seeds, those stark February rose-twigs, there is that hidden which will dwarf the mere differences between one man's skill and another.

But at this time of year the difference between gardeners and me is as nakedly visible as the branches on the trees. For in some miraculous way they slip into another time-scale. I have always been surprised that Dunne did not include Common Garden Time (CGT) among the proofs for his famous Time Theory, which asserts that one time contains another.

For those who live in CGT the four week-ends of March, for instance, actually last about 600 hours. For non-gardeners they do the opposite, they dwindle almost to a non-existent instant – certainly much less than the theoretical 4 x 48, or 192 hours. At one moment, for us, it is too frosty, too undug, or just plain too early, to do anything; the next, we should have had our peas, broad beans, lettuce, potatoes and I don't know what in a month ago, it is too late *again* to do anything about delphiniums, seedsmen are murmuring regretfully to us over old oak counters.

Digging for us is just digging, but proper gardeners' digging, something to do with *spits*, requires an amplitude of approach and preparation only possible in CGT. In the admirable Pan book, 'The Small Garden', by C.E. Lucas Phillips, specifically 'for the amateur', it says 'four kinds of digging operation have to be tackled – plain surface digging, trenching, bastard trenching and ridging.' I suspect that all I do is bastard plain surface digging and even then it begins to get dark after I've done a six-foot strip.

Gardeners don't actually work harder or love gardens any more than I do. They just get into this other time, this CGT. The word *biennial* is a typical CGT word. I used to think it meant a flower that blossoms twice a year (splendid). But it doesn't. A biennial doesn't even bloom every two years. It blooms once – next year. For me this means never because I always find I should have put the seed in last autumn (probably in between bouts of bastard trenching). That's how they justify the *bi* part of it; the whole thing takes two years, then it just dies (they're a dead loss, biennials, really). Now I believe that real gardeners can *step back* in CGT, they can go out now and plant biennials last autumn, in the unlikely event of their having forgotten.

Most of all, living in CGT allows gardeners time in hand for emergency, unforeseen jobs as well as all that routine with trays in the pottering shed, and that bastard trenching. If a tree blows down or a child with an iron spike gets loose on their lawn they have time to cope with the damage. But I hardly ever get on to routine at all, there are too many emergencies – mostly due to birds, with which real gardeners seem to have an understanding; or perhaps birds aren't so quick, jerky, hopping, in CGT, they're more like a slow-motion film and the gardeners can see them coming.

Anyway, a month ago I put six rows of tulips in my biggest bed (I couldn't put them in in the autumn because I hadn't got the dahlias out of the same bed until Christmas Eve). Two weeks ago I noticed six rows of neat little holes, the green shoots lying around, the bulbs gone. What had done this thing? Some terrible kind of armoured slugs? Wild swans? Fairy onion men? Quite by chance I saw the last bulb being eaten by (I might have guessed) a pheasant.

Those great pear-shaped louts know I haven't got a gun. My friend Harblow did make me a pheasant trap, like the wooden skeleton of a great hat, poised on a flimsy stick, which was supposed to fall down on the pheasant when it had followed a trail of raisins to a little heap inside. But the pheasants ate the trail and left the heap inside to smaller birds who hopped in and out without touching the stick. Actually I think the raisins led them on to the tulips.

I had always heard that tulip bulbs were poisonous, but they obviously aren't to pheasants. They sent out invitations, they rang each other up. Come and join us down at old Jennings, for tulips. I think tulips turn to alcohol in pheasants' stomachs, I could hear them afterwards, lying down in the Gritches (scruffy pseudo-orchard behind garden) belching, spitting out the shoots, telling each other uproarious stories about the raisin trap.

So the last two week-ends have been spent putting in six *more* rows (I've got plenty. At least bulbs multiply for me as well as for gardeners) and spreading, over a cumbrous erection of brooms and poles, a huge net; a job which can really only be done by four helicopters, one at each corner.

Real gardeners don't have to net their tulips against pheasants. But I don't think they'll enjoy their tulips as much as I shall, either. (And I know what kind of trench I'd like to dig for those pheasants.)

Evergreen Mansions

ONE OF THE charms of living in East Anglia is that to get to anywhere but London you go by routes that show you a magical, true England, both new and old, like a cleaned picture.

By 'old' I don't mean simply olde. In these rain-washed, hilly, geranium-or-lobelia-filled unknown little towns with whitewashed hotels, in these strange private landscapes of dark parklands or distant wolds, there are plenty of immense brickworks, cement works, distant cooling towers, mysterious forests of derricks (for oil?) on the skyline. Tall ancient or squat modern factories, out of which come lorries laden with sacks and crates, provide livings for people who send their many fair children in green uniforms, by bicycle or bus, to fat calm good grammar schools.

Over a hedge I heard a huge clanking and whirring, and when I stopped to look I saw a perfectly ordinary English field parted by a grand canyon. Over a hundred feet below I could see men working whose heads did not even reach the base girder of a huge excavator. On the base was a tremendous green shed the size of a Baptist chapel, which rumbled round with surprising swiftness behind a jib the top of which towered as high above the field as the base was below.

Clank, whirr, bonk, rumble rumble, groan, the thing worked away at its mysterious task. There was no factory in sight; just this ravaged field and this excavator. Near a place called Thrapston, it was. I think they

105

were getting gold and diamonds out of the English clay, laughing secretly to themselves. How else could they afford a great machine like that, these Thrapston people, unless it was gold?

But there is something else besides mere industry; a greenness, a strength. Cars, maps, geography, the very lines of telegraph poles, suggest that England's spirit is a figure standing in London, looking north, Wales on the left, Manchester up *there*. Cars and ideas flow northwards, southwards, and come back for renewal. But this other England, taken by surprise on such a journey as I made (from East Bergholt to Loughborough; surely I was the first man in the world to go from East Bergholt to Loughborough) – this is the centre; it supplied London, not the other way round, when we were still forming ourselves.

This is the part where we are *other*, where we stopped the Vikings with obscure saints, making Rome something rich and strange. Quite suddenly, quite a long way past this Thrapston, I crossed a kind of Danegeld line, and suddenly it was just modern England again, just another Nato country, worried about exports, full of lorries. I waited for twenty-five minutes behind the widest Wide Load I have ever seen – I think just a vast cube of lead, in a giant yellow box, or a piece of some dam. Three lorries pushing it, three pulling; policemen, flag signalling, queues, bad temper . . .

Ah, but that morning I had come through Bury St. Edmunds, where a notice in the Abbey grounds said

LADIES	PUTTING
GENTLEMEN	BOWLS
SCENTED GARDEN	TENNIS
REFRESHMENTS	CLOISTERS

(Not that Loughborough didn't hold its own, as far as notices are concerned, with its OLD BOOT HOTEL and its TIGER FIRE-PLACE WORKS.) But best of all, on a second-class road with one of those marvellous surfaces that England reserves for chance motorists like me, under weeping trees I caught a glimpse of a classical dream of a house in its own park, and a board saying MANSION TO LET.

Now, you can buy a mansion, if you have scooped up a lot of easy money in something like commercial television, and want to become respectable. Or can sell it, if you've *been* respectable for centuries and are an impoverished aristocrat. But somewhere, in this secret part of England, there are these others; marvellous families – Lord, Lady, three delicate, fine-boned but brave children (two boys, one girl, she

106

rides alone up moonlit, statued glades) a dowager, a mad uncle in Holy Orders (authority on Plotinus, collects musical chamber pots).

These people *rent* mansions. Not for them the endless tax-struggles, the compromises with trade, the devious battles to keep a great national and local name alive. They just appear, from nowhere ('we are Emanations' cackles the Plotinus uncle) and rent this mansion. They are instantly at home. They have never been away, the broken chain is miraculously mended.

Spinet and flute make clear music under *their* tapestries, peacocks call harshly on *their* lawns and terraces, the clock on *their* stables goes again . . . For six months. Then, with no sound, they are gone, leaving nothing but memories of wonderful talk, music, dances. This notice goes up. Then another family comes, and the same thing happens. They flit effortlessly about

> *Dying into a dance.*
> *An agony of trance.*
> *An agony of flame that cannot singe a sleeve.*

There must be quite a lot of them in that country that you do not pass through on your way to or from mere London.

The Dropped Coupé

ONE OF THE more absurd of the motivation-research 'discoveries' is that fantasy, now widely accepted as reality, that a car purchaser equates the saloon with *wife* and the convertible with *mistress*.

This may be partly due to the word itself, which only reached us from America after the war; the progression is convertible – changeable – unreliable – immoral. It does faintly suggest a Jekyll-and-Hyde car-person that goes along sedately, then suddenly winks, leers, whistles, sweeps off head-covering, bows with grinning teeth at some fast woman, offering flowers, chocolates, parcels in red ribbon produced from the boot behind its back . . .

107

But our original English word was *tourer*; a very different matter. No mistress would look at a man in a tourer. She would know better than to waste her wiles on its honest, apple-cheeked, draught-loving, *poor* owner (often wearing steel-rimmed glasses) protected from the keen moorland air only by sheets of celluloid; she would not try to tempt him away from his virtuous routes, his farmhouse teas, waterfalls, ecstasies of rushing wind, blown hair (his own) and humming tyres.

Your tourer-driver was simply a nature lover on wheels, a bird watcher with an engine. He had the cheapest kind of car there was. It was those pallid, urban fellows with little moustaches and two-tone shoes, in their flashy saloons (I'm glad *that* word stays, obstinately resisting *sedan*), who were up to no good.

But the manufacturers, having first made the convertible dearer than the saloon, instead of the other way round, are now one by one either ceasing to make convertibles at all or, at best, replacing the honest, functional metal trelliswork and stout canvas of the tourer with a lot of apparatus that drops furtively right out of sight, not seldom with the aid of strange tiny-growling motors.

What this means in terms of those disorders, such as skidsophrenia, motor attacksya, carannoyia, which are reducing more and more drivers to crazy people who mutter curses to themselves in their mad little private rooms of tin and glass, is obvious to anyone who has ever bowled along with the hood down, beaming at trees, cars, *people*, knowing even in winter, when the hood must be closed, that this moment of communication with the real will come again.

Year by year the attempt to cut off the motorist from air, sky, the great world, is intensified. If you want a car that opens you have to be rich, eccentric, and now, according to this motivation research, morally unstable into the bargain.

But is there not also an effect inside the car factories, less observable but no less tragic? One sees the craftsmen who actually made the hoods, their whole department an oasis of human personality in the huge automated steel barracks. You can't mass-produce hoods; and often the manufacturers, hurrying forward to the apocalyptic day when the entire car is ejected with merely a soft hissing thud, from one enormous machine, must have resisted these craftsmen, stitching away in their quiet, lofty workshop.

Some of them would be of Huguenot descent, from famous old families of *carrossiers*, with forebears who made huge gilded carriages for the Sun King. Others, survivals from the gig and trap age of England, would bring a more red-blooded, popular strain, a suggestion of Dickens ostlers or the tannery of 'John Halifax, Gentleman' – little, bandy-legged, red-faced men, wearing brown bowlers, turning red with speechless laughter at the end of a story in the private bar.

'How does this gusset fit on the reverse placket, Mr. Joskins?' asks a young apprentice of such a one.

'Why, lad,' says Joskins, laying aside his racing form book, 'just nick round the hob with your marling skiver like this, then frank it on the template, so.' The youth looks on admiringly as the knobbly old hands deftly shape the leather. 'You'll learn, lad,' says Joskins; 'won't he, Mr. LeMaitre?'

LeMaitre, the foreman, nods abstractedly. He has just returned from a management conference. I can put some of the younger ones on this Plastik-press they're getting, he thinks, but what about old Joskins, he's been in leather all his life. First it was the trellismen, now its Joskins. Perhaps I can keep Joskins if I give in about the taker-men. (Taker-men are traditional hood craftsmen's juniors who take the completed hood to the assembly line in the main factory.) But now there is a plan, backed by both management and shop stewards, to knock a hole in the wall of the quiet Hood Room and bring the assembly line right through it, together with Muzak . . .

But it's no use preaching to the unconvertible.

Read Any Good Bath Salts Lately?

IT'S A VERY odd thing to be a humorous writer at any time, but it's oddest of all at Christmas, because this is when *all* humorous books come out.

I don't think the publishers think of them as books at all, but as bait.

As the number of Saturdays before Christmas gets relentlessly smaller, there are more and more people whose dazed and confused minds revolve helplessly round one single idea, growing ever more irresistible as their strength fades.

This idea, this concept, is that of *bath salts*.

You have had an exhausting but on the whole successful day; you have got wonderfully appropriate presents for A, for B, for C, and your power of creative choice was still working when you got to the non-stick saucepan, just right for X; the wind-up toy (a bear in a chef's hat that tosses an egg, nodding furiously as it does so) that pleases you, never mind whether it pleases child Y who will receive it; and the well-chosen record for Z.

But now this power is rapidly declining in you. It is five past five. The car is parked miles away, and you are very tired. Suddenly you remember this aunt, this friend at work, this neighbour. *Bath salts*, you think wearily.

These are all very fine in their way, and I mean no harm to the manufacturers. But there is no doubt that bath salts are an ultimate confession of failure, coming even below slippers and handkerchiefs.

People know this in their hearts; and it is because publishers know that they know this that humorous books are used as bait, to get these exhausted people into bookshops.

For the fact is that none of us go to bookshops as often as we should. Those who aren't interested in books fear the shut-in look of bookshops, which in physical appearance often rather resemble shoe shops, with the same regular stacks of whitish, neatish, rectangular things on library-type shelves.

They wouldn't think of going into a shoe shop and just browsing, and they have this instinctive feeling that the manager would stare at them if they tried this with books too.

Those who *are* interested in books, on the other hand, tend to have one particular bookshop that they go to – usually one that just sells books, and not a lot of brass fire-irons, leather holders for the *Radio Times*, china geese, jig-saw puzzles, Plasticine, secateurs, string, raffia, bread-boards and do-it-yourself painting kits as well.

In their supercilious way they overlook the fact that such shops have to sell these non-books in order to survive, and that hidden somewhere among all this plastic junk there still remain possibly several thousand books, many of them doubtless rubbish, but always offering the delightful possibility of some marvellous surprise, some discovery, some work that could change their lives.

Faced with this situation – the tired crowds mumbling *bath salts, bath salts*, to themselves, and the natural and instinctive fear of bookshops – the publishers and the booksellers have this plan to lure people in with humorous books.

All the year round there is, near the entrance of every bookshop, a table with humorous books on it, but at Christmas this table burgeons and grows, into a monstrous mountain of jokes.

Come on in, it seems to say, *don't be afraid. Look, books are FUN*!

I don't think the publishers, or the booksellers, actually hope to sell any of the humorous books. They never advertise them, or so it seems

110

to the authors (although I believe this is true of non-humorous authors as well).

I have often stood in a bookshop at Christmas, watching the people come in, diffident, yet willing to try anything to get away from those perishing bath salts.

I have seen them leaf through the mass products of the clowns; my own included, before putting them down with a small sigh. Cartoons, articles, verse, they stare at it all with deep, puzzled frowns, as though they were working out some algebra.

It is the same feeling I have as when I have to take a piece to our lawyer to see if there is any libel in it; I sit in a brown leather armchair, in this gloomy room full of brown leather books, the lawyer puts on very stern glasses and reads through my fragile little piece without a muscle of his face moving.

All writers, whether they admit it or not, are like Arnold Bennett, who is said to have haunted bookshops with a cheque for £100 in his pocket that he was going to give to the first person he saw buying one of his books; he never did.

The nearest I have ever got to seeing a spontaneous reaction from anyone was one Sunday years ago when my wife and I were having a drink at a pub with tables outside, and the man at the table next to us was actually reading my piece in *The Observer*.

I had my back to him, so I couldn't turn round to look, and my wife relayed his reactions. 'His mouth just twitched,' she said. 'He's gone serious again. He's put the paper down' (despair!).

'No, wait, he's only getting matches out of his pocket. He's picked it up again. *He's smiling.*' Gosh, it was wonderful. It's only happened once since 1949.

No, of course all that publishers and booksellers want to do with our books is actually to get the people into the shops, once they're there they can get them with the real stuff, with the endless, endless talk about sex, betrayal, neurosis, doom, murder, despair; with *writing*.

I once saw a great illustrated feature in *Life*, or some such magazine, called *The Creative Agony of Arthur Miller;* there were lots of photographs of A. Miller, his face contorted, his fists screwed against his temples, his brow furrowed, as he struggled with his next novel or play or whatever it was.

It was like Beethoven howling and stamping behind locked doors as he wrestled with the fugue of the Credo in the *Missa Solemnis,* only more so.

You've only got to try and imagine a piece called *The Creative Agony of Paul Jennings* to see what a marginal position is occupied by us jokers.

Even if it *is* hard to write the stuff (and after all, as Chesterton observed, 'it is easy to be heavy, hard to be light. Satan fell by the force of gravity') nobody wants to know this, And quite right too.

Any good funny piece ought to look as if the chap who wrote it was out in the fields digging beetroot, or building a dynamo, or doing some real, man's job, when he got this idea and, howling with laughter, rushed upstairs and jotted it all down in five minutes and then went back to his real job.

Or is there, after all, a deeper justification for laughter, that wonderful, human thing, in the bookshops at this time? Maybe it has as much to do with Christmas as bath salts, anyway.

A Few Short Ones

STEWARDS ARE AUTHORISED to accept payments also in DRA, LE£, ETS, ESP, EG£, LI£, SOM, SAR, EAS, URP, CRU, ARP, AUS, VBO, INR, PAR, JYE. – Alitalia leaflet.

Is that the Rhine or the Moselle?
We're so high up I cannot tell –
Or is that Dijon down below?
Not only do I just not know,
I just don't *care*. Let countries shrink
While I sit here and sip my drink.
Come, steward, ho! Pour out a jar
And let me pay in ESP, or PAR –
No, look, this thing's a hundred URP
(Not too much soda, makes me burp).
I've just been round the world, you know;
One order's worth a million VBO
Though where it was I can't recall,
And see, this note's no help at all;
It shows, like all of them, the same
Symbolic helmet-wearing dame.
Now, where are VBO's the currency?

Japan? Ah, no, they have the JYE
(JYE ken John Peel, ha ha!). Well, *skol!*
Hey, steward, can't I pay in DOL?
Well, never mind, no need to carp.
Just take this pocketful of ARP.
Drink up, there's time for plenny rounds
To use up these outlandish £'s
Like LE or LI or even EG.
The las' lap of the homeward leg . . .
Wha's this then? Oh, a hunnerd CRU.
Now where the hell was that? Peru?
Or back behin' the Iron Cur.?
I dunno, it's all a blur
I been to Braz. an' Can. an' Chin.,
I flown on planes of ev'ry line.
Less have another. Take these SOM
An' don' ast *me* where they come from;
Use 'em up on gin an' whisk.,
Campar' an' sod', an' champ., an' Bisqu.
Don' wanna land. Less stay up here
Ooray, ol' boy! an' joll' good cheer!
And don' less come on down again
To dreary ol' POU, SHIL an' PEN.

200 Bdrms., 7 Bthrms.

A S ALWAYS IN the tall, high, sad bathroom of a big old English
hotel, I feel a faint air of trespass. Everything is too large and
bare; the huge gaunt bath with its brass taps from which gush torrents
of startling power, unknown in any human bathroom, as if for some
industrial process, the grudging cane-seated chair and the cork mat on
the worn brown linoleum (as though one were having a bath in the
Home Office) – all these seem to be mysterious, oversize, symbolic
objects, not for actual use.

Above all, there is absolutely no sign of any previous or present
human life. Although one's bathroom at home is, by its very function, a

solitary place, it is nevertheless one of the most human rooms in the house, with its familiar toothbrushes, its little pink useless bottles and tubes, its sense of faces and souls having been renewed a thousand times here (and, in *our* bathroom, its five small odd shoes, its plastic buses and helicopters, its sodden teddy bear and pieces of comics).

But here there is nothing. The bathroom is in a back part of the hotel, looking out on to an unrecognisable part of the town (or it would if one were 10 feet high and could look out of the window). I go to it past an open door showing a room with a dowdy settee in it; radio music sounds, it seems inhabited yet looks too humble to be a hotel room. Two women in overalls are speaking a foreign language and laughing softly round a corner. There is an impression of bundles, piles, trays, *stocktaking*. I have somehow got behind the scenes; this is an ante-room, a scenery store, a disused temple. They know I am here, but they make no comment.

(Why do I never see anyone coming from these bathrooms? Am I the only one in this party of journalists that hasn't got a private bathroom? Where *are* all the others, why has it gone so quiet? Who is this man with a creased face and thinning hair, coming out of his room with a secretive look? What is my room number, which is the way back? Who am I? Will they take my clothes away, switch the rooms round, while I am naked in the bath?)

It pre-dates all smart, specially-designed bathrooms. It is just a room with a bath and a lavatory in it. The claw feet of the bath are visible. It is the bathroom of one's childhood, of something even farther off, of an E. Nesbit child's childhood (although no child bathes here, only older, soberly rich business men seven feet long, doffing serious good underwear). There is a low moaning of wind as in childhood bathrooms (we are high up, in an outcrop of the hotel), it moans under the door . . .

The door; ah yes, of course, the bolt, before I start. It is out of alignment with the socket, and will go in only when I simultaneously lift the great Victorian cream door by the handle. Then I have to use both hands to shove it home. At the last shove the bit with the knob comes off. I am locked in, like the famous three old ladies.

I fight off a feeling that the hotel has done this on purpose, it was a special trick rusty bolt, they are taking my clothes away now, waiting to see what I will do. Somehow it would be a surrender to shout out. What words would I use? *Help!* would be absurdly dramatic. Yet if I played it down with *Hi!* or *Oi!* or something equally informal, passers-by would think I was calling to a wife, or was an eccentric of some kind, they would creep away saying, there's a man shouting in the bathroom, let's not get involved. It would have to be something formal, a *dignified* shout. *Holloa! I say there! Er, I SAY, ARE YOU THERE? HUL-LOAH! . . .*

114

Perhaps I can attract attention by running the overflow, they would eventually look up from the kitchens at the perpetual dribble (but no, I hear it going down an internal drain); or by clanking SOS in Morse on the chain (but the frightful roaring gushing from the immense high cistern would drown it). Ha, inspiration! I will tear out letters from toilet paper and spell out a message under the door. After some thought I reject appeals like LET ME OUT or SEND ENGINEER in favour of the simple statement BOLT IS BROKEN. But when I lay out the letters on the floor the moaning draught blows them about even there, so what would it be like where the draught is concentrated under the door, suppose someone came by and found the words BOOB RENT SILK, or LOB NO BRISKET or even O STINKER BLOB?

Suddenly I hear the two foreign women coming, talking and laughing. 'Holloa!' I shout. 'The bolt is broken. Please send an engineer.' It sounds absurdly like a phrase-book sentence, I am half tempted to go on *that bolt is rusty. It is too much. Tell him to come quickly. I shall inform the police . . .*

To the male voice which presently arrives I shout 'will you please bring me a short steel rod not more than a quarter of an inch wide.' This is presently pushed under the door and I push the bolt back from the other side, which is fortunately open (they never thought of that). I feel I have won, and I do not attempt to explain the paper letters and shreds all over the floor.

Come Into the Garden of Weeds

I AM SURE it's harder to maintain a garden in the country than it is in the town. Most town land not actually built on *is* gardens, but here one stands out. All the pests and birds and weeds respect the farmer. He ploughs his field once, harrows it and rolls it, shoves the seed in, the little green rows obediently come up, you never see a weed from one corner to the other, he certainly doesn't get them two feet high every ten days the way I do, and even if he did he would simply pay men to come over in aeroplanes squirting deadly chemicals. He has alarm

115

clocks full of gunpowder that crash off at first light, and many other weapons, but often he hardly needs to use them.

Birds get discouraged by the sight of a four-acre field full of blackcurrants, even if it's totally undefended. It's when, from the wild trees and bushes where they live all round me, they see *my* pathetic looped and windowed fruit cage, with its sagging old net that weighs on my neck when I'm trying to hoe inside, that the word gets round. *Jennings is at it again. Attack at dawn tomorrow. No. 4 Brigade (Blackbirds), one Company of Starlings in reserve.* I *fascinate* them.

It's the same with weeds and all the other things. At the end of the excellent Pan book, *The Small Garden*, by C. E. Lucas Phillips, there is a chapter called *Friend and Foe*. There aren't many Friends, just the Centipede (the Millipede is a Foe, but who has time to count their legs?), the Lacewing, the Ichneumon Fly, the Ladybird and the 'friendly Ground Beetle larva . . . very nimble. Unfortunately it is like the evil *wireworm*, but the wireworm is thinner, deep yellow.'

Apart from the odd ladybird and centipede who have strayed out from town gardens, I don't have any of these. All my ground beetles aren't friendly at all, I can tell by one look at them that they hate me. I don't think these Friends venture out much into the country; they're too scared of the Foes, like the evil wireworm, which greatly outnumber them. Indeed when I look at their awful names – Black Spot, Big Bud, Scab, Ground Elder, I am convinced I have them all; they have dreadful, surrealist, quarrelsome meetings where they plan their campaigns. Like this.

Ground Elder: The meeting is called to disorder.

Scab: Oo by?

Ground Elder: By me. You'll agree I am a founder member of the Muck Up Jennings's Garden Society, indeed I was here long before he came. You may think I'm younger than the Elderberry, but I'm not. I've been here for *ever*, and always will be. I've got my feet on the ground – all over it, not to mention under it. Elder means senior, and as the senior member present I —

Big Bud: Cut it out creeper. Dis is a meetin' of *inseck* pesks, not stoopid weeds.

Ground Elder: The rules of this Society state that 'it is open to all manifestations of nature that shall prevent Jennings from getting his garden organised. The Weeds have asked me to represent them. The birds have sent a message apologising for their absence, as the blackcurrants are on, so that apart from our friend the Unexpected Wind, whom we are very glad to welcome here today, this meeting *is* composed of various species of insect. Whilst always ready to give credit for your stalwart work in furthering our common aims, I would ask you, in fairness, to consider who has done more – the Horse Pox, Tinsy and Old Man's Trousers that absolutely swamped his peas this year, not to mention the work of my colleagues Hellspike, Bloodycup and myself among his strawberries, or Mr — er, Bud, here, with his puny attacks limited to a few blackcurrants already swamped by Thistles.

Big Bud: Lissen, green stuff! Quit dat talk, or me an' de boys (*indicating menacing crowd of Leatherjackets*) is gonna eat up de Weeds too. Whadja mean, *all* manifeskations? Ya want de boids should come too, dem pheasinks an' all? An' de wind dat blew his delpheenums down?

Unexpected Wind: Hwell, and hwhy not? I howl on hollyhocks, *hoo hoo,* hurl 'em down with hullabaloo. Or swish in gusts, whistle and hiss and smasssh his sunstalks.

Codlin Moth: Haw, haw! Well said, old fwuit! Fwightfully decent of you to come.

Scab: And oo might *you* be?

Codlin Moth: Codlin Moth. J. Codlin Moth. I eat Jennins' apples, don't yer know. Then they weally are old fwuit, haw haw! (*seeing Coral Spot*) I say, Cowal, old thing, fancy seein' you heah!

Coral Spot: Codlin, how fab! Haven't seen you since the fab party at the Bramley's. Or was it the Cox's

Codlin Moth: The Wibstone-Pippins, deah girl.

Black Spot: You go an' singe yourself, Moth.

Codlin Moth: Who is this, ah, person?

Coral Spot (sighing): It's my husband I'm afraid. I didn't think he'd be here. He usually just sits at home *stuffing* rose leaves.

Black Spot: You better go away, Moth. Like it says in the book, I'm a *very menacing disease.* An' I got the Greek with me (*indicating Botrytis*).

Botrytis (softly): Anytheenk you say, Bleck. You jist esking me, yis? I got other name in Eengland, *Grey Mould.* I was never eating a Mot' before. But em liking to try.

Leaf Miner: Oh, cut it out, bach! Got to unite against Jennings we have, isn't it? All very well for you to talk it is. The Leaf Miners still have their bitter memories of the bad old days when he hadn't provided a Garden Service at all. Eat nettles we had to then, bach. Now there is a garden, unite to take it over we must. Yes, we must eat Jennings' garden, not each other, indeed to goodness, hallelujah! So I say to you all, Forward With The Pests! (*Singing emotionally*) Y maesteg llandudno gwyn aberystwyth —

Ground Elder: Er, chrrrm, grrrmph! I am indebted to me Right Honourable Friend. Although he speaks from the, ah, maggot side of the House, or rather the Garden, hna hna hna, he has done a valuable service in pointing out the need for unity in this matter. And indeed, in reviewing the past year, I think we may *all* take credit for overcoming the menace of the digging machine that Jennings has bought. As fast as he dug with it (and let there be no mistake, my friends, it *is* a great deal quicker than his spade, leaving him more time for measures against us) we redoubled our efforts with Tinker's Curse, Antipathy, Stinkbane and Theft. In any case, he only had time to dig *between* the rows. In the rows themselves our Intergrowth Service ensured that although he might see no weevil among the peas and beans, it was there just the same. I must also warn you that he has procured a book which indicates measures to be taken against each separate one of us. But, although I do not wish to sound complacent, I do not see how he will manage to equip himself so thoroughly – for Aphis, with *malathion*, for Big Bud, lime-sulphur, for Codlin Moth, *lead arsenate*, for Black Spot, *orthocide*, for –

Cuckoo Spit: No scholuschion's the schlightest usche againscht *usch*, in our schloppy schpittle.

Scab: Oo said so?

Ground Elder: It's in that same book. It says 'inside a mass of frothy spittle is a curious soft creature which on disturbance will attempt to escape by weak hops. Handpick.'

Cuckoo Spit (*smugly*): Yesch, that'sch usch; handpick. Schtormtroopersch, schpeschial asschault schervisches.

Codlin Moth: Haw, haw! Lead arsenate, where will he get that, haw haw! He wants a labowatwy as well as a garden!

Big Bud: An' I ain't afraid of any limey sulphur, neether.

Ground Elder: Well spoken, Mr — er, Bud. And I think we may all say the same. Well, now I just want to say a few words about final plans for the apple and dahlia season, and then we must get down to our main business of our work underground during the coming winter . . .

Abroad Thoughts from Home

THERE IS ALWAYS an element of fantasy in a holiday abroad. Even when one is actually there one feels unreal; instead of one's house, piano, garden, local station, cat, job, past, one has only a few slender travellers' cheques between oneself and nothing, chaos. But at least one is then taking decisions, acting, living; it's during the preparatory period that the whole thing seems crazy.

On the darkest day in February, I saw an advertisement for a house in the South of France to let at what seemed to me the cost of keeping my family anyway (except for about £20 a week anyway) and anyway I would do some writing when we were there, and anyway a lot of people who don't work half as hard as I do manage to go abroad, and anyway perhaps we could let *our* house. And anyway.

I answered it (even though, going to the post, I had to disguise myself to get past the crowd of duns and bailiffs lounging, dicing, cursing and drinking outside our house).

What intimations of disaster there are in the documents one gets for taking the car, those phrase books in eight languages, those international vouchers for use in dreadful emergencies (the Danish phrases all sound as if they'd be useful for swearing in. I've often felt like going into an *English* garage, kicking the car and gritting: 'I have *forhjulet traenger til at blive justeret,* but *dette fungerer ikke ordentligt* just the same.' Actually the first phrase is 'probable answer from a mechanic' – 'your front wheel needs adjusting' and the second is 'this does not function properly').

As for the booklet of vouchers, not encashable, or, tremendous German transaction, *in Bargeld eingelöst werden* (to become lost in a bar of gold? or could it be, frittered away in some bar?) it's the multilingual 'What to do in the Event of an Accident' which instantly suggests an encounter on a hot afternoon on some plain fringed with blue hills, maybe the Cevennes, maybe the Pyrenees. Just as I draw level with a German car parked on the other side with about 18 in. still over the narrow road (we are in no hurry and we came down this little byway because it looked inviting) a French car coming the other way misjudges the gap.

There is a long-drawn-out SKRURRKK-URK-URK, that noise so much more horrible to the car owner than any sudden crash. The

119

Frenchman's car is, of course, scraped on both sides, mine and the German's on one side. The Frenchman, a bald, long-nosed fellow of about 40 in a sweat shirt, instantly starts shouting at me, and the German shouts at *him*, but I get out of my boot the 'chalk, a tape-measure and a camera' which 'should always be carried in the car'.

I am focusing my camera on the 'traces of debris, such as loosened mud and broken glass' when the German starts sweeping it up (he has a broom in his boot as well as the chalk and the rest of it). *'Ein Moment,'* I say. *'Ich muss ein Photograph haben von der'* (consulting form) *'Glasplitter, herabgefallener trockener Kot. (Kot* eh? it doesn't sound as much like mud to me as 'mud' does); but he points down the road and keeps saying something about *huissier.* The Frenchman has suddenly vanished.

Of course, 'In France in the case of material damage call a *huissier.*' It sounds vaguely like some eighteenth-century horse soldier, but on looking it up in the dictionary (also, of course, in the boot) I find it is 'an usher; gentleman-usher: doorkeeper: sheriff's officer, bailiff: beadle.' Well, there will be time enough to start looking for an usher when we've finished our photographing.

We both now observe a silent, neatly dressed man with pince-nez, who has witnessed the whole thing from the shade of an olive tree. We both ask him his 'Name, Christian Name, and Profession,' to which he replies, 'Jean Plon, Equarrisseur.'

The dictionary gives 'one who squares wood, etc. A knacker.' He does not look like a knacker to me. Who ever heard of a knacker with pince-nez? On the other hand, this is agricultural country, more likely to give scope to knackers than to squarers of wood, etc. The German looks doubtful, too. I look up 'knacker' in my *German* dictionary and then say to him *'Ich glaube, er ist nicht ein Schlachter alter Pferde'* (slayer of old horses) *'nicht wahr?'* And what about that 'etc.'? Perhaps he squares something else (terrazzo, in new villas in booming France? cheese? paper?).

'Monsieur, qu'est-ce que c'est que vous équarrissez?' I ask him. He looks as though I had made up this tongue-twister especially to insult his language.

At this point we see two figures advancing down the white dusty road, one gesticulating excitedly, the other nodding judiciously. It is the French driver and a beadle (or usher). The beadle (or doorkeeper) is in a strange fustian uniform, bewigged, with lace at the wrists. He carries a wand with which he taps each of us ceremonially on the shoulder. He signals to the wood-squarer (or knacker), who turns to the fields and gives a low whistle, at which many carpenters rise from

120

behind the bushes where they have been crouching and begin erecting a stand or tribune. Groups of horsemen ride in from the darkening plain. It begins to rain. I turn round; the cars have vanished . . .

But I've paid the deposit now.

⟿⟾

Bad Antimony Drives Out Good

COULD IT BE that 'a technique of exporting ' is a contradiction in terms, that you can't plan it just like that? Whenever one reads about some big export achievement it has a quality of divine surprise, accident, chance. A teenage girl goes to New York, apparently just for fun, and suddenly there are these rough buyers from big stores, women with rhinestone spectacles, falling over themselves to buy a million pairs of red felt stockings from her workshop, an attic in King's Road; some advertising figure – a man with a beard, or an eye-patch – achieves an unpredictable folklore status; British pop becomes actually cruder than American pop, and therefore exportable. You can't plan this kind of thing.

When it comes to the big stuff, if it's good enough it exports itself. Those Japanese shipbuilders didn't go to P. & O.; P. & O. went to them. If you manufacture, say, Jolt Squeeze Rollover and Pin Lift Moulding Machines (and people do), or Double-Headed Semi-automatic Flat Ware Machines and Batt Cutters ('no wet-faced batts, less trouble with slurry marks,' says the leaflet before me), you are up against either countries which make perfectly good Jolt Squeeze Rollover and Pin Lift Machines of their own (and, quite possibly, *entirely* automatic Batt Cutters), or countries full of bamboo and a thousand twangling instruments, where they're just not interested.

Actual export managers, of firms making things like toys, servo-couplings, filing systems, patent roofing materials, are citizens of a realm of chance, quirk, otherness. With drip-dry shirts and workman-like luggage, in a dozen countries they go to patio lunches, office meetings, boring night clubs, they even stay in the homes of their contacts, whose first names they use slightly anxiously. Deep down

121

they are romantics, travellers, hopers; they know it's not a bit of good, really, trying to find a common language with the factory stay-at-homes, still less the Government. They write mournful letters, knowing no one is listening, to *The Times*, complaining about not being backed up.

You would have to *be* an export manager to get the point of this, which was in the Board of Trade Export Services Bulletin (and who knows about it if they don't?):–

> **THAILAND**
> ANTIMONY (Ref ESB/33593/64).
> The following is the full text of an announcement concerning the above requirements.
> AMPHUR WANG-NUA POLICE STATION (Lampang Province).
> Tender for the purchase of 7,004 Kgs. Antimony. Tenders to be submitted on 15 December at 10 a.m.

Gregory Lequesne, a handsome, greying man, is sipping a Tom Collins among a laughing group on the veranda of the best hotel in Singapore, where he is breaking a journey home from Australia. He frowns at the cable from British Antimony. Since his elder brother Morton Lequesne, died, soon after B.A. took over Lequesne Bros., an old family antimony firm founded by their Huguenot ancestor (Jacques Lequesne, settled in Soho, friend of printers), he has felt himself to be on sufferance

'What the hell *is* antimony, Greg?' asks Jim Travers. 'Why don't you chuck it and settle down with me and Mr. Wong here?'

'It suits you, Meestair Lequesne,' says a faultless Eurasian beauty.'Anti-money, yes? I theenk you are not caring about money.'

'I care for *you*, Raka,' says Lequesne. 'Actually it's dreary-looking stuff, but it seems to be in everything. With lead and tin in type metal, with zinc and tin in Britannia metal, whatever that is, with copper and tin and *bismuth* in pewter. There'th no bithmuth like antimony bithmuth.'

All the same, the old excitement stirs. Somehow he has missed Thailand up to now. Seven thousand and four kilograms, that's more than seven *tons* of antimony. He resolves to go himself, not merely submit a tender, if only to annoy that bounder Maxwell, who has taken over as M.D. An old B.A. man, naturally.

Amphur Wang-Nua turns out to be a clearing in charming, hilly, forested country. A smiling man in a uniform with a shining Sam

Browne comes out from the rural, wooden-built police station as Lequesne dismounts from his horse. 'Ah, the so-welcome Englishman! I am Inspector Pramh Panhang. I am glad to tell you the Germans and Japanese merely posted their tenders. But you have come yourself to us. The contract is yours. But first we will entertain you.'

At the alfresco lunch of marvellous spicy foods and heady drinks ('you will like this, Mr. Lequesne. It is distilled from teak bark. It is a little like your *Vieille Cure*'), the police band plays *clong* music and maidens perform graceful dances. 'What's that pile of grey things, Pramh?' asks Lequesne.

'Oh, that is our antimony. Very good. You will like it.'

'But I thought — '

'That you were going to sell *us* antimony. No, look, tender is for *purchase* of antimony. My policemen make it. They have much spare time. There is no crime in Amphur Wang-Nua. Not' (a slight smile) 'since I came here.'

Lequesne looks round at the pastoral scene. 'But — the plant, the equipment? You surely have to roast the sulphide in a reverberatory furnace — '

'We have our own methods, Mr. Lequesne. So you do not wish to buy? It is sad. But maybe you stay here, sell *our* antimony. . .'

So far so lah tea doh

PERHAPS IN 6,000 years' time, when both English and Latin are dead languages only half-understood even by scholars, historians trying to find out what *happened* to English will hail, as Egyptologists hailed the Rosetta Stone, the discovery of a frail, crumbling copy of *Choral Latin*, a booklet published by the National Federation of Music Societies. The cover and introduction will be missing, and with them a vital clue in the words *for the guidance of choirs in the pronunciation of Latin*. The scholars will assume that the extraordinary phonetic words, *keeriay* (kyrie), *kraydo* (credo), *ahgnooce Dayee* (agnus Dei) and the rest, are part of another language, Kraydo-Anglin.

It will be as tantalising to them as Etruscan or Mycenean is to us. They will already know that somewhere in the second half of the twentieth century the written word, after a hectic last spasm of proliferation and formless decadence, disappeared altogether in the face of electronic and visual communication, and that shortly afterwards, in those days of separate 'races', most of the 'white race' disappeared in some unknown disaster. Kraydo-Anglin will be accepted as the language of that confused time.

'We know nothing of the Kraydo-Anglin civilisation,' some professor will write, 'except what has come down to us in fragments of their great epic poem, the *Keeriay*. It was evidently composed after the mysterious Day of Doom (or possible *Oom* or *Boom*) which had ended a previous culture and is powerfully evoked in the section headed, simply *Kraydo*:—

> *Kraydoh een oonoom Dayoom*
> *Pahtraym omneepohtayntaym, fakhtohraym chaylee*
> *et terray, veezeebeeleeoom omneeoom*
> *et eenveezeebeeleeoom'*

(Credo in unum Deum Patrem omnipotentem, factorem coeli et terrae, visibilium omnium et invisibilium). 'Scholars now think that many of the words in this verse are purely onomatopoeic attempts to evoke the sounds, mainly *whizz* (or *eez*) and *boom* (or *oom*), which accompanied the disaster, since most Kraydo-Anglin words are monosyllabic, although in our corrupt text they are sometimes run together. The section *Gloreeah* speaks with primitive directness of the hunger and poverty which followed the disaster (or *Dayoom*):—

> *. . . een ekshelseece Dayoh, et een terrah pahx*
> *omeeneebooce bohnay voloontahteece*
> *Loudahmooce Tay, baynaydeecheemooce Tay'*

(in excelsis Deo, et in terra pax hominibus bonae voluntatis. Laudamus Te, benedicimus Te).

'This breaks down into *een ekshel seece Dayoh*, "one eggshell since the Day"; *pahx o mee nee booce*, "O in my packs there is nothing to drink"; *bohn ay vol oont*, "Even the bone I wish for is not (*oont*)"; *ah, teece loud ah mooce Tay*, "Ah, 'tis loud I cry I must (*mooce*) have Tea"; *bay nayd, eech ee mooce Tay*, "but it is denied, each he's cry he must have Tea." This theme of thirst occurs in other sections, as for example in the line

> *Soopleekahntee pahrchay, Dayooce'*

124

(supplicanti parce, Deus). '*Soop leek ahn tee pahrch ay, Dayooce* "For soup of leeks and tea parched am I since the Day."

'In this same section there are touching hints of a vanished era of comfort and optimism:–

> *Sayd seenyeefair sahngtooce Meekay-ayl*
> *raypraysayntaht ayahce een loochaym sahngtam*'

(sed signifer sanctus Michael representat eas in lucem sanctam). *Sayd seen yee fair sahng* – "It is said ye saw a fair song" (possibly a reference to their electronic visual communications, referred to elsewhere as *Teebee*), *tooce Meekay*, "when all had their own shirts" (or *Mekay*, as these garments were sometimes known), *ayl ray (ment?) prays*, "all wore raiment worthy of praise," *ayn tah tay*, "each was grateful for his own tea," *ah ceen looch aym sahng tahm*, "ah, we have seen in luxury (*looch*) the song aimed at us by tam (rating?)."

'In lines of taut anger the poem bewails the foolishness of leaders responsible for the disaster:–

> *Quee tolleece pekkahtah moondee meezayrayray nohbeece*
> *Quee tolleece pekkahtah moondee, soosheepay*
> *daypraykahtseeohnaym nohstrahm.*'

(Qui tollis peccata mundi, miserere nobis; qui tollis peccata mundi, suscipe deprecationem nostram). 'It is known that there was some connection between the apparatus used in an attempt to get to the moon and the disaster. *Quee toll.* "what a toll," the poem laments, "an attack or peck at the moon, *pekk ahtah moon*, extorts from us if we must all die (*dee*)! How miserable (*meez*) are those who cheered (*ray, ray*), for whom there is now no peace (*noh beece*)." *Soo sheep pay*, "so the sheep pay." *Day pray kaht see o h naym*, "they pray they will never see the name of hydrogen (*h*) again," *no h strahm*, "no hydrogen in the airstream."'

And so on. The professor will get quite a long way with his research, even though the Vatican is still there and there are about the same number of Christians as there have always been. The trouble is *they* won't know Latin any more than anyone else by then. But when someone has the idea of checking the *Keeriay* against the text of whatever universal language is in use then by the universal church they will see that it has only been another way of saying that man had better not be too pleased with himself.

Thurber

I HAVE NO ambition whatsoever that one day on the front of 4 Prospect Place, a tall thin wooden house, like a cottage skyscraper, overlooking Hampstead cemetery, there should be an LCC plaque saying anything but JAMES THURBER DINED HERE.

There is always a curious sense of anti-climax, of contradiction, when one meets an admired writer, particularly one who creates a 'world' rather than just 'characters' (not that Thurber's grandfather, or Mrs. Ulgine Barrows, or Walter Mitty, aren't characters. But people know what you mean when you say 'the Thurber world,' as they do when you say 'the Kafka world,' in fact come to think of it there are similarities). It still seems extraordinary to me that this elegantly grey-suited man, previously always first met in a hotel room where he was changing from one spotless white shirt into another, whom we now carefully guided (for he was blind) down our everyday stairs into our actual dining-room as he talked continuously in a kind of fast growl, was the single-handed creator of that extraordinary, so-familiar territory of bafflement somehow eased by laughter: the Thurber world.

His very name is one that, with his marvellous ear for the physical sound of words, he might have invented himself. It wouldn't be really surprising to learn that his real name was T. Smith or something, and that it was simply given to him to discover that what modern man does is to *thurb*. To thurb is to be soft and vulnerable, though not gormless or a professional 'little man', in a world of sharp objects, to be human among machines, to be peaceful among dangerous maniacs. It is to make indistinct sounds, T.S. Eliot's 'raids on the inarticulate'. It is to be simultaneously purposeful and bewildered. *Furry, burble, disturb, burthen, bother, brother, birth, throb, mother, father, curb, hither, thither, urban, trouble* – all these concepts are involved in the idea of thurbing. A thurber is one who, like the mass of men, lives a life 'of quiet desperation'. Who said that? I looked it up and it was on the same page in the *Penguin Dictionary of Quotations* as Thurber: H.D. Thoreau. The name Thoreau looks perfectly real, as do its companions James Thomson, 1700–1748 (*Rule, Britannia!*), James Thomson, 1834–1882 (*I find no hint throughout the universe/Of good or ill, of blessing or of curse/I find alone Necessity Supreme*), Rose H. Thorpe (*Curfew must not ring tonight* – and we all know who illustrated *that*; the thing is lousy with

126

coincidence), Thucydides (*to famous men all the earth is a sepulchre*), Edward, First Baron Thurlow (*When I forget my sovereign, may God forget me*) and even the Rev. Godfrey Thring (*Fierce raged the tempest o'er the deep*). But the more one looks at the name *Thurber* on the page the less it seems like the name of a man and the more like some kind of function, attitude, atmosphere.

Thurber's world is such a compelling and recognisable one that, like all great artists, he makes one feel that it invented him instead of the other way round. Apart from anything else, Thurber stood for an Anglo-American consciousness and expressed it better than a hundred English-speaking Union manifestoes. The Anglo-Saxons produced the world's first industrial civilisation (if that is the word) utterly cut off from peasant roots. It's only now that France and Germany are going the same way (I keep reading sad articles about frozen chicken in once-famous *auberges*).

In the Columbus, Ohio, where Thurber grew up, fellow schoolboys 'could identify every car as it passed by: Thomas Flyer, Firestone-Columbus, Stevens Duryea, Rambler, Winton, White Steamer, etc.' Everything was already urban, ordinary, unmysterious, offering no place to the poet, the romantic, the inscrutable dreamer, 'and a wanderer who isn't inscrutable might just as well be back at Broad and High Streets in Columbus sitting in the Baltimore Dairy Lunch.' All previous civilisations have offered ordinary men some kind of inherited cosmology – heaven up there, hell down there, man in the image of God in the image of man, architecture with dear human squiggles, music as sung by imagined angels. But now universal cosmology is replaced by individual fantasies. And Walter Mitty can be claimed as the archetypal fantasist of this society.

He is a basic figure to set beside Faustus (archetypal intellect) or Don Juan (archetypal lust). People write whole plays and novels about him now (what is *Billy Liar* but Walter Mitty in three acts?). But for Thurber this was simply one perfect and elegant story (not much over two thousand words) in a torrent of equally acute (and blessedly funny) pieces.

Thurber also made us realise, quite painlessly, that the blue riband of sophisticated humour had crossed the Atlantic for the first time. The ss *Max Beerbohm*, a smart but elderly yacht full of upper-class dandies drinking sherry, but for years the fastest boat on the run, had suddenly been overhauled by this wonderful new liner, on which anyone with a sense of humour could travel free. Both ways. (Who has the riband now is open to doubt. There, as here, less and less wit finds its way into print, more and more into the better TV and radio scripts. If Thurber were a young man today the *New Yorker* wouldn't want to know him.

'It's mostly the childhood recollections of neurotic women now,' he said to me mournfully. And even Ross once called his drawings 'a fad of the English, a passing fancy.')

He was a patriotic old American but I always felt he relished something, fast disappearing now, in the slowness of England, that traditional, backward-looking suspicion of gadgets, that refusal of dock-warehousemen to use fork-lift trucks instead of very old hand-trolleys, preferably with iron, tyreless wheels. The night he came to dinner (and it certainly *wasn't* an anti-climax) he talked a great deal about the longevity of English writers – not surprisingly, as he had been seeing Sir Compton Mackenzie; and he mentioned Eden Philpotts and Wodehouse.

'American writers of short pieces tend to drink Martinis as though the world were going to end tomorrow,' he said, 'and their idea of relaxation is *to wash a Venetian blind*.' A lot of this subsequently appeared in a piece in the *New Yorker*. Thurber's brain was restlessly at it all the time, making patterns against the great white vertiginous abyss of Nothing. When our docks get to accepting fork-lift trucks, any decade now, *we* shall have to face that Nothing too.

He told a wonderfully funny story about those hectic Jazz Age days, when he and his first wife went out to a restaurant with a friend who had recently married a Turkish girl. During the evening someone vomited over a balcony, unfortunately on to this girl. 'Her husband said "you know, it's a terrible thing for a Moslem girl to be vomited on." My first wife said "American girls aren't crazy about it, either."'

In *Babel: the Gate of the God*, by Gordon Bottomley (I am one of three living men who claim *The Waste Land* as a central poem of their experience and still like Georgian poetry, which wasn't *all* written by Sir John Squire) the giants are arguing:–

> Then a lean giant 'Is not a calyx needful?' —
> 'Because round grapes on statues well expressed
> Become the nadir of incense, nodal lamps,
> Yet apes have hands that but and carved red crystals —
> 'Birds molten, touchly talc veins bronze buds crumble
> Ablid ublai ghan isz rad eighar ghaurl . . .'
> Words said too often seemed such ancient sounds
> That men forgot them or were lost in them;
> The guttural glottis-chasms of language reached
> A rhythm, a gasp, were curves of immortal thought.

Towards the end of his life, in blindness (with Helen Thurber always tactfully watching, ready to guide his hand to a glass, to warn about steps) he built (sometimes desperately) intricately interlocking battlements of words against chaos and Nothing. Words became *things* to him, and he built an extraordinary bridge between their thingness, their rightness, and the moral beauty of *order*. *The Wonderful O* seems to me a miraculous combination of moral fable, linguistic analysis, and of course laughter. As he wrote himself, 'the true balance of life and art, the saving of the human mind as well as of the theatre, lies in what has long been known as tragicomedy, for humour and pathos, tears and laughter are, in the highest expression of human character and achievement, inseparable.' The author of those luminous *Fables for Our Time*, the clear observer of sexual warfare, of muddled thought and non-communication, always longed for the sudden wonderful shout of laughter; he never got led into intellectual abstractions, because something remained eternally unspoiled in him. He always had this ambition to write the perfect piece about The Fight In the Grocery Store, even though he was aware that larger things than pyramids of cans may fall about our ears any day.

Let me end with the best Thurber moment I have ever known. It was one of my best theatre moments, too. *A Thurber Carnival*, for a variety of reasons, was a failure in this country. But I think of Betty Marsden reciting *The Last Flower*: perfectly straight, as Thurber's drawings were flashed on a screen. She came to the end:–

> *This time the destruction was so complete*
> *That nothing at all was left in the world*
> *Except one man*
> *And one woman*
> *And one flower*

And there we sat, in front of that child's drawing of one bedraggled flower. There was total, intense silence for a moment, of the kind when your heart is everyone else's heart, you have got into another land. The thing so hoped for, so rare, in the theatre.

Not many people can do that *and* make you laugh. Thurber loved the human race; and it should love him back.

Beldame Elliot: Great Anti-pet

THE DEATH OF Beldame Elliot, for many years senior cat in the Jennings household, has severed an interesting link with the early days of that organisation. She joined as a young kitten in the year of its foundation, and her career covered the period of remarkable expansion which began almost immediately.

That this expansion reflected a policy of which she deeply disapproved cannot be doubted, for it was not in her nature to dissemble. In fact it would have been revealed to those close to her that she had only joined under the assumption that she was to be the sole recipient of all dividends of love, food and comfort – had anyone been able to get close to her; but as a colleague once jokingly remarked, all relationships with Elliot started from scratch and ended with scratch.

With unshakeable strength of character she stayed on after the crisis in her career when it became clear that the expansion policy had won the day. In the event, her unique, superbly professional talent for hatred, her integrity as a small bristling bundle of total dislike for all the other cats, dogs and children who went about their business in the larger premises acquired in 1956, proved to be an essential counter-ingredient, like the dash of lemon-juice in a sweet sauce. Certainly, few who made her acquaintance in her later years, which she spent mostly growling on a shelf (she retired from active life with a small Uncivil List pension some years ago) could have realised with what remarkable success she totally concealed her delightful sense of humour; she had been an accomplished purrer in early youth, but gave it up late in 1952, the year of the organisation's first child.

Hellcat Hateface Elliot was born in June, 1952, the twenty-eighth daughter of Sappho Spitfire Gregory and (probably) the Hampstead Cemetery Cat, a colourful character who later became the first of her own several husbands. There was eastern blood on her mother's side, and the exquisite grace with which she could save anyone the embarrassment of showing affection – arching her back, glaring, walking away from those who foolishly attempted to stroke her – could well have been owed to some delicately formalised old code of hatred. Yet, as the V-shaped cut on one of her ears proclaimed, she never shrank from the more direct, hammer-and-tongs set-to of our

130

western tradition. She combined the two cultures in an amalgam of her own.

Her early upbringing was along conventional lines, and from it none could have foreseen that the playful kitten who came to the small London house, in those far-off days when people still bought fish for their cats, would be a pioneer of the Anti-pet revolution. For as certainly as Robbe-Grillet and Sarraute suggest the Anti-novel or Jimmy Porter the Anti-hero, Elliot *was* the Anti-pet.

Her achievement was the more remarkable in that it sprang from a background with no revolutionary tradition of cruelty to cats. As she herself acknowledged in fastidiously reacting from it, conventional love was all that the organisation could offer her, at any rate in its non-cat personnel. (Some critics, however, commenting on the Anti-pet movement, have noticed that the advent of Barker, the most un-catlike and loving of all dogs, a spaniel, was the final phase in the expansion policy, the final term in the series cats-children-dog; and they have suggested that the very intensity of his love and his desire for love may, *per contra*, have stimulated Elliot to perfect her extraordinary technique of withdrawal.

Will her work live? The two surviving cat members of the organisation, Thomas Tomkins and Captain Dreadful, are still in their formative years. The former, a rabbit-eater by profession, and something of a free-lance (he visits for long periods any other organisation that will give him food) is precluded by occupational somnolence from expressing any attitude at all, whether of hate or love. The latter seems quite ready to hate anyone engaged in eating while he is (or is not), but observers have agreed that this is more greed than hate; and he still purrs. Neither, therefore, is an Anti-pet in the true Elliot sense, and it remains to be seen whether this movement will become a living tradition or, like so many in the past, simply a dead end, the flowering of one rogue personality.

She leaves 33 children, apart from several who predeceased her. (One grandson, William Byrd, died of a mysterious illness, and it was alleged in some quarters that she had put a spell on him; but the case was not pursued.)

T. T. writes: In your excellent obituary of my dear old enemy Elliot, I noticed there was no mention of her prowess in the hunting field. Perhaps I may be allowed to qualify the suggestion that the 1956 move from London was entirely unwelcome to her by recalling her delight in the abundant sport afforded by the country of my forebears.

Though she was a somewhat gruff companion on our expeditions, her sheer professionalism made her a joy to watch. She killed for the pure joy of the thing and never seemed to eat her prey, merely biting off its head and generously leaving the meat to others like myself. She will be sadly missed by hunters and *bons-viveurs*.

Giving up Sailing

I DON'T THINK I *have* quite given it up yet. But summer by summer, slowly, painfully, I am wrenching myself away from the fantasy of being a sailor.

I don't mean a man in a funny hat doing a hornpipe; I mean, of course, a man owing a nice little twenty-foot yawl (would it be? Or ketch? Or sloop? I could draw it, in my mind's eye, I know what it looks like); conversant with tides, skilled in that ultimate ability to do the last twenty yards up to a mooring against a strong wind; able to write this sort of thing – 'so we made a hurried change of sail, from genoa to No. 1 jib. The Rolling Grounds, the Pitching Grounds, and then into the quieter waters of Harwich Estuary by the Beach End buoy . . .'

Hammond Innes wrote that, and I live even nearer to Harwich Estuary than he does. For years now I've been saying 'Well, it's wonderfully convenient living near these estuaries (there's the Blackwater, and the Orwell and the Deben, as well as the Stour), because I want my children to grow up knowing how to sail a boat.' It is true that the eldest has already learnt something; but not from me. She's been on a course. I'm the one that hasn't been on a course, and what I am giving up is the fantasy that I ever shall. (Where are there courses for men of forty-six, never mind about girls of eleven? It's like these grants one keeps reading about 'for young writers' so that they can live on some Mediterranean island and write another novel. Gosh, if I were a young writer I could do that *without* a grant. We middle-aged writers, we're the chaps who need grants, to help with the school fees – and children's sailing courses – let alone getting to Mediterranean islands.)

If I ever get to sail now it will be the children who teach me. I must abandon this picture, lived with for so long, of this ketch (or yawl), my wife handing up a steaming mug of coffee from the galley as we round

Outer Gabbard, Barrow Deep and Galloper (lightships; thank you, Hammond Innes) in a pearly dawn; maybe on our way *back* from a Mediterranean island.

The trouble is that like all dreams it has a touch of eternity, something unassailable, some hint of paradise. That mixture of adventurous joy with wide peace that you have in the ideal sailing dream has as much to do with heaven as with any actual sea or boat. In any actual sailing I have done, as crew in someone else's boat, there has been a strongly unparadisal air of anti-climax, largely due to the realisation that this is no more the dream of sailing than turning over the music for someone is being a pianist.

Yet there are so many sailing men. And these men, quite ordinary on land, have, when you are in their boat, an effortless superiority. There is something about the way they utter those formal cries, *ready about!* or *gybe-oh!*, something about their narrowed eyes, about the way they don't have so much time to *talk* as you do, about the feeling that in the last resort your very life is now dependent on their skill, that gives a moral quality to their superiority. They were more, well, more dedicated than you, *they* didn't just dream about it.

How the hell do they do it? I can understand when it's Hammond Innes, he writes best-sellers. But most people who manage to do all this sailing don't write at all, let alone best-sellers. It's not so much the money, it's the *time* they seem to have. They must all be in jobs where every Friday afternoon they can rub their hands at 5.30, or even 5, and say 'Well, that's it until 9' (or 9.30) 'on Monday,' and absolutely all that time is free for them to drive down to their estuary, do all their caulking and baling and splicing and painting and chandling on Friday evening, and still have two whole days on the water. On *my* last Saturday, a not untypical one, I was still sitting in my study at 7 p.m. trying to find a rhyme for *oblige* (there isn't one).

Of course they too must have wives, lawns, speech days, churches, week-end guests, joint shopping missions, dogs, books, letters, pianos, measles, children's parties, banks, hairdressers, cats, painting jobs, children's bicycle punctures, untidy sheds, other children, and similar time-consumers, like the rest of us. But such is their single-mindedness, their power of organisation, that they still have these huge calm areas of time which they can fill with the graceful and relaxed arabesques of sailing, beautiful curved and organic motions among infinite waters and pure winds, refreshing the soul.

Sometimes, when they are towing their boats down to the estuary, I pass them in my car; *it* is five years old but their cars are older, and I think I have a glimpse of their dedication – maybe they don't care about having a smart new car (as mine, unbelievably, was so recently), they don't throw their money about in this ostentatious way, any honest old thing will do that will get their boat down to the water. And then I have doubts, possibly that is just their boat-towing car, they have another, beautifully new car back in the garage.

At other times I try to console myself with the thought that sailing is a hobby exclusive of all others. After all, I sing. I sing in local groups and in London. But when I come to think of it, the man who sits next to me at the Philharmonia Chorus rehearsals (which sometimes seem to me to be on every night of the week) has a boat of his own. It wouldn't surprise me if they all had, maybe we could have a regatta and races with the Bach Choir on the Solent.

No, people who sail have some secret which has eluded me, and I might as well admit it. Before I finally decided to give up my sailing-fantasy – i.e., only last summer – I bought a book called *Sailing and Seamanship*, by Eric Howells. It was the most practical-looking of the whole row of sailing books in the shop, and if I knew it all I am sure I should not only be able to take up moorings against the wind but right a capsize (*helmsman clambers on to upturned side while crew goes into the water to windward and steps on to the centreboard*), and I should know what sound signals to make in thick weather on a vessel at anchor. (*Ring bell vigorously for five seconds. If vessel is over three hundred and fifty feet long, in addition beat gong at stern.* Who would have thought it, a *gong*?) And I see from one glance at page seventeen that my ideal boat *is* a sloop. A yawl has a second mast right aft, a ketch has a second mast nearer amidships . . .

What really depresses me is seeing that Mr. Howells is headmaster of Melton Constable Secondary Modern School, and Commander B. Lucke, who *edited* this admirable book, is Head of the Department of Navigation, Sir Anthony Deane County Secondary School, Dover-court, Harwich. There just wasn't a Department of Navigation in any school I was at. How am I going to catch up, how am I going to get *away* from moorings, let alone take them up again, without crashing into the rows of neatly moored sloops, catboats, yawls, ketches, etc., belonging to all these kids, who can answer questions like these tests at the back of the book? *Where would you recommend a helmsman to sit when running goose-winged? Describe how you would execute a controlled gybe* (say something sarcastic without moving a muscle). *Explain and illustrate what is meant by the 'Orange Pip Theory' of how a boat sails. What do you understand by Worming, Parcelling and Serving a Rope?* Alas, nothing. It's too late now.

But perhaps, if I ever write a best-seller, I will have this sloop, which I have learned to sail at a special course *for one man,* and I shall have the time because all the caulking and chandling will be done by this ex-Chief Petty Officer. He will have everything ready when we go down to the estuary.

'Evening, Ben,' I shall say.

'Evening to you,' he will say in his blunt way. 'She's all shipshape. I've fitted the Wykeham Martin and the new pintles, and I've parcelled the long splice on the main halyard for you.' He gazes across the harbour bar. 'Tide's taking off. Neaps tomorrow. Reckon you'll be off now to catch the ebb.'

'Time for a drink first, Ben.' We all go into this very clean, bare, white pub. 'Ha, thought you'd be out past Barrow Deep by now,' says the landlord.

'Oh, we're only trying out the Wykeham Martin this time,' I reply. 'The usual, Ben?' The other people in the pub are jolly laughing sailing people, not the dour kind. As we drink, a wide twilight peace descends imperceptibly on the estuary, riding lights begin to twinkle across the calm water. Won't do to stay here too long, we shall never get away . . .

Of course we shan't. I've given it up.

Some Letters Tied with Blue

A FULL ACCOUNT of how I came into possession of the Bacon-Hathaway correspondence must wait, I am afraid, until certain legal questions have been settled concerning land ownership and the status of the archaeological students from one of the new universities who assisted me. It will suffice here to say that from youth I have been interested by the story of Dr. Orville Owen's MSS.

To recapitulate briefly, in Easter Week 1911 Dr. Orville Owen, a prominent Baconian, assisted by the Duke of Beaufort's workmen, made some excavations in a bend of the River Wye. He had, after thirty years' research, discovered a cypher which led him to believe that Bacon had buried certain MSS there. Originally he buried his treasure near Chepstow Castle. Then, later, 'fearing its discovery, he removed it and placed it in an excavation in the mud of the Wye which he formed by diverting the course of the river . . . later, a type of cache

135

was discovered, but then the work was discontinued.' (*Everyman Encyclopaedia*)

Why, one asks? The answer is simple. No wonder the Baconians hastily put the letters back and did not proceed with the work, for they show not only that Bacon did not write Shakespeare, he did not even write Bacon, except for a few of the legal treatises such as that about the *Postnati* of Scotland. Ann Hathaway wrote the plays and Bacon was merely one of many eminent Elizabethan correspondents whose ideas, like any great writer, she ruthlessly borrowed and transformed when it suited her. They seem to have met at a theatrical party in 1598, when the trouble over the Blackfriars site was coming to a head. Bacon was instantly smitten by her dark, mature beauty (he was then thirty-seven, she forty-two), and his first known letter to her is full of the punning conceits which were later to be so refined in the Sonnets (Ann altered most of Bacon's, as may be seen by comparing this pedantic effusion with the mature Sonnet 135).

> *I would I had my wish as thou hast* will
> *I wish my* will *to woo were not so strong*
> *But that for love I needs must conjure still*
> *My full-sailed verse to prove thee in the wrong:*
> *Sweet fault!* Will *not my love, displayed in verse*
> *Trace on your candid brow black furrowed lines?*
> *That which in brows beginneth beauty's curse,*
> *Writ on a page all death's dark night outshines.*
> *So, if thy* will *by* lines *be not constrained*
> *Sith fish by lines are drawne into the net*
> *Still may I hope thy* will *hath not refrained*
> *And* will *for* will *not may be changed yet;*
>> *Who hath a* will, *must learn thy* will *to pray*
>> *Who* hath *thy* will *may hope he* hath a way.

Incidentally the sexual ambiguity of this sonnet, as of some others, explains the curious dedication (*To the onlie begetter . . . Mr. W. H.*, etc.) which has so puzzled scholars. Although Bacon was unable to prevent the publication under the 'Shakespeare' name in 1609, his government connection gave him contact with the monopoly printers, and it was he, by now thoroughly ambiguous, who inserted it, for 'Mr. Will Hathaway'.

Ann's reply, after deftly acknowledging Bacon's infatuation (which was perhaps accentuated by an unconscious desire to prove his heterosexuality), proceeds to turn it to practical use:

'On, Bacon, on! 'Tis a most excellent constitution of Nature that a lover should be jealous of his mistress' *will*. For the will is the mind, saith Bonaventure, that out-argued him of Aquin i' th'old disputation: which is to say, it is not the body. Thus may the passionate coursing of love in his veins, which being corporeal, look you, are but slaves or atomies of the body, be quite enslaved by the cooling operation of this same mind or will, wherein he saith *it is so*, or *it is not so*. Yet I'll warrant you there's not one lacking a man's part, which is, a woman, though she be a very Minerva or Pallas in that same mind, would not as lief you praised her eyebrow as her declensions of Greek or her quiddities of the schools.

'Something more of this, as touching mine own estate. What should a woman do, whose mind can body forth a thousand aery fantasies, giving them shape upon the wooden O, whence with your goodly imagination in their sails they do grow to a mighty dream of the world? For men will but say women's gentle brain could not drop forth such giant-rude invention, such Ethiop words blacker in their effect than in their countenance (for you are to know I began in a most bloody vein with *Titus Andronicus*, for all that after I did follow with many a delicate-fantastical or courtly-comical conceit, love's labour's lost of my prentice youth. But now I begin to have great matter in me, and strain to the bourne and limits of our being).

'Yet could I not prosper under any sign save that of *Will*. 'Tis an honest man. His father was a whittawer, one that doth whiten skins for gloves, of Stratford-on-Avon. He, honest man, to London came and in the like trade prospered – for is he not of the Worshipful Company of Glove Makers, a burgher in fair round belly with good capon lined? And doth he not, as is now the fashion among our burghers, doat upon the company of apish actors, so that neither gloves nor gold can so puff up your whittawer or glove-man with joy as that any whoreson mummer may clap him o' the back and call him cheerly? For I warrant you it were more honour to honest Will that they should suffer him to stride ungainly on carrying a spear and mumble 'What, my lord!' or 'Murder, ho!' or but to cry rhubarb with a very wild and rhetorical rolling of the eye, than to be made Lord Mayor of London. O my prophetic soul! I see the day when it shall be more thus than it is now, when the very mummers shall be knights of the realm; truly, a parlous commonwealth, for if they are brained like ours, the state totters!'

Ann goes on to explain how the Lord Chamberlain's Company, in which Will was a major shareholder, had bought the Blackfriars theatre site but were forbidden by the Privy Council to play there for fear of bringing the vulgar theatre crowds into what was then a fashionable residential area. As a woman playwright in a jealous world of men she had to get her assistance where she could and play one off against the other; and she hoped Bacon might use his already growing influence at Court to get this decision reversed. But we know (see, for instance, G.B. Harrison's Pelican, *Introducing Shakespeare*, p. 77) that in December 1598 the Burbages and other shareholders, all armed, removed the timber from Blackfriars across the Thames to the new site, where the Globe Theatre was duly opened in the following year. It was so named only because of a last-minute error, for the intention had been to name it, in recognition of Will's substantial financial help, the Glove Theatre.

Although Bacon was unable to assist in the Blackfriars matter, his rapid rise in the new Court of James I made him a useful friend to Ann. In a letter written in 1600 he warns her that fame in the theatre, even if not enjoyed in her own name, is short-lived and doubtful:

> When in the Chronicle *I waste my time*
> *And read descriptions of some more first nights,*
> *See, duly praised, the beauty of your rhyme*
> *(They'd praise a lady if you had your rights!)*
> *Then, at your blazing triumph mute, depressed,*
> *I ponder on your lip, your eye, your brow,*
> *Take up my antique pen, but give you best;*
> *The theatre's all that matters to you now.*
> *But all their praises, don't you realise,*
> *Last for a time; then other songs they sing,*
> *Some day they'll look with less admiring eyes,*
> *Some day your skill will not be worth a thing.*
> *Then we, perhaps, will pass more pleasant days*
> *(Although I wonder!) when you lack their praise.*

There are signs of mutual influence here. Bacon's verse has become less artful and pedantic; in this somewhat gloomy sonnet there is a workmanlike attempt to incorporate the everyday rhythms of speech. But there is no doubt about the relative stature of the two writers when we compare this with Ann's subsequent working-up of this homespun material into the well-known Sonnet 106, which I print here for reference:

> *When in the chronicles of wasted time*
> *I see descriptions of the fairest wights,*
> *And beauty making beautiful old rhyme*
> *In praise of ladies dead and lovely knights,*
> *Then, in the blazon of sweet beauty's best,*
> *Of hand, of foot, of lip, of eye, of brow,*
> *I see their antique pen would have expressed*
> *Even such a beauty as you master now.*

So all their praises are but prophecies
Of this our time, all you prefiguring:
And, for they look'd but with divining eyes,
They had not skill enough your worth to sing:
> *For we, which now behold these present days,*
> *Have eyes to wonder, but lack tongues to praise.*

At this period Bacon seems to have entertained hopes of marrying Ann and starting a family. Sonnet 13's conclusion:

> *O! none but unthrifts. Dear my love, you know*
> *You had a father: let your son say so.*

appears word for word in a 1601 letter, one of many on this theme. Eventually Ann grew weary of these insistent proposals.

'. . . *Marry*! 'Tis a vain word. For truly I must marry thee against my *will*! Yet if I marry thee not, how should an issue be got 'twixt the lawful sheets? What, you egg, you bacon, fried-egg lechery, wouldst father a little bacon on me? Nay, 'tis very sure this year will see no baconkin although I may with mine honour unspotted give birth and substance to a *hamlet*' (*Hamlet* was written in 1601). 'And now forbear, the hour is late and I must yet knit up a ravel'd sleeve for Will.'

Truly, the Countercheck Quarrelsome! Indeed, although the friendship was patched up Bacon never really forgave her for this contemptuous letter, and we may perhaps date from this his plan of revenge; to destroy utterly the literary fame of both Ann and the harmless Will.

Yes, Will too was gathering a modest fame, and not merely as a kind of poor man's Maecenas-cum-spear-carrier. Hitherto the humorously tolerated burgher, laughed at behind his back by his wife's literary and intellectual friends, he had quietly developed an interest in science in those last ten years of his life (he had retired from the glove business in 1606). Among the Bacon-Hathaway letters there are also pages from a diary in a third hand, instantly recognisable as that of the signature on the famous Shakspeare Will.

'. . .whether that commerce between the mind of man and the nature of things, which is more precious than anything on earth, may not be the subject of my Great Instauration. I will use induction throughout, and order my axioms so that the most general are not reached until the last. I will perform the office of a true priest of the sense. Now certain idols beset men's minds and hinder these true perceptions. Some, received into the mind from the play-books of philosophical systems and the perverted rules of demonstration, I call the Idols of the Theatre. But it is in no wise to be doubted that the Idols of the Theatre (for that I am married to one!) will not attend to anything I say . . .'

In this, Will was wrong. Ann had at some time listened to his ideas on the doubtful value of mugged-up book-knowledge, for had she not given these words to Berowne?

> *Study is like the heaven's glorious sun*
> *That will not be deep-searched with saucy looks;*
> *Small have continual plodders ever won*
> *Save base authority from others' books.*

Bacon bided his time. As we have seen, he had already been able to introduce the 'Mr. W. H.' confusion into the first edition of the Sonnets in 1609. But he outlived Will, who died in 1616, and Ann, who died in 1623. In the five years remaining before his own death he quietly took over and polished Will's scientific notes and put his own name to them. And with an efficiency we can only marvel at when we consider its effects for nearly three hundred and fifty years, he used his vast government behind-the-scenes influence (quickly restored after his pardon in 1624) to remove all documentary evidence, not only of Ann's authorship of the plays but of huge sections of Will's life (for instance, his name does not appear in any of the lists of dinners of the Worshipful Company of Glove Makers, although he must have attended them. Bacon simply had amended lists printed and the old ones destroyed!). At the same time his intimate knowledge of Ann's mind – a knowledge far more cultivated than that of the theatre people who were her main other companions – put him in an unmatched position for placing subtle hints as to his own authorship.

Why did he commit the truth to this extraordinary hoard by the River Wye? Truly, in solving one mystery we have unearthed another.

The Umbrella Serial (1)

FOR THE READER there are four kinds of book: those one has read; those one hopes to read when one is this old man in a smoking-jacket in some marvellous firelit library (all those chaps one is vaguely aware of – Boethius, Robert Musil, that great Italian pessimist, Leopardi, Leonardi. And wasn't there another rather grand one. Vico?); books one wouldn't read if they were pushed under the cell door after 20 years' solitary confinement – 'The Carpetbaggers,' anything about lesbians or homosexuals, especially French ones, any book in which inarticulate people from some bogus sociological group speak to a tape recorder, any Bon . . .

Goodness, must reluctantly stop to leave room for the rest of this piece, which concerns a supreme example of the fourth kind – books which actually to read would be an anticlimax, books whose mere titles must be allowed to reverberate in the mind. It would be absurd to go to H. M. Stationery Office and buy the *Report of the Standing Committee respecting Umbrella Handles*, even though it costs only 8d.

Like some profoundly still Chinese vase, a title like this is a refuge. One steps into a quiet yet tremendously real world (nothing is more real than an umbrella; it resembles a bat, but bats twink out of sight in the gloaming, you can't *hold* a bat the way you can hold an umbrella – and of course bats don't keep the rain out).

Everyone will have his own idea. Mine is a sort of private television serial – moving but static, real and dreamlike, the same situation endlessly elaborated. I have the clearest picture of the committee's permanent office. It is on the first floor in the vague district between Grays Inn Road and Southampton Row, where the large, smartly painted Georgian houses now turned into offices are interspersed by smaller ones still lived in. There is still a faint sense of neighbourhood; corner newsagents with green fascia-boards, area railings, even an occasional whiff of cabbage on Sundays; the new brutalist block, fences, hoardings, warehouses full of dusty pamphlets, medical accessories, small chromium things. Miles from any park or tree, utterly urban, anonymous. London.

The chairman is Benson Benson, 69, a lawyer, long-faced, prominent cheekbones, gold-rimmed glasses, dry sense of humour. Deep down he thinks there should really be only one kind of umbrella handle, the simple walking-stick-type hook, with a gold band, that is on his own. But strong-faced Thorold Parkson, 56, knows that times are changing. His great-grandfather founded Parkson's Umbrellas in Manchester (my encyclopaedia says umbrellas are manufactured 'mainly in London, Glasgow, Manchester, Paris and Lyons') but today Thorold manages the factory built on Western Avenue in 1937. He has recently been persuaded by his advertising agents to accept a complete restyling, even to the withdrawal of the trademark, famous in the twenties and thirties, of a little drawing of an umbrella with underneath it the words *Famous since the rain of Queen Victoria*. Parkson's wife, Yvonne, is French, daughter of a Lyons silk merchant whom he met on a business trip in 1936.

In the past there have been many heated arguments between him and Eddie Leibovitch, 41, balding, diamond tie-pin, double-breasted suit, who with £100 capital started the now well-known firm of Brollity Ltd. (factories at Edmonton and Hirwaun Trading Estate in Wales), which claims to make 'every other British brolly' and has massive contacts with the big chain stores.

The moderating influence between them has been Roger Preston, the ex-officio member from the Board of Trade, a career civil servant of 34, unmarried. For the past two years he has occasionally taken the committee's secretary, Hester Folsom, 32, to a theatre and dinner, and when alone Hester often takes off her almond-shaped glasses, pats her hair, stares into the mirror and wonders if she really attracts him.

Today, however, Parkson and Leibovitch are united in their hatred of the newest member wished on to them, Kathy Fant, three months out of Camberwell Art School and already a power in the umbrella world. Not only has she insisted, at a stormy meeting, that umbrellas ending in chic little stainless steel hooks instead of ferrules could be hung up to dry; she has rudely denied Benson Benson's mild suggestion that the hooks would catch in the hats or trousers of passers-by by retorting 'Your umbrella handle is a hook, dad, only bigger.'

The usually diplomatic Roger has become besotted with this chit and has arranged to take her to a discotheque. The others are enraged. Until Fant's appearance (everyone, including herself, refers to her thus) they have all taken their elevenses together at a comfortable old-fashioned place up the road, where white letters on the steamy plate-glass window, above the lace curtain, proclaim NOTED FO   THE BEST CUP OF TEA IN THE   STRICT. But Fant insists on a coffee bar near the *Sunday Times* office. This morning, when kindly, rotund, middle-aged Fo bustles up to serve them he says, innocently, 'Good morning, Missee Folsom, gentlemen. Mister Pleston not here?' Hester bursts into tears.

What will happen? Do not miss the next episode. Do not miss the next *twenty-six* episodes.

The Umbrella Serial (2)

EPISODE TWO OF the TV serial based on the *Report of the Standing Committee respecting Umbrella Handles* (H.M. Stationery Office, 8d.). In Episode One we saw how the committee – the chairman, dry, kindly lawyer Benson Benson (69), Thorold Parkson (56), manager of the old-established Parkson's Umbrellas London factory, forceful Eddie Leibovitch (41), who came up the hard way to found Brollity Ltd., ex-officio Board of Trade member Roger Preston (34), and secretary Hester Folsom (32), are shaken out of their routine by new member Kathy Fant (19), with-it pop umbrella designer.

'It's intolerable,' says Benson Benson. 'The fellow's behaving like a cad.'

The committee, except for Roger and Fant (as she likes everyone to call her), are having their elevenses in the café, near their office behind Grays Inn Road, NOTED FO   THE BEST CUP OF TEA IN THE
STRICT (it says this in white letters on the window). Kindly Fo's inquiry after the absent Roger has caused Hester to burst into tears.

'Maybe Mister Pleston soon see Fant not worth botheling about, come back to Missee Folsom, say he velly solly.'

'You are kind, Fo. I'm sorry everyone,' says Hester, wiping her eyes. 'Perhaps he was just being kind all this time, taking me to the D'Oyly Carte and everything.'

'You can take the day off if you like, Miss Folsom,' says Benson Benson kindly. 'We've got to go through the Regional Preference breakdown before we report to the Minister, and I don't think we shall have anything ready to dictate by today.'

'It just ain't true chubbies only go in the south,' says Eddie Leibovitch. He taps a thick file. 'Look here, Mr. Benson. I can show

143

you. I got reports from my boys in Glasgow, Gateshead, Oban, places like that. Look – '

'Let's discuss it in the office, Leibovitch,' says Benson tactfully. Eddie gets up to leave with him, and says to Hester: 'Don't worry, kid. All that fancy talk and them schools he went to don't mean a thing if he goes off with the first bit of skirt that shows up. You want to get shot of him.'

'Uncouth lout!' says Thorold Parkson, who has stayed at the table with Hester. He feels he ought to go with them, even though it will only mean an acrimonious reopening of an old argument, for at Parkson's it is still thought that hooked handles are for men, chubbies for women, with no particular regional preferences, and he does not want the mass-produced Brollity range, with their vast chain-store sales to blur this distinction still preserved in the quality range. But there is something he needs to discuss privately with Hester.

'Oh, Mr Leibovitch is a rough diamond, but he meant it kindly,' says Hester.

Parkson stares moodily into his green tea. 'Look, Miss Folsom – or do you mind if I call you Hester?' he says. 'I agree with him for once. He may well be right about Preston. I – I hope you will not think this is an inopportune moment for me to ask if you would, er, do me the honour of coming to 'The Sound of Music' tonight?'

'But – your wife, Mr. Parkson?' He is married to Yvonne, whom he met on a business trip to Lyons (a big umbrella-manufacturing centre) in 1936.

'Yvonne and I have grown apart. She resents the time I've had to give to building up Parkson's. She's French, you know. She was young and gay when I married her (neither of her parents were natives of Lyons); used to the best of everything, skiing every year and so on. And somehow, over the years – '

Hester puts her hand gently over Parkson's. Her eyes are blurred with tears, or whatever it is in that bottle from Make-up. 'It's kind of you, Mr – Thorold. But you know this wouldn't be right for either of us. You must go back to your wife . . .'

Parkson does take his wife out that night, and afterwards, over dinner at a little place in Soho, they are greeted by Henri, 30 years older now, with delight.

'Oh, Henri, ze place 'asn't changed at all.' Later, over the liqueur, 'Ah, T'orol', I 'ave been so un'appy when you 'ave been cold.'

'Things are going to be different from now on, Yvonne. Chap at the club, my age, started skiing last year, says it's not too old . . .'

The next morning Hester Folsom does not turn up, her first absence since the committee was established. It is Kathy Fant who, when

Hester's phone does not answer, drives round to the bed-sitter in her smart red Mini and finds Hester unconscious after an overdose of sleeping pills, and swiftly and efficiently arranges for medical help. She stays with her till she comes round, and tactfully withdraws when a remorseful Roger arrives for a bedside reconciliation.

She is surprised to find Benson Benson waiting outside in his Rover. 'Er, irregular, of course, but, er, thought I'd better see if she'd be all right. Been through quite a time, you know.'

Tough, brittle Fant breaks down and weeps into Benson's lapels. 'Darling Mr. Benson, you've all been so kind, and I've been so awful.'

'Nonsense, child, we all have to grow up. And you may be right about those ferrules. Got to move with the times, eh? Here, take this handkerchief . . .'

And so on. And on. And on. Till the ratings fall.

⚇

When the Wurlitzer Had to Stop

'Detectives boarded the Shaw Savill liner *Northern Star* when she docked at Southampton yesterday. They will try to discover who wrecked the cinema organ and a double bass when the ship was in Panama.' — *Daily Mail*

GOOD LORD, I thought the Purser *knew* about the Fairfax-Bensons! I mean, if he didn't, everyone else on the ship did. It's odd in a way, but I suppose I was indirectly responsible for the whole thing. We were doing a round at Wentworth one lovely sunny weekday before the Board Meeting of Peabody Marine; both of us due to retire in rotation.

'Look, F. B.,' I said, 'why don't we skip re-election this year? Take a sabbatical. Cruise, perhaps. We've pulled P.M. out of the red.'

'Thanks to the Butibote,' he grunted. I was on the technical side, I'd designed this mass-produced cruiser for the affluent society. Selling like hot cakes.

'Oh, come, old man,' I riposted, 'who arranged the finance?' (He came to us from the insurance world; lot of City contacts). 'Bring Dolly, and we'll stave off executive's thrombosis, the three of us.' I'm a bachelor, knocked about the world a bit, known a few women; and although Dolly Fairfax-Benson is a damned handsome woman I assure you there was no ulterior motive in my suggestion. I'd been a regular guest at Coathangers, their place near Leatherhead, for years.

Extraordinary effect a sea voyage and warmer climate has on a woman. They'd always been a devoted pair, no troubles in their marriage as far as I know, but do you know, we hadn't been out of Southampton a day before something got into Dolly. Of course she'd got herself a whole new rig-out for the trip, bell-bottom trousers, things like that. I gather they're the fashion again now; but by George, it took me back to the 'thirties, when they were called beach pyjamas, gals used to wear them with those floppy hats.

Odd thing was, it took Dolly back to the 'thirties too. Fluffed her hair out in big Marcel waves and all that, and kept asking the bandleader at the ship's dances for old Cole Porter numbers and things from Ginger Rogers films. And one couldn't help noticing she danced a great deal with a passenger called Jago – *Rodney* Jago, if you please. Our kind of age, but one of those tans that make you think he has some lamp at home; greying temples, face like old baby, big flashy smile. Wore blazer, white trousers, choke scarf all the time. Didn't care for him myself, and naturally I could see F. B. cared even less. Out of his depth, too, years since he'd tried to sparkle.

This Jago sparkled like hell, all the time, and Dolly lapped it up. One gala night the four of us were sitting at the bar, F. B. staring glumly into his drink, when suddenly it came to me.

'Rodney Jago!' I said. 'The crooning organist of the Granada Leicester Square. Broadcast every week on the National Programme.'

I could have kicked myself. Dolly's eyes lit up. 'Rod, of *course!*' she said. 'I knew there was something familiar. I was a terrific fan, I thought you were better than Reginald Foort. I shall tell the Captain. You must play at the ship's concert!'

'But I'm out of practice, Doll,' said Jago (I saw old F. B. stiffen at the familiarity). 'I'm what every young idol aims to be – a middle-aged agent. That's where the money is, and it's easier; you don't have to do it yourself!' But it was too late. Dolly told the Captain, and it was all over the ship, people queuing up for his autographs (they were *all* our kind of age). And would you believe it, there was an organ in the ship's cinema, it went blue and pink and had temple gongs and thunderstorms and crying baby noises on it, and went up and down. Just like the old days. Hadn't been used since the war.

'Where the hell does it go down to?' said F. B. 'The engine room?'

'Oh, Don, don't be a jealous spoilsport,' said Dolly. Well, they got this thing going, and one had to admit this Jago knew his stuff. So popular, they couldn't all get in, he was giving three shows a day. The women were all over him, but Dolly was queen. She enjoyed that.

Well, there was an odd twist to the story. When we docked at Panama Dolly went off to some night spot with Jago, and I think I was almost as sore about it as old F. B. We stayed on board and got pretty high, and when he said 'Whyn't we go down there and turn that thing into a Mangle-wurlitzer?' I was right with him. We went down to the ship's cinema (empty, everyone was on shore) and did a real wrecking job. Then we went back to the bar, and who do you suppose was the only other chap there? Jago, looking pretty glum. She'd ditched him for a swarthy type called Gaspar Ruiz, leader of one of those South American bands that wear tight trousers and frilly shirts. He played the string bass and sang. They *all* sang.

She even got them invited on board to do a show. My word, there was one hell of a row when they came on and found the double bass wrecked. Waving hands, oaths, storming off, gent in white ducks from the local police. All smoothed over, though, and the Fairfax-Bensons reunited. But I thought the Purser knew, about Jago busting the double bass, and everything.

Ah, Um, Er, Yes, Eureka!

THERE IS A leisurely, old-fashioned charm about the offer of prizes or money grants for something that the offerer terribly wants to be invented. Such is the £5,000 offered by Mr. Henry Kremer for the first man-powered flight of one mile; such, even more (and not merely financially) is the £70,000 left in the will of Mr. James Kidd, an American miner, for anyone who can offer scientific proof 'of a soul of a human body leaving it at death'.

This takes one back to the days when invention was altogether less grim and technology-ridden, when you could patent any old thing so long as you paid the Patent Office the fee. In the last century a Miss

147

Clara Louise Wells patented the idea (but no very detailed apparatus) whereby 'volcanic heat can be drawn into appropriate receptacles, furnished with tubes, to industrial establishments of whatever kind.' Emily Walker Hunter, of the Bull and Mouth Hotel, Leeds, patented the Preservation of Ferns ('my invention consists in simply ironing the fern in its natural state'). Other contemporaries patented reversible trousers, an aluminium bib for babies with a turn-up that caught the bits so you could use them again, and boots with copper and zinc soles; these, with the weak acids in perspiration, formed a battery which revivified not only the feet but the whole personality of the wearer, although whether sufficiently to counter the physical burden of clomping about with metal soles one cannot be sure.

At least seven people in America believe they will soon be able to photograph the soul. One of them, a Mr. Ireland, says his theory 'owes much to the work of Dr. Bagnall, of England, who, about a hundred years ago, developed a bluish purplish dye to cover a plastic solenoid sheet, and through this he was able to see the aura of material objects'. Many will wonder, as I did, how you could have a solenoid sheet, for is not a solenoid one of those things in your car, usually in the starter, of which garage men speak with that shrug of the shoulders when they wash their hands of anything electrical, so that you have to go to some special electrical place, down a yard, full of brown boxes and tight-lipped men in white coats? 'Ah, it's the solenoid,' they say, and you have to get a reconditioned one. Some kind of coil. Ah, but a *solen*, as far back as 1693, says the OED, was a 'framework to prevent the bed-clothes from touching an injured limb'. Mr. Ireland, it is reported, admits that his method involves hanging over someone about to die and keeping his camera ready, so obviously the subject is under one of these things, only bluish-purplish.

Meanwhile, the typical man-powered flight inventor – let us call him Mr. England – absorbed, with no time to read about such things as Mr. Kidd's will, is deeply engaged with his great flimsy contraption of balsa wood, oiled silk, feathers, felt, nylon and of course piano wire. In fact it weighs almost as much as a piano, although occupying fifty times as much space, it has something of the appearance of a piano that has grown monstrously outwards in some extraordinary vacuum; and at the heart of this piano there is, of course, some kind of bicycle.

On a calm, sunny evening, somewhere in Bedfordshire, this thing is towed by a horse, while two friends gently hold up sagging fins and ailerons, to the end of a secret meadow bordered by woods. Mr. England climbs into the saddle of compressed cardboard (lighter than leather) and clamps round his waist a light but firm aluminium belt which is integral with the whole teetering structure; for this is to anchor his body while every single muscle is involved in work. As his feet pedal, he turns two handles, one at each side. Simultaneously he keeps leaning forward and then jerking back against a felt pad which compresses a spring actuating a clockwork motor; this, together with the handles and pedals, is connected by light and ingenious gears to the propeller shaft. At the same time a rubber bag over his face is connected both to valves which alternately turn a little suction motor continuously with his intake and exhalation of breath. As he gets hot the warm air round his body is conducted to the 'Montgolfier canopy', a little fabric dome which acts as a small hot-air balloon to give extra lift. He steers with one single control, a three dimensional joystick hollow at the end to receive his nose.

Slowly at first, then building up to a kind of gentle twittering rustle, like a small windmill, the blades begin to whir. There is a certain amount of creaking, then – yes, yes, the thing is actually moving. 'Keep going, keep going!' his friends yell, controlling an overwhelming desire to give a little helping push against the first frightful inertia (but this would be cheating). The speed increases. One of the friends, a doctor, takes photographs, which will surely become historic. Then, just as it seems it must become airborne, the figure in the saddle slumps; the machine freewheels gently to a stop.

Willing hands unstrap Mr. England. At first the doctor pronounces him dead, but after prolonged administering of the kiss of life the heart starts again. It is only weeks later, after Mr. England is fully recovered, that the doctor thinks of developing his film, in which there was an experimental emulsion; and there, plain as a pikestaff, is a little bluish shape halfway between a foetus and a gargoyle, just above Mr. England's head; his soul.

Of course it may work the other way round. Perhaps Mr. Ireland cannot bring himself to wait with his camera at a dying man's bedside. After all, why *dying*? If you've got a soul surely there is even more of it while you're alive. He gets his assistant – let us call him Sam – to lie under the plastic solenoid sheet. Mr. Ireland is worried by the thickness of the plastic, Sam by the heat underneath it, for this is summer in Arizona, where it can get very hot. Mr. Ireland says any machinery, such as air-conditioning or electric fans, would disturb the radiations, but he allows Sam a hand-operated fan. He develops ever lighter and lighter plastic, ever deeper bluish-purple dyes, and an ever more subtle shape for the framework; and one day when Sam is sitting in a new version which leaves his arms free, the temperature is higher than ever, and Sam whirls his hand fan, and suddenly moves gently into the air . . .

After all, as Koestler said in *The Sleepwalkers*, most discoveries are made by scientists looking for something else. If you *know* what you are discovering, you can't really discover it, can you? Let's have a little cross-fertilisation. Otherwise you might just as well offer a prize for turning lead into gold.

The Name Droppers

THE NIGHT I met T. S. Eliot, I was at a party full of tall poets. My wife and I came, a little late as usual, to the house of my publisher (that sounds a bit stilted. The pen of my aunt, the hat of my father; the house of my publisher. But looking back, as one can even at the start of a piece, I think I put it that way because it sounds more, well, objective, less as if *I* were claiming to be a poet – as might appear if I wrote casually, right after that sentence about tall poets, 'my publisher's house'. In saying 'the house of my publisher' I am obeying a not altogether contemptible instinct to establish this objective picture of the house, of the person taking our coats downstairs, of the sound of many voices coming from an L-shaped room on the first floor of this London house; the house, as honesty only now compels me to add, of my publisher.)

Going up the stairs is partly like climbing Parnassus, wondering what all these poets will say to one when one gets to the top; and it is partly like that never-forgotten scene in *Citizen Kane*, with its sense of looking up at tall figures who cast shadows on a low ceiling.

Fortunately we find some friends among the lesser poets – smaller, chubbier poets not above, say, doing the commentary to a documentary film, a practice which gives us a tenuous common ground. But even while we are talking I am aware of these gaunt men all round me, a foot higher than I am, although I suppose they can't be really, since I am myself five feet eight inches.

Yeats, surely, was a tall man, although once a poet is dead one somehow stops thinking about his height. The only poet of whom I have an instant physical picture is Pope, simply because he was, of course, not tall, but crippled and small. And he, after all, wrote Augustan poetry in a London more graceful, more elegiac, more a *city* than it is now (what is it now?). Something wild again, a unity merely of streets, drainpipes:

> *Our street is up, red lights sullenly mark*
> *The long trench of pipes, iron guts in the dark,*
> *And not till the Goths again come swarming down the hill*
> *Will cease the clangour of the electric drill*

I don't see MacNeice here, but he probably is. If I find him I shall tell him that I know more actual lines of his than of any other poet in the room. Why does he get these slightly condescending reviews, often containing the words 'Mr. MacNeice's poetic journalism'? Probably written by some tall reviewer, with a private income, who is in this very room (Louis worked at the BBC. I wish I *had* told him now. He is dead, like Yeats. I don't remember him as being particularly tall.)

Perhaps living poets, if they are any good, simply *seem* tall because they wrestle with the wild, with the receding infinite, they tie it up in heroic net-casts of metaphors, they force drastic human similarities on to chaos, they throw delicate wire bridges over the abyss across which we later tremulously follow them.

Of course, although all poets seem tall, not all tall men are poets. Nevertheless I feel pretty certain that nearly all these amazingly tall men here either do not have my anxious desire for the metaphors and compressions to be comprehensible, or else are a kind of men that finds *all* metaphors comprehensible, because of a superior mentality.

One should not be cautious, clearly. Poets should rave. The moment a thing is comprehensible it becomes a little dreary.

Yet these men are not raving at all. They nearly all have upper-class voices. Ha, there is one tall man who is not so much a poet as an editor. He is John Lehmann, and he is, I see, talking to Stephen Spender, who of course is a poet (and, come to think of it, an editor as well).

In this room there should be the beating of eagles' wings. So many tall poets. All the available poets in London are here, and there are some who have come in specially from Greek islands. In fact the whole evening has a very Greek flavour, because the party is in honour of George Seferiadis, who is not only the Greek Ambassador to London, he is also the poet George Seferis; and we are celebrating the publication of an English translation of his poems by another poet, Rex Warner.

My wife and I are introduced to Mr. Seferiadis. I tell him he is the first ambassador of any kind we have met, let alone ambassador and poet. He smiles agreeably and we speak about the *dolmades*, the little

Greek rolls of savoury rice in vine leaves. I am relieved to see that he isn't particularly tall. But then one doesn't think of modern Greeks as tall.

Surely there must be something that unites us all in this room, even the tall critics with their upper-class voices? During a conversation with one of the chubby poets and his wife (we are trying to imagine some other ambassadors, past and present, writing poetry. What kind of verse would the late Lord Halifax have written? Sir Harold Caccia? Ribbentrop? Joseph Kennedy?) I think sadly, at the back of my mind, that I am never going to get into the class of these tall poets and it is this that makes me interrupt to tell the chubby poet of a subway *graffito* quoted in the *New Yorker*: BOYCOTT NON-ACADEMIC POETRY.

It is extraordinary to think that I once read *Antigone* and *Oedipus Tyrannus*, at school. But then, for various complicated reasons, I went into a factory that made telecommunications equipment, where I listened to oscillations in earphones all day long and filled in forms about decibel gain. Another three years and all that Greek would have stuck, whereas now the only line I can remember from either of them means 'thou art blind as to the eyes, to the mind and to the ears.' All the same, that's probably more Greek than some of the tall men in this room have – the poets, if not the critics, for if you are a critic you must know Greek. If you are a poet you must be a poet.

But it cannot be right, all this cultural classification. There must be something that unites us all. And just as I am thinking this there is an extraordinary wave, it runs right through the room. Without needing to be told we glance at the door. There is not actually silence, some social instinct ensures that a little low conversation goes on. But everyone knows, instantly, that T. S. Eliot has come.

I am certain no one in the room feels separated from Eliot because Eliot knows more Greek (or, come to that, Sanskrit), or because Eliot is a critic as well as a poet. All, all of us have looked through the exhaust fumes at the wild world, and, haunted by lost certainties, we have all felt

> *Time and the bell have buried the day,*
> *The black cloud carries the sun away.*
> *Will the sunflower turn to us, will the clematis*
> *Stray down, bend to us; tendril and spray*
> *Clutch and cling?*

He is, I observe, tall. But stooping now, for he has recently been ill. It is shortly after his second marriage, he is leaning on his wife's arm.

How many are here like me, who if asked what single poem had affected them most, would instantly reply *The Waste Land* – and then start qualifying, thinking of the *Four Quartets*? Nightschool lectures, the objective correlative; enthusiastic walks home on windy nights, an overpowering sense of something real about to burst; the kingfisher.

> *From the wide window towards the granite shore*
> *The white sails still fly seaward, seaward fly*
> *Unbroken wings.*

Voices unheard. He is in this room. And he spans the enormous Atlantic, he *is* the West; its trouble and ecstasy.

He sits with his wife on a settee in the smaller part of the L. People are introduced to him. Soon it will be our turn. What shall I say? *You have formed my soul?*

How absurd to be towering over him – he sitting, I standing. He cups his ear, I talk loudly. We are as if on a tiny white stage. Thousands, half seen in the blurred dark background, are listening. We are introduced. I hear myself speak.

'I bet I am the only man at this party who has to leave to catch the 8.30 from Liverpool Street.'

'Oh,' says Eliot instantly, 'where to?'

'Manningtree.'

'Oh, do you know why Falstaff is described as *roast Manningtree ox* in *Henry the Fourth*?'

No, but I've often wondered myself. Of course it used to be a *wool* district, all those East Anglian churches are called wool churches' (shut up, as if he didn't know this already) 'but of course you never see a sheep there nowadays, or an ox. But there is a very good butcher in Manningtree.'

Then my publisher came up with someone else to introduce; some poet. And it was time to go and catch the train.

On Conversation

THERE IS NO such thing as conversation at parties, if by conversation is meant the interchange of ideas, the marvellous mingling of minds by means of words, elegantly chosen, like pieces of mystical Meccano put together into some structure of lasting beauty or significance.

In the greatest conversation in the world, Plato's *Symposium*, it is easy for them to have this beautiful conversation because the guests are all reclining on their left elbows, not trying to stand up, holding a glass and a sausage on a stick. And there are only eight people, all allowed to speak in order.

Just let them try to organise that sort of thing at a party today.

PAUSANIAS: For my part, Socrates, I own that I find pornography boring.

SOCRATES: Have you then encountered a great deal of pornography?

BIG MAN IN BLAZER WITH MOUSTACHE: He loves pornography but he hasn't got a pornograph, ah HAH ha ha, hasn't got a pornograph.

PAUSANIAS (*ignoring this*): No, Socrates, hardly any.

SOCRATES: Now in what may boredom be said to consist?

PAUSANIAS: I should say that boredom consisted in the lack of surprise.

SOCRATES: But is it not in the nature of a surprise to be instantaneous?

LADY WEARING ALMOND-SHAPED GLASSES (*with great earnestness*): Oh, but I believe that a moment can be eternal.

SMALL BRIGHT LADY IN SMOCK: What was that marvellous thing, you know, in Oscar Wilde, when the man says this garden was intended to produce an impression of surprise in the visitor and the visitor says what impression is intended on a second visit?

HAIRY JOURNALIST: It wasn't Wilde, it was Peacock.

SMALL BRIGHT LADY IN SMOCK: Thomas Love Peacock, oh yes.

BIG MAN IN BLAZER WITH MOUSTACHE: Jane love Tarzan ah HAH ha ha.

154

SOCRATES: Let us get back to the question.

PAUSANIAS: I've forgotten what it was.

HAIRY JOURNALIST: What was the marvellous story in Peacock about the man whose wife found him in bed with the maid and said I *am* surprised and he said no, my dear *we* are surprised; you are astonished.

SMALL BRIGHT WOMAN IN SMOCK: It wasn't Peacock, it was Lord Chesterfield.

GLAUCON (*suddenly*): Yes, that is certainly true, Socrates.

SOCRATES: What is?

GLAUCON: Why, that surprise is instantaneous.

SOCRATES (*gratefully, recovering the thread*): So, if boredom consists in lack of surprise, and surprise is instant –

HOSTESS: Ah, there you are, Glaucon. Now here's a young lady who's been dying to meet you; meet Miggy Twimble [at least, that's what it sounds like].

HOSTESS (*to husband*): Do try and get some of them into the other room. They *will* not start eating. Take Socrates with you, he's talking to himself again . . .

In real life, the party is sharply divided into those who have and those who have not. All parties are attended by fundamentally three types of men and two types of women. The men are (a) non-talking, but tall, confident-looking, with sensuous red lips; (b) eager and talkative, with thin lips, but secretly afraid they are talking too much, and wishing they had thick red lips; and (c) just naturally happy men called Billy or Monty to whom something funny has always just happened. The women are (a) beautiful, totally non-talking girls with sensuous red lips and (b) others. Maybe hostesses are right to keep everybody circulating after all. There would not be much conversation at all in that other room if all the (a) men were in there with all the (a) women.

Alone But Not Posh

TO HEAR SOME people talk you would think there were only two kinds of air traveller; Alone/Posh and Group/Vulgar – hereinafter referred to, as they say in contracts, as AP and GV.

The AP traveller is a suave, mysterious man smelling of after-shave lotion, wearing pigskin glasses and equipped with dark matching luggage and a very expensive, light, casual waterproof. Now and again he consults an electronic watch guaranteed to lose no more than 3 seconds every 1,000 years.

He may be really Alone, this lean figure in the well-cut suit, in which case he is quite likely to be some kind of very high-class secret diplomat or spy, perfectly competent to disable five thugs in striped jerseys who set on him in some ill-lit alley. Or he may have a lady AP with him, a haughty dolly with those sucked-in cheeks, smelling of expensive after-chiffon scarves and money. She may or may not be his wife. They have come from some very grand house built of pale stone in Gloucestershire in 1711, and are on their way to a spot of boar-hunting with their friend M. Le Comte. AP travellers are met at the arrival gate by chauffeurs with *shiny leggings*.

GP travellers (in the plural, naturally) on the other hand, are a noisy lot. They all live in the same street in some place with a name like Bog Mills, Cogheap, Bleakbury, Clangbotham or Thrike Moor. They are all 50 and drink beer incessantly. The men wear brown or blue suits with open-necked tennis shirts, the women have fat knees and print dresses and keep shrieking with laughter.

They are on a package tour, of course – or, even worse, a charter flight. And somehow it is suggested that there is something ignoble, something lowering to the human personality, in GV flying.

Well, I dunno. I've done a lot of both kinds. Not of course that *I've* got a 1711 house in Gloucestershire. Far from it. I've got six children. I've got a garden full of nettles and ground elder; our first and probably last washing-up machine has got so that if you forget to turn off the main tap when it has finished roaring and hissing and cementing bits of rice on to the tumblers it floods the kitchen floor two inches deep, and we can't afford another one just now because the garage is going to fall down any minute and the wallpaper is a disgrace in the hall and there is that bit where the carpet is worn and we seem to buy three duffel coats a month and and and . . . well, I may sometimes fly Alone but when I do it's certainly not Posh.

As a matter of fact the boot is on the other foot or, to coin a metaphor it is time we had in the jet age, the wing is on the other shoulder. It isn't only that in GV flying one has the luxury of being with friends or family. It's this very thing of being a human parcel, of not having to think, of having things done for you, despised by AP travellers as sheep-like and sub-human, that in itself constitutes a blissful luxury for me.

Maybe it's something to do with having six children (which no AP traveller would be seen dead with. AP travellers have never even been children themselves; they are born, fully equipped with all that pigskin etc., aged 30). With six children, you spend a lot of your time just *counting*. And trying to remember if the hair brush is in the Big Case. And opening little cardboard pyramids of cream without squirting it all over the place. And saying, Well you can't *all* sit by the window. And re-counting. I've always wanted to persuade some plastics firm to make a modern lightweight version of the old convict's ball and chain, but instead of the ball there would be this light plastic suction pad with which you could clamp say three of them to the wall so they didn't get lost while you went to find the other three, in the duty-free shop or staring at the carousel unloading the luggage of an incoming flight (from Reykjavik). And, oh God, has anybody seen the little black case with the zip, it's got all the money and the passports in it, and and and . . .

Actually, you can't manage much flying at all, even GV, with six children. But even without them, there are occasions when I quite envy the GV parties, with someone to do all the deciding for them. It's not that I can't decide for myself (it's no good the real AP man sneering quietly to himself as he reads this; he's got a secretary who does the real work and finds out what time the dark blue Merc has to be sent to his door. Your real AP man is cocooned from harsh reality by this host of menials.) When I fly Alone *I'm* the one who does all the telephoning and humping bags from Gloucester Road tube station to the Air Terminal up a lot of spiral concrete staircases, because the AP travellers' secretaries have grabbed all the taxis in London.

And precisely because of this I am much more aware than they are of how much there is to be taken off one's shoulders by travelling GV. The whole flying business is such a world-wide, interlocked, delicately adjusted affair – not only the aircraft themselves, but all those radio and Telex messages, controllers on the ground handing over flights to each other, little flags on maps, radar blips, weather reports, showrooms, head offices, floor polish, computers, mysterious red-and-white striped trailers on airfield perimeters, the whole complicated set-up. One false move and you're in Bombay, or you're booked for the 15th of *next* month, or you've lost your little black case with the zip – or, most likely, your flight.

Once I was flying to Manchester. From London. Simple domestic flight, easy as getting on a bus. I was going to take part in the radio programme *A Word In Edgeways*. I got to the Terminal at the time it said, I got on the right coach. On it I met a journalist acquaintance. He was going to Manchester too (or it may have been Bombay, or he had just come back from Bombay. Anyway, he kept on about not having had any breakfast.)

At the airport he said he would set up a couple of coffees for us while I went to find the insurance machine (I'm their best customer. I love flying, in fact I've been up in a hot air balloon too, for this magazine; but I've got these six children. One day some man is going to go to one of these machines and the moment he presses the knob £9,999, in coins all put in by me over the years, will gush out in a tremendous jackpot).

I was, at most, five minutes doing this. When I got back to the coffee place there was no sign of my friend. It was 10.40, and take-off was 11.20. Well, I thought, maybe he's gone to the restaurant or somewhere to get a proper breakfast (he was Scots, after all; they have to start the day with all this porridge and oatie cakes and stuff). I ordered two coffees, in case he turned up, and waited for the flight to be announced.

I didn't read the paper, or do the crossword, or let my attention wander. We know a thing or two, we ANP (Alone but Not Posh) travellers. I kept my mind on the business in hand, I listened carefully to all the announcements. They kept on and on saying with increasing desperation, 'Will Mr. Walsh, passenger on Aer Lingus Flight A 47 to Cork, *please* report to Gate 6.'

Gosh, I thought, they're going to be pretty sharp with that Walsh when he does turn up.

10.45. 10.50. 10.55. They would be calling the Manchester flight any minute now; not one of your fussy, over-organised, called-miles-too-early international flights. Just popping up to Manchester. Chaps do it every day. 11.00. 1105.

I strolled over to the desk and asked the girl if they would be calling the Manchester flight soon.

'It was called at 10.35, as soon as the coach came,' she said 'Gate 7, but it's closed now, I should think.' I rushed to Gate 7. It was in the days when you went down a lot of zig-zag ramps, and I went down one too many, I found myself running on ground level with the stair closing down on me, like the bit under the stairs at home. I rushed back up to where the door was. And there was the aircraft on the apron, its engines already started. They wouldn't let me through.

One thing I found out that day. If you sit all by yourself in a BBC

158

studio in London, connected by what they quaintly call 'a land-line' to a radio discussion in Manchester, totally unable to intimate that you want to break into the conversation except by coughing, it is better to do it under an assumed name (like Walsh, maybe).

In GV travel you are shielded from this kind of thing. Someone else is responsible. Most of my GV travel has been with press parties, where such worries as one has are concerned either with getting a different story from everyone else when you are all going to the same place, or with not drinking so much on the aircraft that one can't last out the subsequent cocktail party, followed by tremendous formal dinner with flowery 'our two-countries-linked-by-tourist-friendship' toasts. Or it has been with about 180 other members of the New Philharmonia Chorus.

Three, four, five times a year we get into some aircraft (sometimes jet, sometimes with eight propellers and wicker chairs and wire struts) and go to Italy, or Spain, or France. Audiences in splendid marble halls and theatres throw down carnations at the front rows of sopranos and give us terrific civic receptions. Our tickets are dished out to us, we are taken everywhere in buses, we occupy entire hotels, and we don't have to *think* about anything except singing and enjoying ourselves. And none of us would change places with the poshest AP passenger in the world.

Little Acorns

LAST WEEK, A school essay by Graham Greene was sold at Sotheby's. Sadly, PAUL JENNINGS had to drop out of the bidding, but he did manage to pick up a cheaper lot, and a few others besides . . .

WHAT I DID ON MY HOLIDAYS
by Greene, G.
I usually get dissappointed by holidays they expect you to be happy but think of all the dead things cast up by the Sea, the first day I found a

dead starfish I took it to my room my Father said Poo it smells why don't you play with the other children in the hotel they are called Simpson. But there was another boy he had a dark face he watched us he said why don't we do something bad.

I asked him where are your Father and Mother he said my Father is with Miss Roberts she keeps gigling why does everyone gigle at the seaside his face wore an expression of disgust.

I always feel everybody is trying to escape from something at the seaside but they dont kno what it is and it makes them gigle they gigle in the hall of Mirrors and they put there faces in a round hole in a photograph of somebody elses Body and they gigle it makes me think of the dead Star Fish.

So I said all right to this boy his name was Lawrence he had an evil face. Let us go and look at the machines What the Butler Saw. He said Greene are you a Baby, I retorted with Spirit 'all right then, I know where the sewage comes out lets go and look at it poo it smells.'

He said nothing he looked at the Sea with Narrowed Eyes. Perhaps you would be happier with the Simpson children he said, it was an unspoken Bond. I know the back way in we can steal in and Drink the communion Wine he said. As we left the beach for the mean back streets we passed an old Man he was preaching his plackard said Repent ye Sinners thats my Father he's an old fool said Lawrence, I had a super holiday.

WHAT I DID ON MY HOLIDAYS
by Beckett, S.

I am going to write this essay on this paper with this pen about nothing because that is what the sea is it is nothing I like writing about nothing it is my favourite word here it comes agane woops   nothing

I think it look even better without a capitol letter, nothing looks more like nothing than Nothing with a captal letter. The sea is nothing strething to an illimmatable horizon. I kept staring at it in Killiney Bay that is where we went for our holidays we always go no change for Million years. I stood at the edge of the water I didn't paddel because I did not want to take my boots off because there were two tramps taking there boots off ugh poo they were waiting for somebody they said. The sea may be nothing but when I paddeled last year, the tramps were not there then, it was cold, so it must be something as well as nothing. I always knew this I bet I shall know it the same when I am Fifty or a Hundred or Two Hundred or a Million.

They were all lepping about on the strand, they shouted what are you doing I said nothing that's all there is here or anywhere else poo those tramp's boots!

160

When the tide came in I walked up the strand a long way, that was the way of it. Then I thought I saw a football in the nothing streching to that ilimmitable horizon. Then I saw it was not a football. I drew near and it was a man's head. I said Can you talk? He said of course I can talk. I have been here a million years. I said can you get out of the sand have you got a body but he started to cry and I went home we had Dublin Bay prawns for tea in the hotel.

WHAT I DID ON MY HOLIDAYS
by Betjeman, J.

We had our holidays this year
In Cornwall, spot to me so dear
The surf boomed in across the sand
And heather blossomed on the land

And in the hotel where we stayed
There was a garden where we played
Some girls were very strong and tall
And I could never win at all

We all had Aertex shirts and shorts
And gosh, I came to hate those sports
They hit me, then away they ran
With 'Yah, can't catch me, Betjeman'

We had our dinner every night
When it was only just still light
The sideboard groaned with HP Sauce
(Each family had its own of course)

And then with feet that seemed like lead
I went up oaken stairs to bed
But to sleep could never go
I heard them jabbering down below

They had red faces and plus fours
They clumped upstairs and banged the doors
(It was a golf hotel you see)
And talked, I felt quite sure, of me

They saw their daughters beat me hollow
I knew what lines their talk would follow
They wondered what that boy would *do*
And just like them I wonder too.

. . . and an Imposition handed in by James, H.

I, since that is the nominative case and one is oneself the actual (how could it be otherwise?) author (yet, again, must not the application of this so made reverend term by the mere accretion of centuries of respect – ah, yes, that at least, respect, whether it be expressed as criticism or as adulation – for the unique, the subjective process of moulding a story, fine-spun out of, as it were, nothing, to one who is already predestined to join that so revered, that so Parnassian group, those very 'authors' but is in fact in all the outward trappings of life a schoolboy, in itself constitute a veritable, nay a fundamental misappropriation of the word – the word 'author', should the reader, no matter how conscientious, have lost the thread, grammatical for all its apparent yet so necessary circumlocution, of this parenthesis, nor let that same reader, for whatever scarcely-examined reason of grudge or incomprehension, suppose – ah, how mistakenly! – that this same, for want of a better, more conformable term, 'author', will by now have forgotten that this parenthesis is of an interrogatory nature of which it will – ah, so certainly! – be asked whether it ought not to end with a question mark, thus?) of these Lines (again, though refulgent poet-glorics hang, as it were, about this word also, their connotation in the present instance cannot, nay must not, be untainted by all notions of a crime, of however inadvertent and unintentional omission) am obliged to confess that unless I can within the ever-narrowing space of words remaining to me, finish (ah, with what pain at its bluntness, its coarse insensitivity) with the congruent verbal phrase *'must not forget my essay'* I shall simply never manage the remaining 199 Lines.

There Was an Old Rhyme

THERE ARE STRONG parallels between the limerick industry and the diamond industry. The first, greatest, most miraculous diamonds were simply discovered lying on the ground, just like that, by some anonymous herdsman wandering up an alluvial river bed. Now, colossal machines drag up millions of tons of worthless rock from which more machines extract minute quantities of the real stuff.

So with limericks. There are the few hard, perfect ones; but because of the form, because it is the one kind of verse that people otherwise totally uninterested in verse can remember – and not least because of the vast soft-porn subsoil underneath the flowers – there is also a limerick industry.

'The Bawdy World-wide Best-seller,' it says on the front of one of the industry's products, *The Lure of the Limerick*, a paperback assembled by W.S. Baring-Gould. 'A fine job of research that left no barrack-room unbugged, no lavatory wall unscanned,' the *Daily Mirror* is quoted on the back as saying (and they can say it again). The blurb also quotes a limerick which, in its ignorance of what rhymes with what, its insensitivity to stress on the wrong syllable, and its jaded, elbow-in-ribs ho-ho, is typical of 90 per cent of the industry's products:

> *The limerick's an art-form complex*
> *Whose contents run chiefly to sex*
> *It's famous for virgins*
> *And masculine urgin's*
> *And vulgar erotic effects.*

(The word is COMplex, not comPLEX, and 'effects' does not rhyme with 'sex'.) As a piece of verse-making, it is about on a level with the one by another collector, Langford Reed, about the Irish city which has given its name to the form:

> *All hail to the town of Limerick*
> *Which provides a cognomen, generic*
> *For a species of verse*
> *Which for better or worse*
> *Is supported by layman and cleric.*

163

Probably BirMINGham, or BaSINGstoke, or AlDERshot, or any place where there have been convivial sing-us-another-one-do gatherings, has as much right as 'LiMErick', for which the claim is made that these verses were first sung at feasts; they were usually impromptu, and followed by a chorus which went:

> Won't you come up
> Won't you come up, I say,
> Won't you come, come all the way up,
> Come all the way up to Limerick?

Frankly, no. Nor is it necessary to find examples, as people have done, in Aristophanes; or, in Latin, in the middle of a prayer of thanksgiving after Communion, as Ronald Knox did; or in *Hickory dickory dock*. The form just grew naturally, like a tree, during the 19th century, even if the best known tender of the young growth *was* Edward Lear.

Obviously in any collection there is good stuff. There is bound to be, just as there are bound to be diamonds in all that rock.

Tastes vary, and perhaps it is not necessary to agree with the ingenious lines of Don Marquis which Baring-Gould also quotes:

> It needn't have ribaldry's taint
> Or strive to make anyone faint
> There's a type that's demure
> And perfectly pure
> Though it helps quite a lot if it ain't.

With the real stuff there is a kind of inevitability, a quality as of something just found lying there, occurring naturally, like the first diamonds – like all good art, in fact:

> There was a faith-healer of Deal
> Who said, 'Although pain isn't real,
> If I sit on a pin
> And it punctures my skin
> I dislike what I fancy I feel.'

> There was a young lady of Spain
> Who was dreadfully sick in a train,
> Not once, but again,
> And again, and again,
> And again and again and again.

Nine times out of ten people are ready to tell you, often correctly, who the author was – Ronald Knox, or Edward Lear, or whoever (Baring-Gould digs up a quite extraordinary number of American professors), but you really don't care. It is just *there*. Sometimes it is obviously ingenious, delighting in words for their own sake:

> *A tiger, by taste anthropophagous,*
> *Felt yearning within his oesophagus;*
> *He spied a fat Brahmin*
> *And said, 'There's no harm in*
> *A peripatetic sarcophagus.'*

That is not in Baring-Gould, although several are which rely on what, he tells us, Clifton Fadiman called 'Co-ordinated Orthography', another word-pleasure. Not only the famous curate of Salisbury (whose manners were halisbury-scalisbury), for which it is of course necessary to know that you say *Sarum* for Salisbury, but also

> *Said a man to his spouse in East Sydenham*
> *'My best trousers! Now where have you hydenham?*
> *It is perfectly true*
> *They were not very new*
> *But I foolishly left half a quydenham.'*

> *A rare old bird is the pelican*
> *His beak holds more than his belican*
> *He can take in his beak*
> *Enough food for a week*
> *I'm darned if I know how the helican.*

Sometimes the great ones are great because they brilliantly encapsulate a bit of science or philosophy, like Ronald Knox's verse on the Idealist thesis that things exist only in the mind of God:

> *There once was a man who said, 'God*
> *Must think it exceedingly odd*
> *If he finds that this tree*
> *Continues to be*
> *When there's no one about in the Quad.'*

and the equally famous reply:

> *Dear Sir, your astonishment's odd*
> *I am always about in the Quad*
> *And that's why the tree*
> *continues to be,*
> *Since observed by, Yours faithfully, God.*

Most people know those, and the equally inspired one on Relativity (by, according to Baring-Gould, Professor A.H. Reginald Buller, a world authority on fungi):

> There was a young lady called Bright
> Who travelled much faster than light;
> She went out one day
> In a relative way
> And returned on the previous night.

Baring-Gould has, in place of *travelled*, the less pleasing *whose speed was*. There are two lesser-known ones of the same kind:

> A scientist living at Staines
> Is searching with infinite pains
> For a new type of sound
> Which he hopes, when it's found,
> Will travel much faster than planes.

> A young schizophrenic named Struther
> When told of the death of his mother
> Said 'Yes, it's too bad,
> But I can't feel too sad:
> I'm lucky; I still have each other.'

Again, Baring-Gould has the less metrical *after all* in place of *I'm lucky*. No matter. What else do you expect in a book including one that makes *Eire* rhyme with *fire*?

> There was an old fellow of Eire
> Who perpetually sat on the fire
> When they asked, 'Are you hot?
> He declared, 'I am not.
> I am Pat Winterbottom, Esquire.'

Har har. If you're going to break the rules you must break them on purpose, and spectacularly, as in the famous one about the Old Man of Japan (whose limericks never would scan) or my own favourite.

> There was an old man of St Bee's
> Who was stung on the nose by a wasp;
> When asked if it hurt
> He replied, 'No, it doesn't,
> But I'm jolly glad it wasn't a hornet.'

166

(I never knew, till I looked it up, that this splendidly anarchic, contemporary-sounding piece of surrealism was in fact by W.S. Gilbert).

Of course the limerick may be on an altogether different level:

> When they said to a Fellow of Wadham
> Who had asked for a ticket to Sodom,
> 'Oh, sir, we don't care
> To send people there'
> He said, 'Don't call me Sir, call me Modom.'

B-G has a Wadham one, but it isn't as good as that. Characteristically, it rhymes *Wadham* with *bottom*.

One thing is certain. Whatever its subject, the limerick reached its final technical form in the second half of the 19th century, when people began to realise that for all the magical charm of Edward Lear –

> There was an Old Man of Thermopylae
> Who never did anything properly
> But they said, 'If you choose
> To boil eggs in your shoes
> You shall never remain in Thermopylae.'

– you could get more of a satisfying, surprise-in-the-last-word pay-off if it ended with a different word. After that, even the late Ogden Nash could not improve on it, tinkering about with something he called a Limick:

> Two nudists of Dover
> Being purple all over
> Were munched by a cow
> When mistaken for clover.

Not his best, eh? Not even in the same league as, for instance:

> There was an old man in a trunk
> Who enquired of his wife, 'Am I drunk?'
> She replied with regret
> 'I'm afraid so, my pet,'
> And he answered, 'It's just as I thunk.'

Baring-Gould quotes a writer, mythical or not, in *The Times Literary Supplement* who was no doubt correct in pointing out that 'the form is essentially liturgical, corresponding to the underlying ritual of Greek tragedy, with *parados* [first ode sung by Chorus on entrance; mis-spelt *parados* in *The Lure of the Limerick*] of the first line; the *peripeteia* [reversal of circumstances, change] of the second; the *stichomythia* [sharp disputation in alternate lines] of the two short lines . . . and the *epiphaneia* [showing-forth, manifestation] in the last.'

Whenever somebody wants to advertise something in verse, his first request to the advertising agency is nearly always for limericks, not always with brilliant results. The moment one looks out on the political scene it is limericks which almost instantly suggest themselves:

> *The Marxist prediction, alas,*
> *Is not what has now come to pass;*
> *The classless society*
> *(English variety)*
> *Means* leaders *who're lacking in class.*

> *An LSE graduate said*
> *'As a student, of course, I was red;*
> *But now I'm with Shell*
> *Let the proles go to hell,*
> *My pension is safe till I'm dead.'*

> *If Britain were only a yacht*
> *We'd be out of this mess like a shacht*
> *With Ted and his crew*
> *Knowing just what to do;*
> *But it isn't, and so we are nacht.*

Or there is the political scene further afield:

> *The stateman's great art, that of fixn,*
> *Would have been more effective in Nixn*
> *If he'd understood*
> *That the bad and the good*
> *Are for keeping apart, not for mixn.*

> *We rejoice that his new model Ford*
> *Can reverse from the chasm abhorred*
> *But are not so clear*
> *When it gets into gear*
> *About what it is driving toward.*

Then there is the cultural scene:

> A modern composer called Fred
> Wrote a piece of which all critics said
> 'We are certain that this'll
> Make errand-boys whistle';
> He thereupon shot himself dead.

> All newspaper boardroom agenda
> Since Murdoch, have had some addenda;
> Must everyone plan
> For the dirty old man
> Who only wants female pudenda?

> An actor said, 'One never wearies
> Of playing in endless war series;
> One offers the nation
> One's camp concentration
> Where even the Nazis are dearies.'

> The comics who go on TV,
> From pressing anxiety free,
> Don't need to hear laughter –
> It's all dubbed in after;
> They laugh as they pocket their fee.

Here is one entitled 'On Reading the Latest Literary Autobiography';

> We have wasted our time all these years
> Reading Homer and Virgil, my dears,
> With no clue in the text
> As to how they were sexed,
> Over-, under-, or bi-, or just queers.

And here, just for the hell of it, is another one that just came to me:

> Said Lot, 'I've escaped from Gomorrah,
> That city of sin, shame and horrah;
> It wasn't my fault
> That my wife turned to salt,
> so I'll marry my daughter tomorrah.'

There is in fact no department of life not capable of being brought within the compass of these mysterious five lines, as bare, basic and essential as the five lines of a music stave. And I don't mean 19th-century or early 20th-century life; I mean our own:

A unisex man who got wed
To a unisex woman, soon said
'We have come to the end
Of this curious trend
And find duosex better in bed.'

O girls, you've no glamour or glitter
Until you find footwear that's fitter!
What on earth is the good
Of those huge heels of wood?
While you teeter and totter, we titter.

A property firm in the City
Destroyed a fine street without pity,
Admitting 'Ah yes,
It's a hideous mess
But the profits we think are quite pretty.'

A last word of warning, however!

Beware of the limerick bore;
From a seemingly infinite store
He trots out more verse
Where the scansion gets worse
But the subject's the same as before.

Hunt the Reader

'**I** DON'T ACTUALLY think signings do much good,' said the young bookshop manager. 'The only really successful one I've known was when I was working down in the West Country.'

'Who was the author?' I asked the manager. 'A. L. Rowse?'

'No. Henry Cooper. And a friend of mine had a queue for the whole two hours for Robin Knox-Johnston. I don't think they come for *writers*.'

I had already been sitting for half an hour behind a table groaning under piles of my book. The window was awash with them. A huge placard adjured customers to 'come and meet Paul Jennings'. Arrows and fingers pointed towards the table. All that had happened so far was that a middle-aged man had come in and asked me 'have you got a Malaysian dictionary?' This was in Norwich, in a very nice shop (there's no such thing as a nasty bookshop, except of course in the back streets of Soho). He thought *I* was the manager. They very often do, because I'm the one that is sitting down.

I don't think they come for writers either. At least, they don't come for me. At the first one I did (in 1952, the Army and Navy Stores it was) a woman came up and started a breathless account of how much she had enjoyed Doctor in the House. It was some time before I could get a word in.

'I'm sorry I'm not Richard Gordon,' I said (who wouldn't be, with sales like that!).

She was very indignant. 'But it *says* so, in the window!'

She didn't buy my book (Oddly Bodlikins, long out of print, like all of them). On my way out after the two hours (ten copies sold, although of course I signed a lot more in case people had mistaken the day) I looked in the window. There *were* piles of his book too, but the placard announcing my signing was undoubtedly by piles of mine.

So why do writers do it? Greed? Not in my case surely. I reckon ten a good score (on a £2 book that's £2 in royalties, Whoopee). Once I sat for a whole day, except for the short break for a very jolly and hospitable lunch, in a bookshop in Ipswich where they really try – they were having a whole week of signings, two writers at a time. I live near Ipswich anyway, but my fellow signer was one of your London writers, very well known, his book had been widely and favourably reviewed. He sold two, I sold one (The Living Village, that was).

Pride? With constantly being mistaken for the manager? With people silently picking up *my* book, my child, leafing through it with a sad, puzzled face and drifting wordlessly away? (Perhaps there should be another table with the the actual books on it, some distance from and out of visual range of the author, so that only people who wanted one would approach him; unless he is, for instance, a TV personality, and they have come to touch the hem of his garment.)

Pride? After the experience I had with my first children's book? This was a new departure, I thought I would be doing a service to the bookshop where I knew my friends, at least, would be going to buy it. I went into their children's department to forewarn them.

'Have you got The Hopping Basket?' I said (all the unsold copies long since thrown down a well by the publishers). A look almost of terror came into the assistant's eyes. 'Who's it by?' she said – like an Ivy Compton-Burnett character, 'in a hopeless tone'.

There is something about a bookshop that prevents one from bawling out one's own name. In an equally hopeless tone I said, 'Well, it's by me.' Before I could think of anything else she went to the boss lady and I heard her ask: 'Have we got The Hopping Basket, by Mee?'

No. Probably most writers at their lonely desks, dream of meeting their readers. (I reckon that the ones who actually buy my books would just about fill the Royal Festival Hall, it would be nice to have a party there, with perhaps a little music afterwards. Cost more than I get for the whole book just for the wine, though, even if they got one glass between four.) Just to meet one person who had actually read and liked the stuff makes the whole thing worthwhile.

There is also one's admiration for the dauntless book-sellers, battling on against an extraordinary kind of active absentmindedness, combined with surrealist unpredictability, on the part of the public who drift into their shops. In few bookshops have I ever watched two hours of what you could call bustling trade, yet there are always rich incidents and stories.

In a Cambridge bookshop, two of those identical teenage girls, with long coats, bobble hats and round eyes of the kind that model in pairs, looking sulky, in teenage magazines, came up to me with a book on elementary karate and said 'haven't you got anything more advanced than this?' and went out when the manager said he was sorry, he hadn't.

The manager of the Norwich shop told me that two women had come in the previous day, and after looking round for some minutes one of them said to the other. 'Oh, this is only a bookshop,' and *they* went out.

It is well known that Arnold Bennett used to haunt bookshops with

172

a cheque for £100 that he was going to give to anyone he saw actually buying one of his books, and he never did. It is as though one was irresistibly drawn by a desire to see the process actually working; this is the centre of the whole process, something magic, a transformation, the point where one's private fantasy suddenly becomes real. It is like trying to watch the exact moment when the kettle boils; one is never looking when it does.

Never mind, at least bookshops are still *there*. Being in one reminds me of Douglas Woodruff's story about the days when as a young man he worked for J. L. Garvin. His study was piled with books, there were heaps all over the floor as well as filling every shelf. 'I ventured to ask him if he had read them all. He said "No; but they're radioactive, dear boy, radioactive."'

It's Everybody's Pidgin

HERE IS THE beginning of an essay by a 13-year old boy which a teacher friend showed me. 'Actually quite a bright boy, and not dyslexic,' he said:

'We hab a nis hodla and wet torcey me dedan mume me sicte lurt lurt to sim in the se the we som big waws . . .'

You have to have been teaching for some time to know that his means: 'We had a nice holiday and went to Torquay (with) my Dad and Mum. My sister learnt to swim in the sea. There were some big waves . . .'

Here is something a bit better, since you expect something a bit better from anyone hoping to do a Music O-level:

'A snarter is a composition written for one or more instruments. When it is written for three instruments it is called a shmpe. The great snarter writer was Betehoven. He wrote 62 pags of snarters. The Phathque op is 13 has three movements. The first is in snarter form. It has expisition, development and decapitulation.'

This is the clearer communication, although it assumes a readership able to make the intuitive jump from *Phathque* to *Pathétique* and from *shmpe* to *symphony* (one must admit this with some regret; *shmpe* would be a very good word for some of those modern compositions, all gongs and cymbals, when you long for them to get to the decapitation).

For an increasing number of people now, this kind of thing is near enough:

'In answer to you avertisment I wish to aply for the tempry posision in your controll labotery. I have two A levels Physics and Chemistry . . .'

Not, presumably, English, although even if this had been among the applicant's attainments there is no certainty that it would have been all that much better. After the brilliant false dawn of universal compulsory literacy there *was* a brief period when everybody knew how to spell *symphony* and *laboratory*, or they did not get very far. But the unpalatable fact is that in order to exercise control over anything as rich, diverse, and full of infinite potential as the English language you need rules. And rules need learning. And the only way to make most people learn them is to bang them very hard on the knuckles with a cylindrical black ruler every time they get anything wrong, up to the age of about 14.

Well, we can't do that any more; and meanwhile the proportion of yacking to writing has increased a thousandfold, a huge flood slubbering all over the precise moulds of the written language and squashing them out of shape. The quacking flow comes out of the walls, from lighted screens, handbags, car fascias, rowing-boats, woods, fields, caves, deck-chairs, trains, lifts, bathrooms, bedrooms, even cemeteries.

Even without a transistor you can almost feel this torrent of unstructured words trembling about you in the air. Sooner or later it will burst through and start babbling in an incomprehensible jumble on wire fences, iron gates and railings, even keys, wristwatches, ear-rings; any bit of metal it can find. Then the next big invention will have to be some kind of portable neutralising box that can silence a few yards around its owner.

Many of the people who do this yacking have grown up in the post-cylindrical-ruler-on-knuckle days. They are dimly aware that somewhere there are, or were, rules. But the few pedants upset about it are not very for*mida*ble to ordinary people; thankfully it is now a super*flu*ous con*trov*ersy, it would be a diabolical liberty to try to make everyone talk proper . . .

Surely the time has come to stop trying to bridge the ever-widening gap between written and spoken English. Why don't we go the same way as they did in Old China, and let popular spoken English go on its own way, independently of the carefully preserved written language?

The more I look at pidgin English, the more it seems to me to offer a vivid, ready-to-hand language which, with a very few additions, would answer all the needs of popular communication. What could be more expressive than 'apple belong stink' for 'onion', or 'gubmint-catchum-fella' for 'policeman'? Or 'grass belong face' for 'whiskers'?

It is said that 'halt or I fire!' used to be 'you-fella you stand fast. You no can go walkabout. Suppose you fella walk-about me killim you long musket.' Rather long-winded for an emergency; but there are enormous longueurs in, for instance, cricket commentaries, which would be charmingly filled by this kind of thing:

Edrich stand longtime he do nutting, sametime ball-fella Lillee tell im field go here go there, he make im one-two-three belong slip. Time we watch im, me ask friend belong me in talk-box, what time him other fella bat belong left hand make ten-by-ten in one-two hour Thursday. You look im in book belong bimeby (book of old records) *Jim. Yes, him book say J.R. Snogsworth belong left-hand, make ten-by-ten leventh day Shower Time* (April) *one-two-six year by Jubilee belong Queen Victoria* (i.e. 1893). *Now Lillee him start run . . .*

And think how much more interesting even humdrum things like the weather forecasts would sound:

Tomorrow you-fella by sunset land (the West) *catch im plenty rain belong sea. You fella in deep land sometime catch sun, sometime catch water, you fix im hat belong head or wind catch im you lose it. You-fella other side belong sunrise you all-time lucky bastard, catchim sun all day, catchim rain in night . . .*

As a matter of fact, when you come to think of it, a great deal of *written* English (if you can describe Government publications as written) would sound better, and could be read out on the media, in this form. Take that booklet on inflation that came through everyone's letterbox the other day:

ATTACK ON INFLATION. A POLICY FOR SURVIVAL. A guide to the Government's programme. *Fight im big debbil, big money get little ting. Make do for keep on living. You follow im walk-about belong Gubmint.*

I don't know, though. Even now I can see the end of it. The mandarins who had held on to the written language would feel, as the generations went by and the gap became ever wider, that their duty was increasingly plain: to bring the glories of our literature to the masses. So they would set to work on translations, beginning of course with the classic passages:

> *To be, or not to be: that is the question:*
> *Whether 'tis nobler in the mind to suffer*
> *The slings and arrows of outrageous fortune,*
> *Or to take arms against a sea of troubles,*
> *And by opposing end them?*

Bin or no bin, you ask im? You tink more good, carry in by you head stone belong string him bad fella throw it, carry im arrows belong bad debbil luck? You tink fight by dem troubles belong sea, make um all-time stop?

On the other hand, of course, they might bring back the cylindrical black rulers.

Is It a Constable?

SEVERAL TIMES IN news stories about the fake Samuel Palmers and other such I have noticed the words 'the Art Fraud Squad'. Everyone has heard of the ordinary Fraud Squad, probing yet another pillar of the City, or Socialist contract-wangling, or Soho, or whatever. But *art*?

I should like to think that we have never heard of them before, because most of the time they are left well alone, in a suite high up at the Charing Cross end of New Scotland Yard, where they enjoy not only a north light but also extensive views of the river from the wide studio windows. In recent years a small laboratory has been added, but it is not much used; for X-rays, carbon tests, pigment analysis and the rest of it, they prefer to rely on the resources of the main Forensic Laboratory.

Grizzled, bearded Chief Inspector Max Prothero, in sombre mood on his return from the weekly meeting of departmental heads, glances up at the motto over the entrance to the familiar, comfortable, shabby old Art Nouveau room before entering. It is from Aristotle: *We must represent men either as better than in real life, or as worse, or as they are. It is the same in painting.*

The quotation, like everything else in the room, dates from the time of the famous Commissioner Horatio Trenton, creator of the AF Squad, the only policeman in the New English Art Club, to which he graduated via evening classes at the Slade, friend of Sickert – and unmasker of famous Edwardian forgers like Dodger Miles ('Dürer' mezzotints), Willie Hunt (the 'Birmingham Botticelli'), and the notorious couple Fay Louise Jenks and Oliver Crompton, whose Vermeer factory at Carshalton deceived half the world's museums.

176

Prothero, surveying the huge room, with four constables and a sergeant working at their easels in the last of the winter afternoon light, reflects sadly that his long fight to keep it this way, with real policemen properly trained in the techniques of copying, is coming to an end. On just such a day 30 years ago Trenton had said to him, 'Imitate the imitators, that's the way to do it! Read yer Aristotle, me boy!'

The sergeant, Dewi Llewellyn, just promoted for his brilliant uncovering of a Swansea gang turning out 'recently discovered' works by David Jones and Ceri Richards, sees at once that something is amiss. 'You been having another battle with the Philistines, Inspector bach, I can see.'

'Light the gas, Dewi, there's a good fellow,' says Prothero wearily, 'and let's have a little Pernod. I need it. You're quite right. The devil of it is, they're so *illogical*, one can't reason with them. You know how I've fought for years to keep this Squad a genuine part of the Yard, with men who have proved themselves as ordinary policemen, passing our own internal examinations here in art forgery. I always resisted intake from the universities, straight into officer rank, after the Trenchard reforms.'

'Have they been on about Constable Dalrymple again?'

'Yes. You know he was one we *did* take from outside, just to satisfy them. He did Fine Arts at the University of East Anglia, wherever that is.'

'But he's terribly keen on the job, and quite content to start as a constable. I'm sure everyone in this room would agree he proved his worth in the Case of the Missing Mondrians.' There is a general murmur of assent.

'Quite so. I don't pretend to understand abstracts; rhythm schmythm, how can you tell one from another? But these millionaires go for them, and it was his discovery that the little yellow square was in the wrong place that saved the art buyer of Neiman-Marcus in Dallas from losing nearly a million dollars, and put Pincher Snodgrass behind bars.'

'I suppose they were on about him having to wear uniform as usual.'

'Yes. Just because he *is* only a constable, and because our establishment allows only one sergeant – and that's *you*, Dewi, no offence! – Internal insist he wears a uniform.'

'But that's not fair! There are plain-clothes men, detective constables, not of officer rank, in other branches.'

'Just what I said. They're only doing this to try and force amalgamation with the general Fraud Squad. They keep saying we just sit about. It's useless trying to explain the need for constant research and keeping up with modern forgery technique, as well as going out after forgers.'

'But we do, Inspector bach, we *do* go out! Cosmo, Cyril here – all of us do it. Shadowing anyone who spends a suspicious amount of time copying masterpieces in the museums. Mingling with the customers in low artists' cafés near the V and A and the Tate – aye, and the Lever Art Gallery in Liverpool, the Barber Fine Arts in Birmingham; even Glasgow.'

'Do you think I didn't tell them all that? But no, they said. Uniform at all times. I asked them, what use would Archie Dalrymple be in uniform with a foot of that gorgeous blond hair, like the aureole of some flaming Pre-Raphaelite god? Tell him to get it cut, they said. Where is he, by the way?'

'Out on a job. Got a tip-off at the National.'

'Was he in uniform?'

'Of course.'

'They'll get away then . . . as usual. Even if he had cut his hair, I asked them, what the hell would be the use of a uniformed policeman with close-cropped fair hair in a low artists' café? That's *your* problem, they said. I tell you, Dewi, sometimes I feel like – '

The bell beside the candlestick telephone shrills urgently. Wearily Prothero picks up the earpiece. Then he stiffens as the hasty whispered message comes through. It is from Constable Dalrymple.

'Archie One here. Sir, we were right about that woman copying the Botticelli *Annunciation*. She finished it today, and I followed her to a mews flat behind Harley Street.'

'Where are you now?'

'In the telephone kiosk opposite the BBC. I think they're going to scarper. I had my cloak on over this damned uniform, but it must have opened as I ran, they saw I was a policeman. Their look-out man followed me. He's waiting in Riding House Street. I think I saw him aiming a Biretta till he saw me looking. Can we get the nearest squad car on to him?'

'We'll handle this ourselves, Archie. Stay where you are. Stare him out, with a hand under your cloak as I taught you, he'll think *you've* got a gun.'

Prothero puts the phone back on the hook. 'Come on, men,' he grates. 'We'll show them whether the Art Fraud Squad are real policemen or not. Here are your truncheons. Dewi, get the horse into the hansom straight away.' Past experience has shown that this vehicle, once owned by Horatio Trenton himself, cuts a way through the traffic – as admiring motorists pull to one side – with a speed impossible to mere police cars. In no time, filled with the burly and determined men of the Art Fraud Squad, it is clattering along Whitehall to the rescue of their comrade and the apprehension of yet another forgery gang . . .

At least, I hope it is. If not they might just as well be *ordinary* policemen, mightn't they?

Putting the Best Fetish Forward

L IFE IS FULL of surprises, but honestly I never thought I would be surprised by an advertisement by the publishers Routledge and Kegan Paul. But there it was. In the *Times Literary Supplement,* no less:–

The Sex Life of the Foot and Shoe
WILLIAM A. ROSSI
From earliest times the foot has played a direct role in human sexuality; William A. Rossi examines the realities of foot and shoe eroticism practised by almost all of us whether consciously or unconsciously, and gives proof positive that the words foot and shoe are part of the language of sex. £4.75

Routledge and Kegan Paul, who would have thought it! How serious and businesslike they sound, with all those hard consonants – hardly like publishers at all; one can imagine a sign, glimpsed across some waste land in Birmingham, over a Victorian brick factory, saying ROUTLEDGE & KEGAN PAUL BROS WIRE ROPES CRANKS & SCREW BODGERS. It has been no surprise, knowing they *are* publishers, to see that most of their books are solid serious sociological stuff – Durkheim and chaps like that.

It's easy enough to imagine the magic day when Chatto met Windus or Secker met Warburg – obviously all Oxbridge people with a foot in the culture world already, it simply needed the magic conjunction of their names for it to be blindingly obvious that they must set up as publishers, it would all have been cheerfully arranged over a laughing lunch.

With Routledge and Kegan Paul it must surely have been altogether a more serious matter. I myself see Routledge as a man in his early sixties, looking rather like Kipling, with an iron-grey moustache. In the late 1880's, after a working life as an accountant in Chicago, he is returning to England having inherited a Leicestershire estate from a distant cousin. On the White Star liner he strikes up a rather earnest friendship with Kegan Paul, European representative for a rapidly-growing Kansas-based firm of agricultural machinery makers.

Kegan Paul, a muscular, hard-featured, close-shaven 42, shares with Routledge an enquiring Victorian-agnostic social conscience. When the ship docks at Liverpool the two men look down from A Deck on the swarming mass of Irish and Polish emigrants waiting to board her. 'The western world is in ferment, Kegan Paul,' says Routledge. 'I believe there is a need for a new publishing house which should examine the problems of which we have been speaking.'

'By heaven, I believe you are right, Routledge!' exclaims Kegan Paul, and so the famous house is born . . .

And suddenly, the bright young men take over, there are fierce board-room arguments. 'Sociology, that's a good steady text-book trade, I admit,' says one of them, 'but if we want to expand and go places, we'll need some sex in our list, like everybody else.'

Even so, is there not a lurking suspicion that the blurb-writer has made a mistake? *Is* shoe eroticism practised by all of us? It's a well-known but surely not very common perversion. And when it comes to words that are 'part of the language of sex', or of anything else, you can't beat the *Oxford Dictionary of Quotations*; it has twenty-nine references under *foot,* and only three of them have the remotest suggestion of sexiness:

> Her f. was light (Keats, *La Belle Dame Sans Merci*)
> Keep thy f. out of brothels (Edgar in *King Lear*)
> Nay, her f. speaks (Ulysses in *Troilus and Cressida*)

– and in that last one Ulysses goes on, having pointed out already that 'there's language in her eye, her cheek, her lip' to say, after that foot bit, 'her wanton spirits look out, at every joint and motive of her body'. In other words, the foot comes pretty *low* in the list of sex-stimulants.

Most of the other quotations bear this out, even if you allow the letter f. its suggestive pre-Tynan significance:–

Caught my f. in the mat
f. and hand go cold
f. – f. – f. – sloggin'
f. is on my native heath
Squeeze a right-hand f. into a left-hand shoe
The Forty-Second F.

Nor do the *shoe* entries seem much more exciting, they are all stuff like

dame has lost her s.
for want of a s.
one, two, buckle my s.

No, surely what we have here is not a Routledge and Kegan Paul social study job, but a novel; a red-blooded, rip-roaring, H.E. Bates kind of novel, set in that timeless Mummerset inhabited by his Larkin family; and The Foot and Shoe is a *pub*.

The story has all the ingredients of a best-selling sex comedy thriller. Everyone is surprised when Henry Stinton, a VAT Chief Inspector, ten years before retiring age, at the height of his career (though not of his sexual powers, for he has been impotent for some years), throws it all up to become the manager of The Foot and Shoe at Abbots Farthing.

Although this remote village is notorious as the scene of two unsolved sex murders, and at the start of the story has acquired further prominence as having the highest illegitimacy rate in the country, Cynthia, Henry's nymphomaniac wife, is not pleased by the decision, since it will take her some sixty miles away from her current infatuation, Rodney Farquharson, a young government scientist working on an investigation into the problem of nymphomania for the Ministry of Psychiatry.

The dislike between Cynthia and the locals of Abbots Farthing is mutual. 'Har, me dear, I'd rather go ferretin' along of 'ee than George Dicey,' says one old regular, Amos Turdley, about a week after reopening night (The Foot and Shoe has been closed for six months after the unexplained disappearance of Dicey, the previous landlord).

'Ugh, how I hate their awful gnarled hands, which they can't keep to themselves,' Cynthia says later that week to Rodney, on his sheepskin rug (she has gone up to London, ostensibly to choose curtains for the saloon bar). 'And most of them don't even drink beer, they have something called a Crimley Ginger.'

Rodney raises himself on one elbow, not even noticing her strong white thighs for once. 'Ginger, did you say? By George, Cyn, that's interesting. I've a good mind to come down next week-end.'

'Rod, there's something I've been meaning to tell you. I don't think we'd find Henry so – well, so complaisant. I don't know whether it's that damned country air or what, but something seems to have happened to him after all these years. At first I thought he was only besotted with this woman that always wears floral hats, a big wheel in the W.I., Mary Bridd, she's a widow, they all call her the Merry Briddo, it's that kind of place. But last night, when we went to bed . . .'

Cynthia does not see the thoughtful look that comes into Rodney's eyes – nor, of course, does she hear the call he puts through to Inspector Framlingham of Dabchester, or some such name, after she has left.

In fact she will only see him alive for another five minutes. When, the following Saturday, he does arrive at Abbots Farthing, Henry is down in the cellar tapping a new barrel. Rodney enters the bar, kisses Cynthia briefly, orders a Crimley Ginger and goes out immediately after drinking it.

Five minutes later Inspector Framlingham, waiting in a lay-by in Bare Knuckle Wood, hears a girl's piercing scream. Rushing up to the short-cut path to the village that runs through it, he is just in time to rescue the girl, her dress torn and everything, feebly trying to hold off Rodney, who glares at him with red, lust-inflamed eyes and then suddenly collapses dying, as an unseen hand flings a knife accurately into his back from behind the sinister, rustling trees. With his last breath Rodney pants ' . . . couldn't help it . . . Crimley Ginger . . . aphrodisiac . . . Bridd.'

When the Inspector reaches Mary Bridd's house she and Henry Stinton are digging feverishly in the back garden. He removes his pipe. 'Mary Amelia Bridd, née Crimley, I arrest you for the murder of George William Bridd and of George Dicey. Please do not disturb George Dicey's body any more. It may be used in evidence against you, as may anything further you say. Henry Clark Stinton, I arrest you as being an accessory to these crimes. You discovered, from your examination of George Dicey's VAT accounts, that he was receiving large sums from Mary Bridd, whose father, the proprietor of Crimley's Breweries, had handed on to her the secret formula of the world's most powerful aphrodisiac, by threatening to reveal it to another brewery in which he had an interest. You then . . .'

H'm. Good title, that would have been. *The Sex Life of the Foot and Shoe,* by Paul Jennings. Well, I know one publisher I shan't be able to sell it to now.

✦

The Last Cuckoo?

D EAD SIRS – I have wathed absolutely it; instruktions on your pink ticket which tells me:

Instruktions for Setting-up this Quarter-hour Cuckoo Clock.

Clock must absolutely be kept upright, when winding the chain of the casing.

The clock is now suspended on the wall. To this purpose is provided hole on the back wall or a carrir-wire. The nail may only be so long as not touching any wire.

The pendulum is now being hung on the wire loop protruding on bottom of caling whilst the weight is suspended on the fool of the clock-chain. Now push the pendulum.

The cockoo is calling once every quarter of hour. Avoid turning backward the painters. When the clock advances too quickly, push the pendulum dish towards the bottom, when the clock goes too slow, push the pendulum disk upward. To displace the pendulum disk, absolutely take oft the pendulum from the wine hook.

Please wath absolutely that no wire is being damaged or bent on the clock. Should case arise that the chair is gliding off the wheel, please put the clock to the head and get gliding again the chain across the wheel.

With clocks having a closed box the back wall is to be removed and the paper above the bellows pair es slowly to be taken away.

These are the incidents which have lowed. I can bend my pen to relate you, that there was a big cursing of th in my house wich had a peacfull till your clockoo-cuck arrive!

I must speke truely to you. I by self is not wanting to suspend on the wall cluckoo-cock any where in my house which has a lot of clocks in it already, with an electic one (silent) and not using my soul jump out of its socket every quarter of an hour with a bird popping out like a mad one with cockoo, cockoo, to drive a nail through the head!

I have tripped in your country by meself for some vacancies in my youth, and admired the maiestic panoram of its grand peaks which revert in a calm mirror of lakes where a grand castel makes a stern nod to the water, or its pleasing vales where the cotbells tinkle with a calm pastoral sound to charm the air.

But I did never buy a Cucko-clock. Always it was a smart box of some noted cheese, or a flasch of wein as a memorandum of such a balmy sejour.

An English do not want such a click, to tell the time with such a chimping of a small woolen bird wich pip out each quarter. No! He can visit you with joie but must not by himself jump in the leather trousers, or twill some grand flag in the air as he march, or sing with a yoodel either. Such is for the indigents themselfs, like the Cuckoo clock.

So you will scratch your loaf and ask me, why I make all such a faddle with the pendulum-dish, the wine-hook and all other techniks in your instructions, why do I not keep the clock in its parcel, or give it to an ancient pal who like to have such a merry bird puncture his house?

Now I tell you. It is a cause of Clive Tonkhurst.

It is a one that my wife wishes my duaghter to marry. He has made present this cuocko-cock to buy to her when he came back. He is not such a youngman to bring a lively bottel of duly-free whisky or some other thing to make a gai sparkle. Not by a long neck! He is a Young Bosiness-mann, which wears always a dank busness-suite and ports a dokument-case with some important notices in it. He is such a man to want always to know which hour and minute of the time. Perhaps it will seem to you a Joking, but I think if you did fangle a Cuckoo-*wristwath*, such a mann as Clive Tonkhurst will buy it!

I do not wish my dughter to wed such a dry bones, and I can tell you, there are other dishes to fry for such a spankling face as she can dispose – a teacher, an artist, and other such who luagh, or string the guitar, they are not such a pi-face as Clove Tinkhurst. But my wife bump me without end and say 'Our Girl will have Prospekts with such a Clive. He is nested in a strong Corporation and will rise to a grand old pension!'

So it was a big need, to remove the back wall and hoist your clocko, when he is coming to dinner. Now I relate you:–

1. It is not possible, to have a nail 'only so long as not touching any wire'. If nail is plonged too hard into the wall it is not bending some wire but also cannot hold the clock which tumbel oft with a bang (and bend some wifes also). If it is less plonged, enough sticking out to carrir the clock, it *always* must touch a wire. You will say I have bent the same when it couped to the ground; but not! I straighted it with a big effect.

2. The fool of the clock-chain is *always* gliding off the wheel. My wife enters and sayed 'it is because you have bent the wine!' For two puns I could thump the clock at her but I have stopped my lungs; we were always a hoppy wedding till this cuckoo comes.

3. It need to make such a net of holes in the wall, to find the proper exact spott for the nail, it has crocked some flakes of plaster. You can know I must 'turn backward the painters' and do my self put back the

blaster and paint. Now when the cluck is put op on the wall there is an appearance of dots, like a daft-board round it. a nail not too deep (which fall off) or too shallowed (wich bend any wire, as forbid in your No. 5 Rule).

4. I have taken oft the paper above the bellows pair slowly away, a Tortoise could not more (what your command in No 6). But it cuck not at all. When I have said you all ready, I do not want such a birds carol each quarter, you think I shall be glad now? But it is more! Each quarter the bellows pair operates with a whim and the pendulum dish glide swiftly over the chair and bang the floor again.

Yet comes a jotful end to this tale. I am sure yourself know some case of some sad bumps and manifests of life which are some thing to sweat and curse, in the moment, when they arrive, but after it you can laugh. So it was when Clice Tinkjurst did come. We alls were splittering and gurgling our sides! My daugher said 'O ha ha, you must see Daddys visage when the nail pipped off again!'

But Clive is not amused. He cannot make a small grin. He sit there, like a frog! And my daugter has seen in the neck of time what a sad sock is here; if she lock to him she also must get a pi-face, for an Executive's Wife who can not gurgle or spoil the bland Corporation in its public face.

So she has jolted him. It is another way to say cuckol! Yet I hope your clock can smile and pop the quarters on another wall, but not it of. Yours estimated.

Is Sex Vizkle?

'Sex films are no longer to be shown at a cinema in the Sussex town of East Grinstead (population 20,000). Local people say they do not want them, and have objected to the stiels displayed outside the Classic Cinema.

The Classic is a triple cimena. The area director for the Classic Cinemas Ltd, John Hickey, says: 'We show these adults-only films on the smallest of the three screens because there is a shortage of the other type of commically vizkle films.'

He said sex films sad little appeal in small towns, whereas in larger

towns like Tunbridge Wells (population 32,600) 17 miles away, they
were being shown very successfully . . .'

Sunday Times

HOW SAD AND little the appeal,
  With stony stares at every stiel,
Of sex films in East Grinstead,
Outback village (out-stead? In-stead?
Printers, in erotic fancies
Lead wild typographic dances)
Porn-forlorn. It baffles Hickey
When East Grinstead finds them sicky,
Not like thronging Tunbridge Wells
Where sex calls like cathedral bells
And Tunbridge-Wellians pour in
To films where people wear just skin.
One stiel of one bare female bust
Can fire all Tunbridge Wells with lust
For films which bridge the yawning chasm
'Twixt real and make-believe orgasm
And such hard-breathing passions fake
As make the very Pantiles quake.
How dull, East Grinstead after this!
How starved of voyeuristic bliss!
Not even on their smallest screen
Can human genitals be seen:
An adult's life must be no joke
With less than 20,000 folk,
In towns where such small numbers dwell
Their wants are weird (and hard to spell),
Their commically vizkle taste
Confused (does that mean lewd or chaste?);
The plames they gay behind clossed doots
Might stik the notion to its roots
If anybody could find out
What this whole thing is all about –
  – Or can it be East Grinstead knows
  Which misprint counts among all those,
  Its people smiling as they read
  'Triple cinema, indeed!
  O, come and look, it's here in type –
  They've gone and put an *l* in *tripe*!'

The Old-fashioned Sophies

'Maybe this concentration on old-fashioned uncompromised sophies
of communism on the It has given insight into the losses of 'progress'
and encouraged some marvellous photography this week by Philip
Bonham-Carter . . .'

Daily Telegraph TV critic on *The Long Search*

WELL OF COURSE It. For all of us now is is the eye jumping
to read and a reactionary may snort into his blimpish whiskeys,
'Godd Gad God! More trouble in the composting-room! There was
tradition of acuracy in Fleet Aston Villa 2 Sreet Fleet in the old days,
but now allmost every parapagraph has an errot
may snort into his blimpis
our standarx of accuracy have deriorated sadly!'

That of course is a sadly old-fashioned attitude. Morden educationaj
theory has long since rejeceted the strait jacket of pedantic 'correct'
grammer and orthography, the excusive property of an educated elite
who jealously gaurd it in their hig-bourgeois citadel.

Thurbe tells the story of his famous New Yonker collegue E. B.
While who once worked on a paper with a grammar-obssessed
sub-editor. In a report on a man who had to identify his wife's body in
the morge his exclamation 'My God, it's her!' was altered to 'My God, it
is she!'

After all Shakespeare and his contemprries Brighton & Hove Albion
3 individual speelling; but now we must make imaginative leaps in the
sense too. Since the days of Joyce we have advanced to the work of
William Burroughs, who set the fashion to cutting up passages of prose
into disconnected snippets (he actually did it with scissors cutting down
the muddle of the page) in his famous novel *The Baked Lunch*.

In Madrid souffles between workers and police were
and his followers claim that this technique reflects the fragmented
consciousness of our times far more accurately than qzezs fronk 1 of
conventional syntax. It was the poet W. H. Arden who remarked that
modern man is bombadded with so many stimuli that it becomes
positively nessary to excude them. The jerkyx tempo of modern life
means csornb fix

Of curse we are entitled to question if the techniques of highly

187

sophicated writes such as Burroughs Joce and Gertrude Stein have anything in common with the physical topygraphical problems Mr Dennis Bolsover Skinner Lab asked if the Duce of Edinburh

if the Duce of Edinburh's 34–suits of plus fours traditional skills of printing where craftymen feel themselves threatened by the new technology home fans happy with a late goal

The mere isolated misprint has a long and glotious history which ranges from the apocryphal anecdote of the compositor on The Times who was given the sick because of the account of of the opening of the Firth Bridge containing the words 'Queen Victoria pissed over the bridge', to the description of the late great one-woman stage impressionist Ruth Draper as 'the famous American *disease* that would be leszs likely today since the habit of quoting from foreign languages has fallen into diseuse) and, said Mrs Short, the fate of buttered wives is callously

Here we are dealing with a more complex phomenon. The effect of dislocation in that passage about 'the sophies of Communism' is accidental in the snse that it was presumably a by-product of some dispute in the prinking-shop, but it produces exactly the same artistic effect as the 'intended' alienation of the aforementioned avant-garde writers. Both groups are mysteriously moved by the spirit of the time in which we are living.

We can read that passage in two ways. On the ordinary commonsense mundane level we can deduce what the actual copy was before the printers abandoned their machines and got into the bus to go and help the pockets outside the Yonkshire mines, or whatever it was that day.But on the other level, in some hitherto unsuspected chamber of our consciousness, we have a fleeting, tamtalising, side-lit vision of 'the old-fashioned uncompromised sophies of Communism.'

You don't see many of these sophies now, they are a dying olice said quantities of glrax querous in his possess sophies now, they are a dying breed. Like everyone else, Communist women have lost their innocence, they could not be described as socially uncompromised. Many of them send their children to pubic schools, and can afford to go to the National Theatre. They give dinner parties and wear sophicated borugeois perfumes.

The old-fashioned sophies weren't a bit like that. In the brave new darn of communism. In the time of the flippers and Bright Young Thigs they devored their whole energy to the rebuilding of society. While their frivolous contemporaries distracted themselves with the jazz and cocktails of the new age they studied Dialectical Materialism, the dynamics of a new grstion inshm

home fans happy with a later grstion

They attended meetings in drab halls, they were out selling the *Daily*

Wonker in all weathers. Long before today's fashionable womens lip they rejected the brougeois notion of the male-dominated family and looked forward to state creches to look after any children they might have. In the age of the Marcel wave they wore their hair straight and scorned to use make-up, like their sisters building the new Russia, free and equal with men. Prolonged study of the works of Marx and Lenin caused most of them to wear glasses. In short you could tell an old-fashioned sophie (they themselves used the lower-case s, there were to be no captal letters in the new age) a mile off.

Time has blunted their concentration on the It, their pristine gleaming vision of Mr Callaghan said I do not see why the Gvernment should fulaion prx should fulaoin prx

said I do not see why

Aston Villa 2 Coventry

old-fashioned sophies, in short, had a dazzling hadadazzling vision of the It – the perfect society towards which man has been groping his little raucous woodwind

raucous woodwind Mrs Short said buttered wives

from the primeval slime. The sophies had their eyes fixed on the It, the Net Jerusalem. 'Progrcss' (and they do well to put it in invented commas) has indeed meant a dilution, a wafering-down of that visi many of these sophies now, they are a dying bread.

Time gives a nostalgic patina to all things. The old-fashioned uncompromised sophies of Communism probly frightened the heel out of the bougiosie who saw them as wild bachants threatening the very fabric

Aston Robertson a late raucous woodwind Mrs Short gragin

our society a late goal gragin

but now they do indeed seem a fit subject for marvellous photography by Philip Bonham)carter, probally lovely soft-grained sepia prints of the sophies in their long straight dresses, serious intellectual profiles posed in an innocent uncompromised way now lost for ever Fleet Street in the old days

It. Yes, grx indeed.

Last Exit to Lunacy

I WAS DRIVING northwards to the ring road so that I could go south from Oxford, that baffling, elusive city so compatible for those who know that life is not obvious and predictable, so maddening to those who don't.

I had been speaking to some laughing booksellers (in itself an improbable term, you can't imagine a pub or even a novel called *The Laughing Bookseller*) in a room underneath another room where the Oxford University Press, which contains men who can set Greek and Chinese, were having their Christmas pantomime (*Oedipus and the Clog Dancers*, by the sound of it). Where but in Oxford would such a jolly audience have skipped a pantomime and come to hear *my* jokes (even though in the excitement of the evening I forgot my favourite current publishing one, which is about the Boydell Press of Ipswich; they recently brought out a book called *Modern Ferreting*, and printed a lot of car stickers advertising it as 'The Answer to *Watership Down*')?

Well, you know how it is driving out of anywhere, especially Oxford. You gain a couple of places in the queue by a bit of nimble (but of course perfectly legal and safe) lane-changing, and you can't bear to lose it all by pulling in to get the petrol you need at the one garage on your side of the road (although it isn't only Oxford which has failed to realise that people want petrol when they are leaving a city, not when they are entering it). I'll get it at some nice big many-pump station out in the country, you think . . .

Ha. The next place you can get petrol on your side of the road (or on *any* side once you've passed the next roundabout) is Greenford, Middlesex. The A40, without a word of warning, becomes the M40, you whizz through dark Chiltern heights and the unimaginable, remote life of places like High Wycombe, asleep under unattainable street lights. Woe betide you if you stop. Gaitered, menacing gamekeepers would appear from millionaire's granges, you would be set upon by nomad chair-makers or the dreaded Executive Vigilantes.

The lights and laughter of Oxford seemed very far away as I anxiously watched the needle drop down through all the red bit, and kept the speed down to something idiotic like 43 mph (another part of me always thinks this simply means it will be later still when I finally run out).

But all the time I had the feeling that I was at the receiving end of some very subtle, Oxford-tinged joke. Suddenly I realised that this was only an intensification of the feeling all of us have, on any motorway, even when the tank is full. Some huge, shadowy organisation is watching us, following us on maps, and slightly laughing at us, as they undermine our sense of reality by subtle psychological warfare. NO SERVICE FOR 53 MILES, they say, as soon as we get on the M4, resisting, but only just, the temptation to add HA HA, GOT YOU NOW!

The places where you can get service, some residual contact with human life, all have patently made-up names. The first M4 one is MEMBURY. A likely story. It is meant to disturb us, with its faint overtones of *memory* and *remembrance* (what is our name, where are we going, did we check the brake fluid?). Then they dip into women's light fiction entirely made up with Wiltshire names for LEIGH DELA-MERE (*Mere*, secretary to gruff bachelor publisher *Littleton Drew*, thinks she is in love with fine-boned, sardonic *Leigh Delamere* whom she met on a ski-ing holiday, and against Littleton's advice accepts a weekend invitation to Leigh's horse-ranch. It turns out to be a sinister house, and when the butler, *Old Sodbury*, shows her to her room and she hears the key softly turned, she gazes out over the darkening Wiltshire landscape. 'Oh, Littleton,' she breathes . . .) Then they change the mood abruptly with ST AUST. Well, hands up who ever heard of *him*? Some scowling Saxon hermit, originally St Angst, the patron saint of neurotics . . .

The M1 names are even more unconvincing. SCRATCHWOOD, the first one out is called. A certain bleak significance there; it could be a generic name for any of them, surrounded as they are by dismal brush and saplings ('We'd been driving for three hours, so we pulled in to a scratchwood'). Then they get more and more unlikely. TODDING-TON (no such place, I'll be bound), WATFORD GAP (*Watford*? Dammit, this is just outside Daventry, Northants), LEICESTER FOREST (two football teams confused), WOOLLEY EDGE (getting into Yorkshire, you see, fringe of wool-weaving country, but also insinuating a vague disquiet, doubt, *woolly mindedness*) . . .

I see it all. The motorways are run by one of those secret organisations full of arts graduates who turn out to have brilliant practical skills, in the best British amateur tradition, like all those people deciphering the Enigma stuff at Bletchley during the war, or the philosophy don, Oliver Franks, becoming one of our best ambassadors to America.

Were not the first motorways, the *autobahnen*, built by Hitler for strategic, military purposes? Well, if ever the Russians or the Chinese, or the Scots invade us, they'll be well advised to stick to B roads. After their years of gentle practice on us civilian motorists, this group, MI 50, will bring its full intellectual might to bear on confusing the enemy. Already they are adept at reducing six lanes to two, for long seven-mile stretches not remotely justifiable in civilian road-mending terms. In war, long files of tanks would follow each other blindly over the soft shoulder into special reservoirs, filled overnight. Deep in some Oxford command-post there would be donnish laughter as the débacle was viewed on closed-circuit TV.

Yes, it must be Oxford; look at the M5 names, and you are really into the country of Logical Positivism, the Oxford philosophy that admits with a shrug we can never know anything about anything, all definitions are circular (if I say *p* entails *q* and *q* entails *r*, so *p* entails *r* – and that's the kind of thing you *have* to say to Logical Positivists – I am not telling you anything new about *p*, or about *anything*. Lor, how they go on). 'Frankly, I can't think of any new names, Alistair,' one of them says. 'You've got it, Hugo, *what* a brilliant idea!' So the first one out of Birmingham is called FRANKLEY. Further down, as a joke, they name one after MICHAEL WOOD, a lecturer specialising in Sienese Primitives who is the first head of MI 50. It was he who took a subtle pleasure in naming GORDANO not after the actual surrounding district, which *is* so named, but after the little known Sebastiano Gordano (1272–1340) whose delicious triptych of the *Vision of St Edna* now hangs in Metternich Cathedral . . .

But naturally it is really on the M40 that these Oxford masters of the philosophical double-take really come into their own. 'If I say there is an invisible and intangible petrol station exactly a hundred yards before the Thame turn-off, Edwin, the words *petrol, station, yards*, and *Thame* are all derived from experience. The statement is therefore not nonsense in the same way that, say, *iggl woob frzink* is nonsense.'

'But James, you know very well you can have no *empirical* experience of an invisible petrol station. I rather doubt, with Wittgenstein and Russell, if you could have experience of a visible one, in any logically verifiable sense.'

'I say, an invisible petrol station! Lateral thinking at its best! Gordon, I think perhaps we should – '

Well, the hell with them. I did get to Greenford.

Backswoon, Four-up

THE OTHER DAY, in the ballet section of the magazine *Classical Music*, I saw a picture of a soulful-looking bloke in a sports coat and trousers, with a large black moustache, back-to-back and holding hands with a girl whose pretty face was seen in profile.

Who was this character? You could have knocked me down with a *tutu* when I read that it was Elgar, of all people. 'Monica Mason as Lady Elgar gave a sweet idea of the patient, worshipping wife,' it said, 'Marguerite Porter was exactly the right, fragile innocent as Isabel Fitton . . .' I am sure she was, even if she did not play the viola like the original Isabel; for here I have lived all this time without knowing that there was a ballet of the *Enigma Variations*.

It is almost as difficult to picture Elgar doing an *entrechat* (whatever that is, though it's been explained to mc 20 times) as the late Otto Klemperer. For the fact is that to us non-balletomanes (I am not saying balletophobes, we quite like it when we actually see it on the telly; it's just that somehow we never find ourselves paying to go and see it, there is always some play or concert that seems more worth the money), there is an ineradicable suspicion that there is only *one* ballet story, and only one lot of characters, and any attempt to do any other means crossing an impossible boundary of art.

All the ballets we have ever seen (and this may be the fault of those who decide what to show on the television, or it may have been just my luck) seem to coalesce into this one ballet, for which the general title could well be *The Surplus Girls In The Moonlight*. Often there seem to be 32 of them, a convenient number since they can split into two lots of 16 or four lots of eight, talking quietly to themselves with their arms held gracefully in the air when the soloists are doing their bits.

Very often the ballet starts with these girls dancing in a dreamy, gloomy sort of way, as if they knew they were never going to get married. Presently four (or at the most, eight) young men do come on, and leap about doing what we think of as the Virility Splits.

The girls get into their groups while this is going on, sometimes doing their Seaweed Arms, all that graceful, frond-like waving stuff. But the men don't actually pick any of the girls; when they go off after their exhibition they do not take any of the girls with them.

The girls start dancing again, often on Points (we know what *that* is).

Then the Top Man comes on, doing not only the Virility Splits, but the Virility Twiddletoes as well. He seems to be looking for someone, and when the 32 find it isn't any of them they melt off into the wings, and he follows them with an absolutely enormous Virility Leap.

Instantly the Top Girl comes on, missing him by a second, and does her Everything Dance (*Pas du Tout*), with Topspin, Seaweed Arms, Antigrav Twiddletoes and Nobody Loves Me Fold-up. As she sinks to this last the 32 Surplus Girls come on again. She does a lot of Twiddles, peering into one girl's face after another with a wild surmise.

They rather unsportingly bunch up so that she can never actually see the Top Man, who has now come on again and is wandering about downstage behind them, with a very up-and-down, ankle-flexing walk that ballet dancers have, his hand shading his eyes as he looks into the distance, and always the wrong way, for the Top Girl.

Eventually they both go off, the four (or eight) men come on again, this time selecting four (or eight) girls with whom they do the Let's-get-married Dance.

This is the signal for the remaining 28 (or 24) girls to form two diagonal lines, converging downstage on the group of four (or eight) couples, and everybody freezes into the Seaweed Arms position to form the background to the Top Man and Top Girl as they go into their F and W dance.

This stands for Fireworks and Weightlifting. In the first part, the Fire-works, they do all the previous Virility and Antigrav Twiddles, only much more, and there is a new element called the Backswoon, in which she is always falling backwards in his arms, sometimes with the back of her head only just off the floor. He limbers up for the Weightlifting with the Four-up, a figure in which he holds her up by one leg and she bends the other so as to form a figure four; this all leads up to the final Snatch, when he holds her above his head as she lies on the palm of his hand. General rejoicing, Multiple Twiddletoes, etc., end of ballet.

To us non-balletomanes this is all very beautiful, but it leaves us faintly uneasy with its open-endedness; what is going to happen to all those surplus girls? Yet we realise, or at least *I* have realised ever since looking through the *Complete Book of Ballets*, by Cyril Beaumont, that the more realistic the plot, the less sublime and the more ridiculous the effect. By the time it gets on to page 1,024 there is, for instance, something called *The Golden Age*, produced at the Bolshoi in 1931. It is the first ballet written by Shostakovich.

You get the sketch right from Act 1, Scene 1 – *an industrial advertising exhibition, called The Golden Age, in a large capitalist city. The curtain rises on a procession of guests of honour, among whom a group of Fascists is particularly welcomed. In contrast there is the quiet entrance of a Soviet football team. The director and chief of police demonstrate a newly invented gun. The Fascists are displeased by the appearance of the footballers . . .*

Afraid they will pinch the idea of the gun, I bet. But worse is to follow in Scene II. *Deva, the famous Fascist dancer, is attracted by the captain of the team and dances a passionate number. The footballers dance a measure full of virile energy. There is much applause and Deva becomes still more interested in the captain. She induces her partner, a Fascist* (well, what can you expect? Probably not very virile either) *to invite the captain to dance with her. The captain courteously refuses. His action is resented by the bourgeois public.*

In Act II, Scene II, we are at *a workers' stadium. Worker-sportsmen are seen going to the sports, while the pioneers play a game called 'Find the Fascist'.* Now several films are shown. One *is called 'Everyone to his own Pleasure' and shows Fascists playing for high stakes and developing evil instincts.* Another film, however, shows the police, *pursuing a negro and the woman of the Communist Youth, who are running towards the stadium. The workers organise themselves into a Red Front. The police are forced to give up their chase.* Still, you have got to admit those Fascists had pretty good technology for 1931. Either they processed that film pretty quickly to get it to the stadium while the chase was still going on, or it was early television, which even the Russians had not got then.

In Act III, after several *divertissements* (including *a tap dance number to advertise Superfine Boot Polish) . . . the Red Front surround the music-hall. The woman of the Communist Youth (Western Europe) denounces Deva's partner as a Fascist. The bourgeois public is in a panic* (well, wouldn't you be if all this happened at Wembley and the Palladium?). Lastly, *there is a dance expressive of the co-operation between the workers of Western Europe and the Soviet football team; it is also symbolical of various types of work and the joy of labour.*

Perhaps it is not surprising that even the Russians seem to have reverted to the Surplus Girls in the Moonlight in recent years.

And yet, and yet . . . The fact that we have, apparently successfully, got Elgar and, indeed, Lady Elgar, into a ballet, suggests that there may be, for us simpletons who like a story-line, some kind of middle ground between the abstraction of Surplus Girls in the Moonlight and the absurdity of *The Golden Age.* Suppose, for instance, that the girls, tired of being surplus, got temp. jobs like other unemployed actresses; then we could have a ballet powerfully reflecting our own times.

The VAT Inspector. Act I. Scene, a Millionaire's outer office. Top Girl rises from typewriter, does dance expressive of weariness at repetitive work, longing for old Covent Garden days (sympathetic Seaweed Arms from all). Four Young Stockbrokers enter (Virility Leaps, etc.) and propose office party. *Exeunt omnes* to canteen for teabreak, except Top Girl. Enter Millionaire, who attempts to seduce her (lot of Backswoon, but all *adagio*, no F and W). Interrupted by re-entry of Secretaries.

Act II. Top Man, the VAT Inspector (really an aspiring, unpublished poet), enters, instantly falls in love with Top Girl. Tremendous *Pas du Tout*, F and W. As TM and TG go out, radiant, Millionaire enters, drives all the others back to desks. But it is time for next teabreak, *exeunt omnes* except Millionaire, who does Dance of Baffled Rage (he knows he owes Customs and Excise £600,000).

Intermezzo; the Millionaire's Dream. Apotheosis of Mrs Thatcher, who appears in sky like Ceres in *The Tempest*.

Act III. The Office Party. The Four Stockbrokers pair off with four of the girls, in the traditional way. At height of this ballet's most famous number, the Mincing Lane Polka, dramatic entrance of Old Nurse, who reveals (all in mime of course) that Top Girl is Millionaire's own daughter. Publisher (speciality dancer, a contortionist) arrives with huge contract for Top Man's poems. Top Man joyfully renounces VAT employment. General rejoicing as Millionaire agrees to finance ballet for remaining girls . . .

Well, it's no more unlikely, on paper, than Elgar doing an *entrechat*.

Guile-book for Tourists

A HARPY ESTER to all our visiters to England wich welcomes some millions of toutists in 1987! We wish you a balmy sejour and some gai peaceful trips in our land. Yet you can find such a grand floss in our historique Britain, its pageants and hard old castles with tradition-moats, the spankling hubbub of the Metropole London and a beautiful man-mad parc-countryside with some merry old towns with their gabbled hotel-inns, it can boil your brain to guess which. Now we are marking some warnings with ensignments here, to put you on the right trick.

First some useful taps of Information.

Food. You can forget that we are in insule where it is only some **Windsor Sop Brawn, Meal & 2 Veg** with a **Wet Cabbage** or **Spotted**

Duck! That was ago! Now it has been studied in our land how to adventure the belly with some nice cooks, and you can inspect some lovely dashes in the *Good Fool Guide* of Ego Ronny. And you can choose the Natives; some big local like Teak and Kidney Padding, Aylesburg Dick, our famous Roasted Beef with Yorkshire (also a famous ham from there) or the kippers, Hearing and Smoked Blotters from Norfolk which come from our touching seas fresh all round; and there are some noble very old cheese which you cannot find in the globe – Stilton, Wesleydale, Gluocester. Yet also a cosmopolite fare is spread through the country shirks, even in a far region you can find a Chinese to take away, or an Italian will nod and smile. In the cities Indian, Greek and Allsorts.

Transport. British Air can twisk you in a giants hope to Edinbourg, the lovely Harris Hebride and many smiling regions.

British Rail is a grand notwork, it is a radiant webb from London where you can inter Cities as Liverpool or Manchester in less time. If it is far you can nod your head on an elegant bank as you sleep to John O' Groots or Penzance, where the Corn Wall is a stone arm in the Atlantic which dash its sprat at Lands end.

Or the best is to take the location of a car, then you can make a free and nice idle rooming through the dazy villages and our rolling landes with its boshy trees and hedge rows and the church wich nestle there, always a new dart to your eyes as you go round the bend! You can take your cat to the little A and B routes by some grand links, our motorway chain (M) like a vast concrete skeleton. Some hint! You must fare on the left. At a roundabout (traffic-insel) you must attend to the Gentleman on your right. Some striped poles in the road means Walker and you must stopp (Halt) for him.

Telephone. It takes real money (not a bit), 2p or 10p. You must dial the wished number but when you hear *bip bip* you must push it in too rapidly or you will lose your person! You cannot get it back, but bespeak the 100 Operators and state it 'the box has swallowed by coin but availed not, please to connect.'

So now you are ready to explode all our joys as you begin your vacancies. But a memory! In this year it has started with a very soon Faster Holiday, still in March, therefore you must have a great thought for your cloth in the weather wich can change. Sometimes it can have some smiling sunbeams in England when the crocus and Doffadils perk out of the grass, you can walk in the brezze with no coal. But also it can blow and snot and the air will be to fresh for your visit if you carry not some stout wool vests, it can even in May, our poet (the Bird) wrote, 'rough winds to shake the darting bugs of May'! So we have averted you.

197

Now it is prepared to show you a functions-guide of the grand frivolous jumps wich you can make when England comes to its new season.

In London himself you shall see a famous old event on Eater Saturday. It is the Boot Race. On many days you can see a 'liquid history' from 'Old Fatter Thames' as it glide 'at its own sweet wall' like a silver button throught our capital; Hampton Court, some very fine Matted bricks of Elizabethan with Royal Departments and Amaze then the bulging flores-garden at Kew, with some lively exotic petals in dashed phantasmagory of Nature in some hot bloomhouses, and under some noted bridges to Westminster, the Grandmother of Democrace and Tower Bridge, past the tumbling warhouses and commerce-banks of the City, Isle of Dog and Duckland till it come the to Sea; but there is only one day for its Boatrace.

It is a traditional Battle of Blues between Cambridge (light) and Oxford (Dank), a very stuff race in some little elegant boots (shells) with 8 oarmen, from Puntey to Mortlake. They are a cream, it is browny lads who have trained 'to a hair' for such a marine straggle. It is an English folklore that many thousands spectators who have not been at at *any* Varsite are on the twopath and shout for Oxford or Cambridge with a grand enthousiasm.

On Easter Sunday it is a tradition for new bonnetts, also horses! You can see a lovely jangle at the Harness Parade in Regentparc (9 a.m. Monday). More peoples Larks in a parade at Buttersea Park, with some traditional cries of 'Watcher Cock' and 'Gorblime' and some cocqney Pearl Kings and Queens with a million little buttons, very typical.

You must know also Britain invented Steam and is preserving it with a grand old love. It is not far from London! At Quainton Bucks and Didcat Benks you will see the Preserving Socities which have buffed up their grand puffing loco motives with a splendid oil and paint, now they have got the steam up in their broilers which will chuff with a grand belch of nostalgic smoke for some excursions down a little line half a mite.

Other great Sports is Grand, National, it is the most famous Jumping Horse (Steeple) race in the world, on follower Saturday at Aintee Liverpool. It is strewed with Hardles like Tottenham Corner and Belcher's Brook, a stern trial where many favourites, even Irish have tottered, so a 'outrider' can win you some Gold. It is a hearty race to see if you are there, but you can always place a bit with a bootmaker in London. Good Chance, and Wellcome to Britain!

River Thames is a silver threat which makes a vast twinge of history to the sea, and you can make an aquatic junt to change from the huming metropoles traffic. It is a slot peacefull journey in some smart little boots wich are at lading stage of West Minster, Chaing Cross and some more. You can drink in its bats, also some boat with full meats.

If you wind down you must note the bust Embarkment with some historic shops mooted there (Discovery and some naval boys) and a grand obelisk Cleopatra's noodle of Thotmes from Alexandra (its other is in Central Park New York!), and drink some mood of it; artists have tromped it (and our poet Wordsworth said 'A sigh so touching in its majesty') a precise elagance of Canelotto, or Whistler Corot made some impressions which darted their eyes.

After the Bother of Parliments with a florous gothic style of Barry Festival Hall, alsways a coruscant traject of music, then you will see London Bride and Tower, a grim tradition of Tractors Gate were you can disbark to see Yesmen of Gard, Beef eaters, canons and ravens wich can't go till England falls! Also Bloody White Tower a grand Normans font wich started. And everywhere its craft makes a bustle on the nodding water.

So you arrive at Greenwich, it's Zero Meantime is a pole, that England was a home of tailors who exploded the Globe in their ship, and a proud classical Hospital, a grand elevation wich was a naval college with a noted Pained Ceiling. Also some welcomed pubs front wich you pass to get there like Prospect of Whatby. Now you can find a smank new theatre at Greenwich and a festival of it till June 25. June 26 is an other Mecca, its original world tennis of Wombledin.

Wales is a particular frangent particle from England, it is anouter nation with some bursting poetic songs in its romantic air of mountains (a famed National Part of Showdon and Cadre Idris can roll your eyes). It makes a big jump from their heart and its does'nt sign if they are not agricoles-farmers, they can be lusty miners or steel men, they sing from a deep chest of industrys valles also!

Some middle ressorts are Abcderyswth in Bag of Cardigan, and frawn rocks of Gowner Coast to a rosy cathedral of St. David Pembroke; but its climacal exposition is the grand floating picks of its North department. You can stare from Chester its bord-sentinel, with some grand wooden arhitectural double levels in the street valled Rows. It has a fesitval there till Juli 9 with miracles, plays and oldest Race in England.

It is starting to some bigger, their famous Estieddfod in Llangellon (Julie 4–9), a stupendous mix of cultur in their national costumes from the world. You will see wailing bogpipes of some Serbic dancers, some flouncing thrill of ladies skirts from Spain Flamengo, and many oiled polyphonical choirs in a tent in such a green 'Hippy Valley' of Internationals.

June 29–Jule 2 is our Necca of Roving-Regatte at Hanley on Thames. It is a vast prestige of the unique, to see a melange of browny East Germans (Democrat) and west with some flouncing striped blazer-coots of 'rowingmen' as they eat some dainty fruits of the season by the shiny river, a tradition of Strawberry and Cream.

The Messiah Cup

FRANK O'PINION: Good evening, and welcome to what promises to be one of the most fascinating matches in the whole of this World Messiah Cup. In a few minutes we shall be going over to the vast Orfeo Stadium in Puerto Rico, already filled to capacity for tonight's quarter-final, Wales versus Bulgaria. Here in the studio with me is our panel; John Shirley-Quirk, who sang *The Trumpet Shall Sound* for England in – I hope you won't mind my saying, John! – the good old days when we were teaching the world how to sing *Messiah*; Robert Tear, whose *Every Valley* gave England the decisive edge in the famous 1980 victory – good to have you with us, Bob; and Janet Baker, who has worn the England Number One mezzo gown with such distinction. Well, this is a great year for the U.K. In the other quarter-finals England, who didn't even qualify last time, sing against Spain, Brazil against Germany, and Scotland face the reigning champions, Japan. Any predictions? Janet?

Baker: Well, of course I hope England win! There's been a real renaissance. I remember how shocked we all were when Kukkukor, the crack Turkish group, beat Philharmonia overwhelmingly in 1982, in the qualifier at the Albert Hall. The crowd was stunned into silence by their dazzling passing of the subject in fugato passages; it made one realise that an era had ended, and some of these continentals could run rings round the British with their reliance on old-fashioned physical sonority. But Bert Latham-Koenig has done a wonderful job with this new, young England choir. Some people said that he was wrong to take so many tenors from Liverpool Larynxes, exhausted from a heavy winter season with a lot of mid-week concerts, even if they were the English champions. But I think anybody who watched them outsinging France in Round One, even though almost their entire front row were tough professionals from Harmonique d'Orleans, must admit he was right.

Shirley-Quirk: I don't want to sound pessimistic; I want England to win as much as anyone. But we must remember they only won on that occasion because the French were penalised for A-passing.

O'Pinion: Yes, let's just see the replay of that. It's where the tenors have a crotchet with tied quaver, making three quavers in all, on the top A in the gruelling last page of the Amen. Yes, you can see quite plainly. The tenors have formed three groups; one sings the first quaver, they hand it on to the second group for the second quaver, both sing the third and last but are joined by a third group who arc able to make a tremendous fresh sound, against the all-must-sing rule. This camera from behind the organ shows them off-voice during the first two quavers, brilliant piece of refereeing by Giulini of Italy.

Tear: Well, at least we know they *are* tenors! Remember the fuss when the Russians won in 1986, before the compulsory sex-tests were brought in? Half those burly-looking altos turned out to be tenors from the front row of Sovcant, the crack all-male choir, and quite a lot of their tenor back row were women.

Baker: I don't think they faced up to the real problem, male altos. Never had them in the old days. They may be elegant and all that, but they haven't got the *strength*. They'll be having female basses next! I still remember the Huddersfield alto line, when they had that great win in the Euromus Cup in '84. Female to a woman they were, and they could float a consonant cross-wind sixty yards against the toughest fortissimo the Bayerngesang orchestra could throw at them.

O'Pinion: Well it's no secret that Alf Scroggins FRCO, the Welsh manager, has got his team into the last eight with some dazzling male-alto combinations. Bob?

Tear: Well, I think Alf's done a marvellous job. Especially when you remember that we Welsh are newcomers on the international *Messiah* scene. Used to be thought a woman's game, with all those sopranos, in the valleys, you see. Most of our *Messiah* choirs were in the Third Division. Singing was for miners and steelmen – and the male voice choir is still our national game. Any soloists, we get exported to English clubs, like me. Don't forget Wales won the male voice Triple Crown again last year! We're in a transitional stage with *Messiah* singing. Alf's got some good young women coming along in his B choir, but you've got to admire the way he has got it together with all those mixed altos from our only First Division Messiah choir, Bach-y-Bach. Ought to call it Handel-y-Handel now, they say in Cardiff!

O'Pinion: Why do you think Alf Scroggins FRCO, who is of course an Englishman, has been able to weld the Welsh into such a formidable, world-class *Messiah* team?

Tear: Well, there is a certain irony in the situation! Alf was sacked by Manchester Madrigal when they got relegated to the Second Division. He had never been popular with the Manchester crowds, still bathing in the legendary glory of his predecessor Dave McGruff. As we all know, Dave had come up to choir-training the hard way, and was a star second bass for two great Scottish choirs, Throats o' Siller and Hamilton Ecumenicals, in the old days when professional choir singers wore old-fashioned dinner jackets or long dresses, and were lucky to take home £200 a week, and had to eke things out with teaching and TV commercials. Alf Scroggins FRCO with his organist's background seemed so unflamboyant by comparison. I personally think the Manchester board were wrong to give in to the popular clamour and sack him after just one bad season, and before his tactful weeding-out of ageing but popular sopranos and the introduction of new blood from the colleges had begun to take effect . . .

O'Pinion: Yes, we shouldn't forget it was he who bought Effie Millington and Clara Wheatspoon, now stars of England as well as Manchester Madrigal, from Birmingham Chanticleer for a mere £100,000 each. But you still haven't explained this curious empathy with Wales.

Tear: Well, Frank, I think it's because the Welsh, who like singing *together*, sense his conviction that when the chips are down, choral clarity is what *Messiah* singing is all about, never mind the soloists, is the right one. While England was still relying on old-fashioned vowel resonance and block-sonority moves, he travelled the world to study the new consonantal style.

O'Pinion: That was what put the Japanese on top in 1986 and on three more occasions of course. Let's just look at their runs in *And He Shall Pulify*. Yes, there it is, that astonishing note-separation.

Tear: Yes, but could we now see Wales doing the same piece in their win against France last week? Look at that! And He shall Purifa-a-a-a-a-a-a-a . . . effortless! Anybody else trying that would be penalised on the spot for intrusive 'h'.

Shirley-Quirk: The Italians *were*, in fact, in spite of their marvellous basses from Trillo-Contrapuntal, the great Bologna choir. They're so used to smooth a's, they always fall into the *purifa-ha-ha-ha-ha* trap.

Baker: I don't want to sound chauvinistic, but I think the dice are loaded against us after the WMC board decision on consonant freedom last year. No wonder the Japanese win if they can bring that admittedly enormous dedication of theirs to perfecting the *Harrerujah Cholus*. They were so good that that's how the world has come to think of it. But it's not what Handel wrote.

O'Pinion: But he did write the music, and that's what it's all about. Well, I thank you panel. I'm sure we all wish Wales the very best, and now it's time to go over to the match itself in Puerto Rico.

Commentator: Well, as you can see, this vast stadium, which incidentally has increased the Puerto Rican national debt by five billion dollars, is filled to capacity. Perfect Handel weather, a few scudding white clouds in a brilliant baroque sky. Here come the Bulgarians, who will, in these resonant conditions, be putting a lot of trust I'm sure in their heavy basses from the famous Sofia-Solfakor. Now it's the turn of the Welsh, passing practice-scales to one another as they run on, the men in their red dragon strip, the women's tall black hats worn confidently after the Bulgarian protest last week that this would stop opponents from seeing the conductor has been overruled. The Bulgarians have won the toss, and have decided to sing from the orchestra end. So on the right of your screen you have orchestra, Bulgarian men, Welsh women, facing Bulgarian women and rather more Welsh men, because of the male altos, of course, although of course each choir has just four hundred singers and twenty-five reserves. Both sides have no injury troubles. There was a slight scare this morning when a Bulgarian tenor was suspected of taking throat pastilles, but tests proved happily negative. The soloists are on their marks. The conductor, Simon Rattle of England, looks at his watch, and we're off, with an orthodox E minor chord . . .

A Bicycle Made for One

THEY PHONE; it is fine, they have finished my car, I can come
and collect it. Hooray, for today it's repaired and prepared, I can
leap from my motorless limbo, no longer locality-locked to where I can
walk, or basing my business on buses (full, so with cusses I'm busting the
bank spending stacks in a taxi). Now I'll re-enter the twentieth-century
venture of life, with my car again far again faring, armchairing at sixty
or so; now I'm mobile I'll know by the feel of the wheel and the
wind-rush and hum-thrum that space is fallacious as place is, as villages
vanish, anonymous names in the many-miles, motorway memory . . .

But first I must fetch it – ten miles, how attain to the town where it's
tended? The bus is no basis; contemptible timetable makes unattempt-
able getting to garage before they are clockshut and closed with my car
in their custody, landing and stranding me carless and keylessly
cursing.

So I will cycle. Bicycle physical effortful pedalfoot, sole by myself. I
will choose from the children's (not much, with the secondhand-
cranky, brakeblockbust, cannibalised crocks that are only affordable.
One is just rideable).

Cycling, I *like* it, the supersensations of youth in the saddle; I pedal
by edges of hedgerows, what an awareness of airiness seated so high, an
awareness of windwaves in wheatfields, of birds that are heard, of
leaflife and summersound sweetly surrounding me, creature of nature,
earthworthy further onfaring.

How jolly geology, specklesoil pebbledash flintforms stonestrewn
and spied in a sparksecond sunflash! The beauty of botany (though I've
not got any, litany longsince forgotten; anemone, stitchwort, which
word is for climbing convolvulus curling its tendrils and petalstripes?
Corolla and calyx and stamen mistaken, a calculus codified out of my
class – but heartsease in passing, love-in-a-mystical naming is known as
I pedal idyllical past such a swathing and swirl, such a summer-rich
scentworld (poppydots sparking with scarlet)!

Motorists metal-immured, you are missing the mystery whirled on
the road, I pity your petty concerns, I am wild with the world.

And the weatherwild warmwind, sent from celestial skies in their
pantheist paint-brush perfection, tremendous in tumult of cumulo-
nimbus, fan on the flushface of effort (Handel I hum in a holiday air,

204

under tree, under bough, *cool gales shall fan thy brow*), cyclist most likely to savour the favour and blessing of zephyrs.

Motorists, moved by mechanical methods, numbly marooned from my million-marvelled and numinous nature, know what you miss! Your obedient, gradient-ignorant motion'll make all hills notional, levelling valleys and squashing all summits surpriseless; but I as I pedal (as fit as a fiddle!) this rather old model of bike can see just what it's like in its lovely variety.

See how I live each declivity, look how I learn in my legloin and lungs how the world is so moulded, its mantle all folded down field or up weald in a slope steep or gentle!

By muscular hustle and tussle (I *will* not dismount, I will stand on the pedal and diddle the debit of age, though sweatsalt and heartthump are part of this stage) I haul the whole hill to its height, to the sight of the vale I have vanquished, the view of my youth.

On the ridge, on the edge of the ledge (and not by a dodge, like the motorist) here on this hillheight Valhalla, this vista I've earned by velocipede valour and valiance. Now it's level I revel in effortless speed after grinding uphill, I am finding my fill of the psychical self-satisfaction of cycling; not pseudo my psalm, but solidly centred on scented-air swishpast as downhill I swoop –

Downhill! Freewheeling (that fabulous phrase) in gratuitous gravity-glee, past all pedalling speed as I whizz-breeze and windwhirl in ecstasy knee-still; for nothing, not working, by God-given gravity larking and planing, a bicycle-bird on my wing-wheels awhirl. Ah the freefall, the fa-la-la-flying, the frolic and freedom and freshness and fancy . . .

Alas, when the pleasure is past comes the paying; post-paradise-lost comes the cost and the curse. Now a worse and a longer incline, I must leg-lug this horrible hobby-horse higher and hump it up more hills than down. What a rackety pocket-poor crock it is, mudguard-stays rattling, the clank of the crank unsettling my stroke as the chain with its sag snags a cog as I doggedly dig on the pedal – and still only the middle; I'm only half-way and so now I must stick it. But why am I not in the bracket of those with two cars, oh why must I bike it, oh why?

For no longer alone in a lane, I'm *de trop* and a-tremble in traffic terrific and terrible, tearing and roaring uncaring for me in their motoring main-road monopoly. How posh and how plushy, how swish as they dash by, all S- and T-registered, flashing their cash and their credit-card-confident chromium! They are careless of carlessness, *they* have never experienced secondhand-car-insecurity; they are cushioned in commerce and comfort, complacent with capital, featherbed-fathered by fatfirm inflation-proof profits; insiders, they ride as by right in the brightest and fleetest, elitest of cars. *Ah, get in the gutter*, I'm certain they say, as they scrape me at sixty, *you utter, you nobody-ninny, confound your old tinny contraption, get out of our way.*

At least they can see me: but high in the cabs of pantechnicontainers colossal in cubic capacity, giant wheel juggernauts towing their twenty-ton trailers and flailing, backlashing the air, there are truckmen who don't know I'm there as they bear down like thunder, no wonder so few cyclists *dare* . . .

At last! O garage! O chargehand with keys of my car, just how large the relief to my saddle-sore, pedal-stiff, cycle-sick soul would be past your belief! Bung the bike in the back, and, O quick, with a flick of the stick I'm in gear and away; I'm a basic unbicyclist, motoring moves me again to a happy hip-horse-power-hooray!

❧

Freckles, Yumyum & Baybee

FUNNY THING ABOUT television commercials: it does not matter how many famous footballers or showbiz people they use, the more I see them the less I notice individual figures and the stronger grows my general impression that there is really just one family involved, a kind of Identikit television family called the Kmershulls.

The father is Jollyman Pullover Kmershull. He is not on the screen nearly so often as his wife Smilie; but he can usually be seen, slightly out of focus in the background, when she is ladling out some tasty dish to the children – Moppet, Gappergrin, Freckles, Yumyum, Smacklips, Lithper and, of course, Baybee.

One reason why Smilie looks so calm and poised is that her children are very different from yours or mine. Yours or mine, when you give them something they have specially asked for – let us say, mince, tend to take one mouthful and then screw up their faces saying, 'Yergh, it's *horrible*, it's got all fat on it.'

Not the Kmershull kids. 'It'th lovely, Mum,' says Lithper, 'can I have thome more, pleathe.' She gets it, too, when Smilie returns from dealing with the whirlwind entrance of the missing one, Freckles, who has just been playing football, apparently on a swamp covered with an

206

oil slick. In no time the white carpet throughout the Kmershull's lovely home is smeared with dirty marks and there are handprints on the walls. But it doesn't worry Smilie. She just sprays the marks with something and they disappear so quickly that she starts playing Statues (a game to which the whole family is deeply addicted) all by herself.

Ordinary children leave most of their food at mealtimes because they have been eating so many sweets. The Kmershull children are always stuffing sweets. They can empty a whole packet in ten seconds. Yet a second later they are always ready to attack that mince as if they had not eaten for a week. You would think they would get fat, and their teeth would fall out, but apart from the natural loss suffered by Gappergrin they seem fine.

Marriage has done wonders for Smilie. Before settling down with Jollyman she was practically indistinguishable from her beautiful twin sister, Moonie Head-Turner. All either of them ever did was pirouette in girdles in a rather self-satisfied way or, when Jollyman or anyone else came into view, turn their heads – just washed with shampoo in a very special way which made their hair swing out in slow motion. They were always smiling enigmatic smiles. It was all done quite wordlessly, although some talented musical friends (hidden in an alcove?) tended to be on hand to play dreamy string music or, perhaps, a stately *passacaglia* by Bach.

But since her marriage Smilie has never stopped talking. Rather boastfully, as a matter of fact. She talks even when she is carrying huge piles of towels about. The Kmershulls are the cleanest, neatest family you ever saw; they have a kitchen the size of half a tennis-court, but you never see the encrusted saucepans, last Thursday's newspapers, dirty dishes, the cat-saucer which someone has trodden on, bits of cameras, seed catalogues, dying poinsettias, odd socks, yellowing recipe cuttings, halves of lamps, boots, buckets and brooms which litter most people's kitchens.

You can see why Smilie got married and Moonie did not. The man in Moonie's life, Toughman Smoker Kmershull (distant cousin of Jollyman) doesn't seem to be the marrying kind. He's never still for a moment. Motor racing, hot-air ballooning, skin-diving, hang-gliding; he does it all, and often Moonie is waiting for him, even in the desert, with a drink.

No doubt the Kmershulls, like all families, have problems. They cannot be very happy at the way Jollyman's younger brother, Pusher Kmershull, known to his friends as 'Elbows', is shaping. He may have a good head for drinks, but he had better watch it. Whenever he goes into a pub, half a dozen rather rowdy friends greet him. He elbows his way through quite rudely, leering at the barmaid. He always seems to buy huge rounds of drinks, and he never smokes anything but cigars, which seem to attract very expensive-looking girls to him.

You are never quite sure where (or indeed *if*) he works – or for that matter where Jollyman works, but one wonders as he smiles meaningfully at his wife over a cup of some beige drink before a fire they would be well advised to damp down a little before retiring. They always seem to have a new car – getting into it, or popping out from under it – and smiling like hell. They are always just off to another holiday in some West Country village where the postman smiles at everyone from a wobbly bicycle. Where do they *get* all this money? From us?

∾☙∿

Lines Composed in Increasing Desperation in a Multi-storey Car Park

WHERE THE HECK is the deck where I left my car?
From A (for Anxiety) up to G (for Gigantism) – all the letters there are –
There's none to answer my appeal
Where the hell is my automobile
Where the hell does it dwell? I cannot remember the number
Of the floor or bay. The ticket is here in my pocket
But where did I park it and quit it and lock it?
You horrible car park, hark, as I stumble and ladenly lumber,
You car park, careless as, carless, I search your interstices,
Functional junctional concrete, cold and uncaring,
Curse your computerised lack of attendants and courtesies!
(That's a crime of a rhyme, but to hell with the niceties,
No poet rightly should be put
To trudging round these decks on foot):

> Listen, reticulate maze inarticulate, lacking direction and bearing,
> My *car*! My carrier! Far beyond price it is!
> It links me to life with a linkage umbilical
> Each time I start it, a small thrill (or thrillicle)

Leaps through my limbs; I am active, galvanical,
Part of society, working, mechanical,
The whirr of the starter's the start of my life,
Then I'm a man, with a home, and a wife,
And a job, and some kids. Then I know that I *am*
Since I move – or even when stuck in a jam
I am part of the world, as I sit at the wheel
I'm mobile, I'm car-borne, I'm ME, I am real . . .

But now, you static production-line, of vehicles only identical
In not being mine; you human-rejecting conventicle,
Anfractuous, tortuous, maze that is driving me crazy,
Perspectives of pillars perplexing me like Piranesi,
Skeletal, wall-less, blown through by winds from the dockside
And smelling of rubber and oil *and*, of course, carbon monoxide –

See these men with pigeon-hole minds,
See how easily each one finds
His car, and settles in the seat;
Switch on, and *vrrooom*, and *tout de suite*
He's off, and gives no thought at all
To me, pressed flat against the wall,

Irrelevant *revenant*, ghost in a concrete machine, pedestrian-pathetic
In your arid rectangular gridwork a bungler peripatetic;
Am I doomed, like the Wandering Jew, to wild-eyed searching
eternal,
An Ishmael-outsider, on foot, in this stock-piled car-stack internal?
O where is my chromium-homium, luxury-leathery car,
My cushiony-comforty, distance-diminishing farer-afar?

O God. D7, D8, D9 –
Why, *look!* This one! It's here! It's MINE!
I'm sure I passed here twice before –
But quick! Get in and slam the door
And get the damn thing into gear
Before it can re-disappear.

And the Parsimonious Peasant

'I CAN'T THINK why no one has yet written a sci-fi/horror story about a motorist, haunted by a nameless fear, who stops at a lay-by and when he opens the door there is *nothing*, just empty black space all round the car. He can still see the road ahead through the windscreen, and the usual vague misty fields are visible on his left through the nearside window, but he knows that if he opened it there would be utter emptiness on that side too. He hastily shuts the door and drives on, perhaps seeking desperate assurance from the car radio that an outside world (of sorts, full of people called Ken and Amanda Blooth, of Wiggin Flats, who would like to hear the Desperadoes singing *Ah Wannabee Joojooo*) still exists . . .

Well, it would be one of those stories easier to start than to finish, but it would surely touch a chord in any motorist whirling along detached from all reality – or worse, lulled into thinking that only *he* is real. Part of the awfulness of any accident, even the one with the small dent in the boot, the bits of red plastic from someone's rear light, is the shocked realisation that the other car was real and had real people in it.

At all costs we have to remember there are people out there. The trouble is that this means watching them; and I don't know about other motorists, but I find that the more I watch them the more they all fall into categories.

1 **The Hairy Fool** – Psychiatrists are always going on about the car being a virility surrogate for all drivers, but this is the only one of whom this is actually true. He really works at it. In winter he has the window open (and indeed, if it is a convertible, the hood down) and wears a white shirt open at the neck. There is something about the way he drives behind you, as you are fourth in a line passing a bus, that suggests you ought to get into the inside lane for him. Often *he* gets into the inside lane, and if you won't let him out he pursues you for miles like a dodgem car. He probably has some name like Jed, or Buck, or perhaps Ray. He has this theory that it is cissy to use headlights, especially at dusk, especially when he is passing a long queue of cars coming out of town towards you with dipped headlights, so that it is very difficult to see him, especially as his offside sidelight does not work anyway.

210

His reasons for eschewing headlights are exactly opposed, psychologically, to those of

2 The Parsimonious Peasant – Nothing will persuade this man, probably called Amos or Jabez or Silas, that it is anything but a criminal waste of electricity, or candles, or acetylene, or something, to switch on *any* lights, no matter what louring thundercloud, sheeting rain or dense fog obscures the sun, until the time given in the paper for lighting-up. No, stay, he is far too mean to buy a paper, he reads them at the public library, if there is a free car park near enough, on his way back from collecting the rent, recently doubled, owed to him by some starving widows; he has all the lighting-up times up till December 31, 1999, in a well-thumbed manual he picked up at a jumble sale for 2d. 17 years ago.

3 The Manic Depressive – As he rushes along, I imagine him shouting and singing the *Ode to Joy* from Beethoven's *Choral Symphony*. Then, utterly unpredictably, not because of any traffic conditions, the tempo changes. Suddenly he remembers the appalling phone bill, or maybe one of those how-normal-are-you? sexual surveys in some magazine or other where he has deduced, from the answers on page 39, that he is on the verge of impotence; or maybe simply the thought of British Leyland comes into his head – something infinitely grey and depressing, anyway – and tears start to his eyes, a fearful lethargy seizes his limbs, and with blurred vision he just manages to keep going at that awkward speed just too high for third gear and too low for top. Then, just as you are going to pass him, joy breaks through the gloom with equal unpredictability, and he leaps forward.

Quite often, however, he slows down on nice straight bits, and speeds up on corners. He is not *trying* to stop you passing; he is far too much involved in the lurches of his own personality to be aware of the existence of anyone else. In this he is the opposite of

4 The Blocker – I see this man as the junior partner of a firm in which the senior partner, a jolly, whiskered, ruddy-faced, laughing fellow, is in rude health, popular everywhere, unlike this lantern-jawed bloke (somehow you can tell he is lantern-jawed even from behind), who is despairing of ever taking his place. Or he is henpecked at home. So what he does, especially at weekends, is set out without any particular destination in mind. He waits until he sees a car – yours, in fact – which he knows to have a top speed and acceleration slightly less than his own. On long straight stretches, with nothing coming the other way, he goes as fast as he can. The moment there is light, oncoming traffic he slows down; indeed at any but the gentlest of curves he changes down to get round. He goes slower and slower, until he can see you swinging about impatiently behind. He actually has a scoring system, which includes

211

ten bonus points if he can get you to blow your horn at him. The moment another clear straight comes, of course, he is off like the wind, with something as close to a smile as you can get on that kind of face.

5   The Urban Leveller – He combines some of the Parsimonious Peasant's miserliness and the Blocker's bloody-mindedness with a curious dash of irrationality. Basically, he thinks that city driving is a mechanical affair and that initiative should be punished. He is firmly against the use of two lanes, even when these are clearly marked with a dotted line. He drives astride it, and if he *has* to move out for any reason and then finds you, quite legally, coming up inside him, he cuts across your offside. If you are behind him on the outside lane, he disdains the electricity-wasting, nervous habit of operating his turning-right winker when stopped at the lights until they are actually green again.

6   The Round-Britain Ford Transit Van Race – This is a gruelling test of skill and endurance known only to a band of mad *aficionados*. They are often quite old vans. They can be of the same year, 1970, as the one which I hired, new, fitted out as a kind of maxibus, to drive my entire family across Ireland to live in a castle (for this very Magazine, in fact), so I know what expert souping-up must have gone into them to make them capable of getting past me, either on the open road when I am nearly flat out myself, or in traffic – which obviously does not present the problem, with such a broad vehicle, for these nippy (but not at all aggressive) drivers, that it did to me.

Sometimes the vans bear the name of an obscure laundry, but usually they are quite unlabelled, and the back doors are tied shut with sisal rope so that they can get in . . . who knows what – a grand piano, a billiard table, a garden shed? There are probably load conditions laid down for some extraordinary rally in the Midlands which only they know about.

7   The Return from Cousin Aggie's Funeral – Much against his will, Horace has been persuaded to get his car out on a weekday (it is one of those cars that look brand-new although they are in fact seven years old; he polishes and maintains it every Saturday and goes for little runs on summer Sundays). With his wife Bertha in the front seat, and his wife's sister Mildred and her friend Miss Tomkins, two white-haired ladies, in the back, the car is coming back from the funeral; there is a smell of mothballed furs. Mildred is developing the well-worn theme of how marvellously the third sister, Our Elsie, manages with all those children (Horace and Bertha have none, and Mildred is not married) and what a crying shame it will be if Aggie has not done right by them in her will.

The sudden reduction to an even lower speed outside an Underground station is due to Horace's indecision between the pleasure it

212

would give him to stop and say brusquely 'this do for you, then, Mildred?' instead of taking her all the way home, and his fear of the row with Bertha ('you know Our Mildred means well') if he does any such thing.

8   The Man Who Beat, Perhaps Even Welcomes, Inflation – He has a fat, low sort of car, capable of such enormous speed that he gives you no impression of crowding you as you get going on the outside lane when you are out of the limit. With courteous, undazzling lights, he waits till you have passed all the people you want to pass and drawn in; then, wheeeesh, he effortlessly leaves you, doing at least 40 more than you are. His car is quite muddy but clearly has many little purple lights, grained walnut surfaces, possibly a fur-coated, slightly exotic woman with high cheekbones who does not speak much, not needing to. They own a huge toy firm, or he is a gold smuggler. Something right out of your league, anyway.

There are a whole lot of categories. Just as every human face reminds you vaguely of some other human face, of someone you know, so does every motorist behave or look like one you have seen before. There are definitive books about categories of the human face, and drivers too are a field for scientific classification. **The Dwarf** (where's his head, then?); **The Desperate Smallholder** (battered green vehicle rushing out from country side road, wife is having a baby or they have suddenly run out of nitrate); **The Gearbox Wrestler**; **The Father of** (apparently) **Septuplets**; **The Dreamer**; **The Homespun Vegetarian Commune Van**; **Mr Why-Worry** (dent in his wing was two years ago at least); **The Salesman Who Never Smiles** . . .

But one thing you are never going to know: not what **their** categories are nor what they think of you so much as whether they think of you at all, whether they know you are there, until they or you – *look out, you idiot* . . . good thing I've got good reflexes . . .

Love You, Hate Your Dog

AH, ABOUT 12.30. Then we can have a nice peaceful drink before lunch and catch up on everything. *Be nice to see them again. And surely they won't bring that damn dog after what happened last time.*

Yes, well thank goodness it didn't go septic, ha ha. Bites very often do. *I suppose they really DO believe it wasn't their awful Rex that bit me when they were fighting. As if Fred would. Fred didn't bite the drunk that wandered into the back garden that time, why should he bite ME when some frightful aggressive red setter suddenly appears in OUR house? Or, from a canine standpoint, HIS house?*

No, I suppose you can't. *I BET they can't get a dog-sitter. That Rex bites THEM if they make a sudden movement, let alone anyone fool enough to dog-sit.*

No, I suppose you can't. *Why the hell not? Other people, equally devoted to their dogs, manage to bring themselves to leave them in kennels. Whenever we've picked up Fred after leaving him in kennels he's always looked brushed and clean and in better condition than when we left him, and indeed seems to have made friends. Kennels get INSPECTED these days, for God's sake. There's some kind of diploma, kids who actually like being surrounded by all that yapping and yowling work for years, for kennel-owners with the same inexplicable patience (and when it comes to monsters like Rex, fearlessness) before launching out on their own. It's no good going on as if all kennels are a kind of canine Auschwitz-cum-Dotheboys Hall.*

Well, they're the kind recommended by the RSPCA, you know. Off the floor, out of the draught. *What kind of bed do they want for a dog? A four-poster, and a room-service bell for Chappie snacks in the middle of the night?*

Well, yes, of course it depends what you mean by a cage. *Anybody would think they put them in a meat-safe. There's plenty of room for the perishers to run and jump about – and that's AFTER they've been out for proper regular exercise, which is more than that fool Rex can count on, which is why no loose object weighing less than two pounds can be kept at a height of less than five feet in their house, otherwise he'd either crash it off with the huge swishing tail by accident or gnaw it to pieces on purpose, even if it was made of glass.*

Yes, I remember you told me last time. *If I had a dog like Rex and it lost its bark for three weeks after one night in kennels I'd put it in once every three weeks even if I wasn't going away. When Fred barks it is at least at some tangible person or thing, but Rex can bark for hours out of a kind of abstract frustration, on a higher and higher note, gerrau gerrau gerrAU, as though there was some kind of dogs' crossword puzzle he couldn't complete and all the other dogs had and were laughing at him.*

OK then, about 12.30. Oh no, *they* won't mind. *They'll take one look, arch their backs, and we shan't see them the whole week-end. WHY is it taken for granted that Rex has a thing about cats? Fred gets on well enough with them, in fact he often sleeps on the same chair with one of them. What's so undogly about that, how does going for cats make Rex more of a 'proper dog'? If he gets out of wherever we have to make sure he is while we're feeding the cats, whom we shall have to coax in with absurd-sounding high-pitched calls of WEEDLE WEEDLE WEE COME ON LUBLY THUPPER, COME ON BLAST YOU, in the rainy dark outside the shed where they are probably sitting, Rex may find out to his cost they have a thing about red setters who keep going gerrau gerrau gerrAU.*

OK then, about 12.30 . . .

Hello, welcome, welcome. No, not at all. The traffic's hellish on Saturdays. Oh, poor you! Well, we've never taken Fred a long way in the car, perhaps *he* would in a traffic-jam too. No, don't you worry, we've shut Fred in the back room for the moment, they can get used to each other later on. No, honestly, I'll just get a pail and some Dettol, better clean it up now, it kind of impregnates the whole car if you don't clean it up straight away I – children, DON'T LET FRED OUT, I told you. Yes, in a minute.

(From back room): Grak grak grak GRAK, grak GRAK, grak grak grak GRAK.

(From car): *Gerrau gerrau gerrAU GERRAU.*

Hello Rex. Good boy then.

GRRRRRRRRRRR GERRAU AU AU AU GRRRR.

There you are boy. There, he's thirsty. Good old Rex then. I – darling, I TOLD you not to let Fred out!

A gerrau a garrawow a GRAU GRAF GRRR A GRAK grak GERRRRRAU.

I expect it's because Fred was on the lead. *Although why Fred should be on the lead in his own house I don't know, why isn't Rex on the lead? What's Fred supposed to do, go up to him and say, I daresay you'd like to wash your paws, then we'll have a little scamper, eh?*

Well, I suppose he's not used to another dog in the house. *Why should he be? I'd like to see how Rex would behave if we ever took Fred to them. On second thoughts, I wouldn't like to.*

Later on, darling, when they've got to know each other. Put Fred in the other room just now. We'll just let Rex sniff about a bit and get used to us. He's – darling, it's all right, he won't bite you (*I hope*). But don't make sudden movements, be gentle with him (*why, for God's sake? He's bigger than the child, why can't he be gentle with HER, or with anybody else for that matter?*). Yes, it *is* a lovely coat, isn't it! They brush it every day. (*More fool them. I've got better things to do.*) Yes, it's called a red setter (*ought to be called dead setter really, it makes a dead set at anybody it doesn't like, which on the whole means everybody*). It's a game and shooting dog (*or was originally, unless it had to be put down because of a genetic streak which made it bite sheeps' legs off, and it gets very angry living in urban conditions where it can't find any sheep so it has to make do with people*). Yes, it is funny, now you mention it, we live in the country and have a town dog and they live in the town and have a country dog (*or maybe it's some sort of compensation factor, this is their connection with Nature in her more bloody-minded aspect*). . .

Grak grak grak grak grak grak grak grak GRAK grak grak GRAK.

Well, perhaps we'd better, we can't really eat till they've settled down, can we? But let's get our drinks first. Darling, the ice has melted, would you go and get some more from the fridge. Mind you – DON'T LET THE CAT THROUGH!

GERRAU GRRR.

SPSSTCHKSPKOW GRRAUU yow yow YOW.

I say, sorry about that. Oh, I don't think cat-scratches go septic. They don't even on people, let alone dogs. William's a terrible greedy, I expect he thought Rex was eating from his plate (*as a matter of fact he was. Unlike dogs, cats can leave a little on their plate and come back for it when they feel like it, a fact which Fred learnt to live with long ago*). No, there isn't a vet in the village, I'm afraid. All country vets live eight miles away, it's not like London where there's always one just down the road. But I daresay we could get some kind of antibiotic from the chemist, he'll be open at 2.15, in a minute or two. Poor old Rex, I *am* sorry (*God forgive me, I'm glad. That'll teach him about one cat anyway, even if the other IS hiding in the shed*).

Grak grak grak gragGRAK GRAK GRAK.

All right Fred, gently, now. This is Rex, *you* remember. Ye-es, that's right. Now you've all got a drink. Ha-aah, well. Cheers, everybody. Well. I hear David's getting married. I'm –

Gerrau gerrau grrrrr.

All right Rex, *good* boy Rex (*evil-tempered neurotic lout Rex*). Good boy Fred. See, I told you it would be better when they were both off the lead. Now nobody take any notice of them, just relax about it, they'll be OK. Oh, don't worry about that, there's plenty more gin. I'll put this one on the mantelpiece for you.'

216

Will they marry before David qualifies? Well, if she's working, I suppose – well, darling, that's the way dogs always get to know each other, sniffing like that.

Grak grak grak. Grrrrrrrrr-AU.

Now Fred. (*And now Rex, only more so. Surely even you must be satisfied by now that Fred isn't a bitch you dismal sex maniac.*)

Grak gerrau aaarghgrrrr grrr YAG YAG a GRRRRRR gak gak GAK . . .

All right Fred, if that's the way you feel (*if that's the way Rex feels, he was the attacker*) you'd better stay in the back while we eat. Come on everyone, no harm done, thank goodness. We can catch up on everything while we eat.

Gerrau gerrau gerrAU.

They'll get used to each other in time. Well, sit down everybody, it's all ready. Really it's ridiculous how long it is since we saw you. We musn't let it be so long again . . .

And next time they come I'll put FRED in kennels.

Moscow Belongs Tae Me

LIKE MOST ENGLISHMEN (and, I wouldn't mind betting, a fair number of Scotsmen), I have a generalised idea of Robert Burns as one of those marvellous poets who make their own rules *after* giving ample proof of their ability to write within the old rules, in his case with lots of perfectly straight stuff about girls with names like Chloris, Clarinda, Delia ('Sweet the tinkling rill to hear/But Delia, more delightful still/Steal thine accents on mine ear').

When it comes to the vernacular with which he soared to freedom, celebrating everything from the wee sleekit tim'rous beastie to the domestic virtues of *The Cottar's Saturday Night*, where the mother is pleased to see that the boy friend Jenny brings home is 'nae worthless rake', and after a meal of 'halesome parritch, chief o' Scotia's food' they sing hymns ('compar'd with these, Italian trills are tame'), he does make you feel how much better this all is than everybody just staring at the telly; and there were all those de'ils and witches too, and drink, and women, and life; Tam O'Shanter stopping to look at a new witch being enrolled in the local Sabbath, dancing in a rather short garment, a cutty sark, indeed the only one worth looking at ('a winsome wench and walie') among the other rigwooddie hags who only managed to grab his mare's tail before he escaped over running water . . .

But, well, there you are. Rigwooddie, what it mean? My edition has a glossary from which I can learn that a *spleuchan* is a tobacco pouch, a *jocteleg* is a large knife (from, it says, *Jacques de Liège*, whoever *he* was), *mashlum*, *meslin* and *maskin-pat* all mean teapot, *red-wat-shod*, a word that's going to come in very useful, means 'walking in blood over shoe tops', *waff* means shabby and *waft* means woof; and so on. But it doesn't give *rigwooddie*. It doesn't give half the words.

I thought this might be because they are still in current use. But now I have tried out on three genuine, paid-up Scottish friends the following verse from *Address to the Toothache* (and I admire anyone who can make verse out of that, as, in the present state of my personal and the nation's finances, I warm to one who can write a poem called simply *Ode to Ruin* beginning *All hail! inexorable lord!*')

> *Adown my beard the slavers trickle*
> *I throw the wee stools o'er the meikle*
> *As round the fire the giglets keckle*
> *To see me loup:*
> *While, raving mad, I wish a heckle*
> *Were in their doup.*

Not one of them could tell me what a doup was, and how it could be made worse (since that's obviously the sense of it) by having a heckle in it. There is that about the human mind (or about my mind, anyway) which, faced with an impenetrable passage like that, seizes on the first association, however remote, and builds on it a construction at once elaborately, fantastically detailed and totally unreal, like a fairy castle. For me it was *giglets*. From God knows where in my subconscious comes the word *gigot* (Fr.), a leg, as of lamb for instance – perhaps still in use in Scotland from Auld Alliance times.

Instantly the picture forms of the poet so raving mad with toothache that he fancies that even the roasting giglets (lamb chops) are cackling (or keckling) with laughter to see him loup, i.e., to see his face swell (I just happen to know, *truly*, that Louping-ill is a genuine disease of sheep, together with Quarter-ill, Felon, Bradsot, Pulpy Kidney Disease, Strike-ill, Vinquish, Turnip Sickness and Wool on the

218

Stomach); frantic with the pain he hurls the nearest things to hand, the wee stools of his own children, out of the window at the meikle (an ingenious device of slatted wood and iron use in eighteenth-century Scotland to dispense fodder to sheep in snowy weather) and wishes that the lamb chops were part of live sheep again so that they could have a heckle (a very painful kind of sore throat, cf. *hack*) in their doup (throat, obviously).

This picture is only slightly altered when I find from the O.E.D. that *giglet* meant 'a wanton woman' in 1625, although by 1725, 34 years before Burns was born, it had come to mean merely 'a giddy romping girl'. It almost serves him right, having toothache, if he gets these giddy romping girls in the moment his wife (Jean Armour) is away visiting friends in Peebles; probably the kind of girls that had a heckle in their doup already, no wonder he threw stools about at the dismal anticlimax of it all.

This is not part of another feeble attempt to laugh at a great poet through mere ignorance of the language. I bet I'm as moved as any Scotsman by some of the songs – say the four perfect verses of *Address to the Woodlark*, and when it comes to things like the *Epistle to Major Logan*, no amount of ignorance can prevent a general picture from emerging of a jolly, hospitable old boy:

> *Hale be your heart! hale be your fiddle!*
> *Lang may your elbuck jink and diddle,*
> *To cheer you through the weary widdle*
>   *O' this wild warl',*
> *Until you on a crummock driddle*
>   *A gray-hair'd carl.*

What I *am* questioning is how, if so much of him is inaccessible to his own compatriots, let alone Englishmen, the Russians can be so mad about him. Last year, in the *Daily Telegraph* for January 26, it said:

More than 100 Scotsmen and 100 Russians celebrated Burns's 219th birthday at a Moscow hotel. The Scotsmen brought 2 cwt of haggis, 22 cases of Scotch whisky, a piper, and a Scottish preacher with them by plane, and they were joined by Russian admirers of Burns.

That's 228 lb of haggis and 264 bottles of whisky, for not much more than 200 people – 10 lb of haggis and rather more than one bottle of whisky *each*. That's a hell of a party. You can't imagine more than 100 Russians flying to a Dostoievsky evening in Glasgow (or, perhaps more likely, a Tchekov evening in Edinburgh) bringing 22 cases of vodka,

2 cwt of caviare, a balalaika player and an orthodox priest, if there are any still out of jail.

Of course there's a lot of stuff about liberty in Burns, but not so much as in, for instance, Shelley or Byron, and you never hear of 100 Englishmen going out there with 22 cases of claret, 2 cwt of roast beef, a violinist and a free-thinking curate. In fact there's quite a lot of Burns that one can't imagine going down well there at all, like

> As the wretch looks o'er Siberia's shore
> When winter-bound the wave is
> Sae droops our heart when we maun part
> Frae charming, lovely Davies

– not to mention his song against Whigs, and therefore presumably *for* Tories.

Doubtless on both sides in this party there are serious academic philologists, Professor This and Academician That, who can discuss for hours why a daimen-icker in a thrave is indeed a sma' request for a mouse to make, or how one crummocks on a driddle. But what one has to remember is that Burns, as well as a poet, was an *exciseman* (even if in a lowly grade) and a freemason; and he must have combined the qualities of both in developing, and passing on to initiates through the generations, a mysterious way of getting whisky past any customs, anywhere.

You've only to think of the standard Russian hotel, with those huge elderly women sitting mysteriously at little tables on every landing, looking out for the slightest impropriety, to imagine what would happen to a party of 100 ordinary tourists who tried to get more than one bottle each of duty-free into the hotel (they took 264, remember) and a small mouth-organ, let alone bagpipes and all that haggis – even making the unlikely assumption that they got it past the Customs.

The moment the conversation-hum in the ornate, old-fashioned private dining-room with its Ionic pillars, bobbled table-cloths, potted palms, heroic murals and the rest of it, rose above a certain statutory level – a whispered word over the house telephone from one of these women, a fleet of plain vans at the hotel entrance . . .

But not if they're celebrating Burns. Because of something he passed on, some technical, frontier-passing secret of the brotherhood of man, these marvellous gatherings are possible, nothing whatever to do with contemporary politics. They don't have to make speeches sucking up to Big Brother, like Boss Evans on Radio Warsaw or Mr. Buckton in that citadel of freedom, Prague. They just sing and drink and toast the sonsie ('pleasant-looking, jolly, fat') haggis and the Immortal Memory, secure in the knowledge that *Freedom and Whisky gang thegither* far into the night, without caring *how* rigwooddie the women at the little tables on the landings are. Good luck to them.

❦

The Unacceptable Bass of Capitalism

'Oh, our Pyongyang,' sings the chorus in one revolutionary opera. 'Beautiful is the red socialist capital. With boundless joy we have come to the Pyongyang we have always longed for. Our leader is here in the revolutionary capital, which is the fountainhead of all our happiness.' – *Time*

I'VE ALWAYS WANTED to write an opera but I've never had the time. Till now, that is, when rock, with its limited number of soon-learned vamp-till-ready chords, and the Chinese type of social opera where you don't have to bother with harmony at all, since it all seems to be in unison, are obviously going to coalesce into an art-form immediately accessible to anybody.

It's a commonplace that nothing is too absurd if you sing it. Even in the days when opera was a kind of intellectuals' luxury, Wagner began a whole cycle with three girls called Woglinde, Wellgunde and Flosshilde (or it may have been Flosslinde, Woghilde and Wellginde) singing under water, and producing nothing like the unrecognisable glub-glub sounds you get if you actually try this. In Puccini's *La Fanciulla del West* one of the characters is called Wowkle, Billy's Squaw. In the opera made by one Albert Wolff from (admittedly) Maeterlinck's *The Blue Bird* there are singers called Light, Bread, Joy of Being Just, Father Time, Sugar, and Fire.

I myself, with the rest of the Philharmonia Chorus, learnt *Turandot* (for which *The Gong Show* would be a good alternative title) in which, as I am sure you know, there are three men called Ping, Pong, and Pang. At one point Pang sings *Ho un giardino, presso Kiu*, which means 'I have a garden near Kiu.' We had a ravishingly beautiful bit calling on the moon

221

to rise. Because we love the beauty of it? Not on your life. It's because when the moon does appear it will be time for some poor bloke to be beheaded. (The only opera that isn't about people who are unbelievable, or trivial, or both, is *Fidelio*, and we've done that. However.)

But this Pyongyang or Pekin stuff is a different matter. What have Pyongyang and Kim Il Sung got that London and Mrs. Thatcher haven't? Let's face it, we're pretty low on political opera in the west. The Tories are lowest of all. There are plenty of left-wing plays, and even a left-wing anthem, that dismal *Red Flag*. Maybe the Tories should get in first with this medium.

ACT I

A group of self-employed stockbrokers, shopkeepers and estate agents, refugees from the brutal and tyrannical regime of socialist-controlled Liverpool, are making their way south, led by Watson-Smith, who still wears on his tattered pin-stripe suit the faded medal of 'Salesman of the Year, North-west Region' for his insurance-selling exploits after leaving a safe job as a manager for the Prudential, which has now been nationalised, like everything else.

As they pass through the ravaged countryside of Warwickshire, littered with dead cows because no one on the nationalised farms will look after them, they sing of their hopes of joining Margaret the Liberator, who has freed great areas of the south and is now head of her troops, at the outer gates of London itself.

An aged cotton-forwarding agent, Congleton, declares he can go no further. But Elsie, once a cosmetics buyer for Marks and Spencer, enters triumphantly with some money she and some other girls got by capturing a village post office and Giro bank, and revives him with it.

'How beautiful are your eyes when you have done a great deed for capitalism!' sings Watson-Smith, but Elsie sternly rebuffs him for thinking of such personal matters until their great aim is achieved. Acknowledging his error, Watson-Smith leads the people in singing: 'Soon our conquering feet will march down Throgmorton Street, Lombard Street, in the heart of our glorious city. Onward, brothers, till our proud flag is raised on the Stock Exchange itself!'

ACT II

As the group prepare to pass through the dangerous neighbourhood of Birmingham, Coventry and Wolverhampton, along the grass-covered but recognisable route of the M6 and M1, never certain whether the ruined tower blocks contain snipers of the powerful socialist barons, Cholmondeley, an old motorist, sings, 'When I was a young man, O beloved road, my TR7 never left the fast lane. When will those years return?' He is being sternly upbraided by Elsie for thinking of such personal matters until their great aim is achieved when distant shots are heard and Sprudgett, bleeding from a flesh wound, runs panting on to the stage.

He warns them that the M6 is thickly ambushed and offers to lead them via Sutton Coldfield to the A5. 'Who are you, stranger, with your Birmingham accent?' sings Elsie suspiciously. 'I am Sprudgett, the famous Tory gas-fitter,' he answers proudly. 'A traitor! A spy! Bring back the death penalty! Hang him!' sing the crowd, and Watson-Smith himself suspects a trap. But Congleton, who is now fading fast in spite of repeated injections of money, with his last breath sings of his recollection of Sprudgett's appearance at a Conservative Conference at Blackpool in 1971 ('or was it Brighton in 1959? But O my friends, I adjure you, trust him'). Congleton dies and after a moving lament for him the group move on, picking up a large number of recruits in Sutton Coldfield.

ACT III

Outside Watford the group are challenged by a Tory group led by Chalmers-Petrie, who is at first suspicious of their claim to be Tories at all, so ragged has their appearance now become. His attitude changes after Elsie has sung to him of the hardships they have endured. They are conducted to an enormous shopping centre and fitted out with new clothes and given Barclaycards with which to pay for them over the next eighteen months. Watson-Smith sings, 'How glorious life is now our troubles are ending, and I have a new pin-stripe suit.' Elsie sternly upbraids him for thinking of such personal matters until their great aim is achieved. Chalmers-Petrie sings of the famous Tunbridge Wells Rising where Margaret the Liberator began her campaign. They agree to sink their differences as they march together, singing the Song of the Five Clearing Banks, to Hampstead Heath and the final victorious entry into London. 'O London, sacred Temple of Free Enterprise, now at last you are free again. In the name of Adam Smith, Professor Hayek, Keith Joseph and all our heroes, hear our joyous tramping feet, hear our voices as we salute her from a million throats. Long Live Margaret The Liberator!'

There you are. Shove in a few guitar-type chords and Pyongyang, here we come.

Old Golfers Never Die

'... AND OTHER LEGENDARY heroes of golf, tomorrow evening,' I heard the telly voice say. I was in the next room, as one tends to be during those ever-lengthening 'glimpses of tomorrow night's programmes'. (Do you sometimes get the feeling that they are taking ever longer bits out of tomorrow night's programmes, in fact all the best bits, so that in the end the *whole* of tonight will be taken up by tomorrow, then bit by bit they'll start shoving in bits of the day after tomorrow, till in the end we are completely out of phase with the calendar and we're seeing Wimbledon on Christmas Day and Michaelmas is February 22nd and the Pope has to change us all on to the new Johanno-Pauline Calendar, which the whole world will observe except Russia, which won't go on to it till the year 2052, and of course Ireland, in 2137? However.)

In any case, as I was saying, when you documentarise legendary heroes you merely diminish them, so that they always turn into actors with costumes usually involving fur and horns and metalware. What you should do with legendary heroes is read about them; that's what the word means. *Legendum*, to be read about. I don't see why any exception should be made for golf. So. Read on.

All over the world the legendary golf hero turns up in folklore. You can read about *Brassey* (the old spelling) in *The Heliotrope Fairy Book*, one of the less known in the series edited by Andrew Lang. He was an Irish giant, feared by all golfers in the time of King Padraic O'Guinneaiss of the Seven Clubs of the Land of Connacht.

Now the King was sad in those days, for his favourite son, Colm of the Iron Club, had gone out, on a fair morning of sparkling rain, four years and three years ago, to play at mountain golf. Mighty men they were in those days, who used stone balls the length of a man's fore-arm in diameter, and the clubs were fir saplings banded with iron, and every tee was a mountain top, and every hole was a dried-up tarn.

Now when it was the year of the King's turn for the Hosting of the Sidhe he was exceedingly sad. And the O'Bryan of the Nineteenth Hole, a handsome, red-haired warrior whom he had met at the Wexford Amateur Championships and invited to that court of his in the far western land, beyond the falling rain of the sunset, said to him, 'Why are you sad, O King, when the great feasting halls of the golfers should

224

be getting ready for the warriors to come and drink deep from the horns, and tell many tales into the night, of seven-league drives, of spells against *ruaighinn*, the Evil Spirits of the Rough, of the golden age when Machamlet, Captain of Sligo, did the Eighteen Consecutive Holes In One, in the dawning of the world?'

'Ah, O'Bryan, Lord of the Fairways,' said the King sadly, 'I cannot raise a scratch side of my own, let alone play host to visiting ones. Do you not know that the giant Brassey devours all of our young men, even the bravest, who have gone to the mountain course to seek tidings of my son, Colm of the Iron Club, who went out to play four years and three years ago, and has not been heard of from then till the ending of the world?'

'Oh King,' said the O'Bryan, 'If I find your son, is it the hand of your fair daughter, Grania of the Third Green, that I may ask for?'

'That you may,' replied the King, 'but I must warn you, many heroes of golf, as mighty as yourself, have gone on a like quest and never returned. How will you succeed where they have all failed?'

But the O'Bryan smiled to himself and replied, 'In four days and three days I will return, and your son Colm of the Iron Club with me, and all the others who have disappeared.'

With that he betook himself to Culann the Smith. 'Make me,' said he, 'six stout spikes of iron, while I can still say it, for I am going out to the mountain course, either to conquer the giant Brassey and return in four days and three days, or to die in the attempt. Make the spikes to fit solidly into my seven-league golfing boots, three on each one, and let them be as sharp as a woman's needle.'

Culann did as he was asked. When he had got the spikes the O'Bryan went to the first hole with his enormous Iron Driver. 'Ho, Brassey, come forth!' cried he, as he addressed the granite ball, as big as a pumpkin. but he heard naught save the sound of his own voice echoing round the mountains. So he holed the great ball in one. And at the second tee he shouted, as he addressed it, 'Ho Brassey, come forth!' But he heard naught save the sound of his own voice. And so he went, and when he was not shouting taunts at Brassey he was singing and holing in one, for this was in the morning of the world.

But at the sixteenth hole the ground trembled, the sky grew dark and Brassey appeared. 'I will seize you by the left leg and throw you into the sea!' cried he in a voice of thunder.

'That you shall not!' said the O'Bryan. He dug the spike of his left boot into the ground, and Brassey pulled till he could pull no more, and fell back in exhaustion, whereupon the O'Bryan again holed out in one. With three steps the giant caught him up. 'I will seize you by the right leg and throw you into the sea!' cried he.

'That you shall not!' said the O'Bryan. He dug the spike of his right boot into the ground, and Brassey pulled till he could pull no more, and fell back in exhaustion, and the O'Bryan holed out the seventeenth hole.

At the eighteenth tee the giant caught him up again with three steps. 'You shall not escape me again,' roared he. But the O'Bryan took off both his boots and flung them straight at the giant so that all the spikes pierced him. That was the end of him, for he was killed and turned into the great green mound above the bunker on the eighteenth that may be seen to this day. And when the O'Bryan did his last drive the stones lining the fairway turned into brave young golfers, and the youngest and handsomest of them all was Colm of the Iron Club, for the O'Bryan had broken the giant's power . . .

Some detect in this famous old legend a dramatisation of the triumph of the Iron Age over the Bronze (or Brass) Age, the perpetual human lament at increasing sophistication and nostalgia for the simple glories of an imagined past. But there are many variants. In the Norse epic *Galfsang* the hero Niblik has to slay the fearsome dragon Bunker to rescue the Green Princess, and the dragon becomes a heap of sand. In the North American Hopi cycle Kleek, a young pro warrior, prevented from advancement by jealous older rivals, eventually earns the respect of the whole tribe by defeating, with cunning ruses, two demons called Mistaneesi-putt and Godda-mit (figures almost identical with the Boghi-Pa of Persian legend). Even in China, when the Emperor Fu Zle questions the strange warrior Ho Lin Wun . . . but it is difficult to know when to stop; the legends of the past are almost as tempting to quote as the programmes of tomorrow.

My Average Lady

NOT BEING AMONG the millions who looked eagerly for the traditional re-telling of the heart-warming old Christmas tales in such films as *The Sting* and *Where Eagles Dare*, I saw only two holiday programmes that could be described as jolly. One, of course, was *Charley's Aunt* and the other, even more of course, was *My Fair Lady*; and being as enchanted as ever by the latter I wondered yet again why this and *The Boy Friend* remain the only two musicals, compact of joy, style and, above all, *life*, that I would go anywhere to see, done by anyone – sailors, nuns, amateurs, convicts or (in the case of *The Boy Friend*) about 60 children at the school on an enormous American air base, and very good they were too.

Perhaps a good musical has to sum up a decade, and there is always one that does it best. *The Boy Friend* encapsulates the twenties. *My Fair Lady*, based on *Pygmalion*, which was written in 1912, encapsulates the Teens, perhaps, as *Major Barbara* (1905) does the Tens, too remote from us now for becoming a musical.

Possibly we aren't ready for a musical encapsulating the Seventies yet, although given the way nostalgia is getting ever closer to our heels I doubt it. But since the social attitudes to speech have been completely reversed, so that anybody who doesn't sound demotic (and preferably provincial) let alone anyone who talks posh, is a non-starter in the media and in increasingly large sections of commerce and industry, how marvellous it would be if the genius of Lerner and Loewe could be added to that of Shaw in a reversal: *My Average Lady* . . .

PROLOGUE
The saloon bar of the Space Buyer's Arms, local pub of Basinghorn Gelber Watson, a smart advertising agency. Barry Iggins, an account executive who read philology at Norwich, is so fascinated by the conversation of two debby-looking girls that he has his tape recorder on.
Razor-cut: Ay weddn't geoh ight with him agen for a thigh'zn pigh'nz. Tooo middle C.
Blonde: Eor wale, Ay spayze you know what you're dayng, dorling. He's *laded*, efter orl.
Razor-cut: Oeu yaiss. But Aym gayng to be laded too, dorling.

227

Blonde: Dorling, yaw fawther didn't even send you on a secret*airial* cawss. Deddeh sed to myah –

Razor-cut: Eow blawst, it's pissing with reen, and Ayve got an awdition.

Blonde: En *awdition*? Whet *faw*, dawling? (*they go to the pub doorway*)

Razor-cut: Wale, not for taping. I'm gain grind to a film studi – *texyah! Texyah!* (*hailing a taxi*) Eow feck, they're all engeeged. Texyah!

Iggins joins them in the doorway

Iggins: Within five miles of Haslemere, I should say. Then Benenden.

Razor-cut: High dare yaw! What are you dayng hengin a rind with thet teep recorder? High did you know I was at Benenden?

Iggins: I am a student of phonetics. I've no doubt an illiterate upper-class girl like you thinks a phoneme is an Italian radio programme, if she thinks at all –

Razor-cut: If yaw say pride of yawself, why daynt yaw get mya texyah?

Iggins (*cheerfully*): Anything you say, honey. Taxi!

A taxi instantly pulls in. He hands the girls into it, bowing sardonically.

ACT I

Barry Iggins's pad, a large attic flat in Pimlico full of cushions, very explicit posters, and electronic equipment. The Razor-cut Girl, now revealed as The Hon. Lavender Hope-Meldrum-Hope, is listening to a playback with Iggins and his friend Lance-Corporal Pickering.

Playback: The reen in Speen stees meenly in the pleens. As an ordinary hicewife . . .

Iggins turns it off angrily

Iggins: You see, Pickering? I picked this girl up in the worst part of Mayfair. Just listen to those vowels of hers –

Lavender: What's wrong with my vials?

Iggins (*ignoring her*): And this is the creature I intend to get into a TV commercial as a housewife. But I'll do it, Pickering, I'll do it.

Pickering: Garn, bet yer a handred quid yer carnt. No' in free munfs.

Iggins: You're on. (*To Lavender*) Well, come on, you bedraggled Hunt Ball begonia, try again.

Lavender: The reen in Speen –

Iggins: no, no, *no*! If there had been a *Mrs* Walter Pater that's what she would have sounded like. You –

Pickering: Aow, cam orn Barry, less gdarn the Spice Byres navva pint.

Exeunt Iggins and Pickering

Lavender (*sings*):

Jost you wait, Berry Higgins, Jost you wait!
You will faynd we hevnt finished with you quate!

If you think the upper classes
Cawnt manipulate the masses
Because they cawnt speak common, you're too late!
The blood thets in may veins
Is of men who owned the manes
End the fectories thet made our Britn Great
When with dividends tremendous
We were such terrific spenders;
Don't think socialists can end us –
Jost you wait, Berry Higgins, jost you wait
Till we've got the people's eccent on a plate!
If you find our lips still curl, it's
Because we've been to Berlitz
And can make *well* sound like *werl;* it's
Too late, Berry Higgins, jost you wait, Berry Higgins, jost you wait!

ACT II
*A big football match. Iggins, Pickering and Lavender are in a group in the
middle of the terrace. The excited crowd sings*

Oh, what swearing
At everybody wearing
Colours of the other side!
Each punk and rocker
Knows it's not in soccer
That we take such manly pride;
What a lovely caper
Throwing toilet paper
When our side has scored a goal!
If it's theirs, a bottle
Is a wepping what'll
Take a bloody lovely toll . . .

Lavender (*excited, shouting*): Go on, Kickisbluddy ankles, gerrimoff,
gerrimout! Gwon gwon gwon! (*Iggins looks expressively at Pickering*)
Heah, I say, I say, that was orfside! (*There is a shocked silence around her
as she lapses into U-talk in the heat of the moment. People nearby in crowd,
staring at Lavender, whispering to each other*) Heah, orfside, I say, she
said, I say . . . (*Pickering looks expressively at Iggins*)

ACT III. Scene I.
A TV studio. Lavender with a pile of sheets, in front of a washing machine, being interviewed by a character in a sharp suit.
Lavender: Aow, yerss, defnitlee. Yerss, qua a diffrence, iss efsa much why'er. Aow yerss, this wonn defnitlee . . .
Scene II
Iggins and Pickering in the control room, singing joyfully

We done it! We done it!
We never thought we'd do it, but we did!
She will surely scare the pants 'n'
The daylights out of Rantzen
We done it! The fun it
Will give to GBS's ghost
To find that the normal
Is now no more than formal
But just the way you hear spoke most
And the teachers now speak as by pupils they are bid . . .
We never thought they'd do it, but they did . . .

I could have wrote all night, but there isn't room for any more.

Saw Points

IT IS REALLY amazing, in a country with the rich oral tradition of England, that so little research has been devoted to popular tags and sayings, of which many are particularly relevant to seasonal turns of the year, particularly in spring.

Although Peter and Iona Opie's classic work on nursery rhymes does overwhelmingly evoke a pastoral, pre-industrial past (*Cock: Lock the dairy door, lock the dairy door! Hen: Chickle, chackle chee, I haven't got the key*, etc), there are plenty of references to TV and pop stars and other modern subjects in their later work on children's playground rhymes; in fact I picked up several myself when I was doing a book called *The*

Living Village – e.g. Donald Duck, washing up, broke a saucer and a cup. And as for graffiti, half the population of England got that little paperback about them for Christmas

Yet here we are, with this huge stock of modern folklore lying all round us, uninvestigated, uncatalogued, the subject of no thesis. All I can do here is give a few examples from this huge untapped field and hope a few real scholars will get at it.

All situations and all seasons are covered, but, as I have pointed out, spring, perhaps not surprisingly as it is *the* great crisis and turning point of the year, is the commonest theme. It is true that some of the rhymes do still deal with the ancient rhythms of the soil. In Gloucestershire they say:

> *Was never pest*
> *But came out best*

and a Lancashire variant of this runs:

> *When Jim bought patent pesticide*
> *'T'wor crop, not bloody pest, as died.*

Many of the 'nature' saws, however, reflect the shift from the farm to the suburban garden, now that this is the basis of a multi-million-pound industry. There is a marvellously terse expression of the Englishman's traditional suspicion of brightly-coloured seed advertisements in:

> *Brighter packet*
> *Bigger racket*

and the well-known marital division of labour (recently confirmed in a survey by the commercial firm Mintel) is noted in:

> *When May wind blows*
> *All nature speeds*
> *When husband mows*
> *'Tis wife who weeds.*

Other rhymes in this field display an age-old wisdom born from centuries of gardening experience:

> *Pigs will fly and dows will speak*
> *When shears re-sharpened last a week*

231

and of course the well-known

> *Mower lent*
> *Blades all bent.*

   Increasingly, in the modern world, the coming of spring means, especially for the weekend driver, the release of the car from its winter bondage in the garage. First the machine itself must be seen to:

> *End of maying*
> *Start re-spraying.*

and

> *Drain not anti-freeze too soon*
> *Better wait till end of June.*

   There are scores of examples dealing with the journey itself:

> *Go to Chichester, try to get in*
> *End up Jones in loony-bin*

said to recall the legendary motorist Albert C. Jones who, driving from Brighton to Southampton, resolved to see Chichester Cathedral. Three times he arrived at the market-cross where it becomes 'No Entry', turned left, drove past three full-up car parks and found himself back at the roundabout where he had started.

> *Damn the seaside for a lark*
> *Even if you get there, nowhere to park*

is on a similar theme, and another interesting variant is

> *When springtime traffic loud doth hum*
> *AA men take hours to come.*

Sex and weather retain the prominence they had in the older rhymes:

> *Girls in spring beware of chaps*
> *In open cars, with woolly caps.*

Many rhymes reflect the changing values of our society, especially where the young are concerned:

> If a baby's going to come
> Tell the Doctor, not your Mum

Cadbury, Beerbohm and Rowntree, in a little-known paper read to the New Eugenics League annual conference at Grimsby, state that this is a shortened version of a rhyme current in the Home Counties as early as 1977:

> Doctor, I am getting stout
> I've come to you to have it out
> To a dentist you should go
> If your tooth is hurting so
> It's not a tooth, you darned old fool
> I'm pregnant, though I'm still at school
> The Hippocratic oath, that's flat
> Would not permit a thing like that
> I'll report YOU then, OK,
> To the new-style BMA.

As for the weather, the English fantasy of ideal, godlike figures who spend the year in whatever country the sun is shining in finds expression in:

> Come spring with merry sound of bee's
> Returning to us yearly
> Where the sun is, there are these –
> Boycott, Botham, Brearley.

There is also the age-old fear that a fine spring will be 'paid for' by a cold summer:

> After fine Cup Final Wembley
> Cricket cold and shivery-trembly.

Perhaps the most remarkable evidence of this ability of our oral tradition to absorb new ideas is in the amazing abundance of sayings concerned with our new role as a tourist country:

> Weak pound, strong dollar
> Grab the Yankee by the collar

or, in a Shakespeare Country version:

> *Stronger dollar, weaker pound*
> *Yanks are thicker on the ground*

and from the same area:

> *St George's Day, come wind blow hard*
> *Pour rain never stopping*
> *So them that come to worship Bard*
> *Spend more on drink and shopping.*

(This is recited three times at midnight by the Stratford Chamber of Commerce.)

Economics, of course, are another basic theme.

> *April Budget never yet*
> *Brought down anybody's debt*

or the succint

> *Miner's strike*
> *Buy a bike.*

Also

> *When will the angels come to town?*
> *When Budget brings the beer tax down.*

But the tourist theme keeps recurring:

> *When cuckoo calls in meadow sweet*
> *Cash will flow in Oxford Street*

and

> *Heathrow Tube train, go away*
> *Cab can earn ten quid each way.*

Nobody ever suggested that all these old saws were meant to give poetic *pleasure*, charming though some of them are. They express something real, deep in the experience of the people. They are part of a continuing tradition, and perhaps we may end with one which brings an old traditional phrase right to the centre of our life today:

Red the sky, and red the sea
Is red the whole world going to be?

You Can Always Switch Over

DIANNE IS BRITAIN'S main hope for the women's butterfly backstroke. A schoolgirl of fourteen, she is still at school. Totally dedicated, her father has given up his work as a lampsmith at 5 a.m. when her day begins, driving her thirteen miles to the nearest full-sized

crowd of students in many clashes with police, although the release of the tourists seems unlikely if the hostages held by the police cannot be exchanged for the kidnapped ambassadors. Today's claim by the police that a terrorist hostage was shot by a tourist guard can only worsen terrorists between relations and the government. Tony Benn, News at Ten. Meanwhile at the United Nations

oh, a 23. That leaves him with a 17 and double 6, fortunately one of the best shots in Wally's locker. Unfortunately for this brilliant lad from Nottingham

we asked Mr Bladbloom, Apex manager in Gothenburg, what had *happened* to this load. He told us that when Carson Peabody, whom he had not met, sent the order to transfer it to the *Global Conoffex*, he had no idea what the cargo was, or that the Rotterdam agreement with Mitropoulos had been signed *before* the ship left Haifa. We asked Mr. Mitropolous about this, and he told us

I love you when you're away, and when you're here I'm not sure. Does that sound silly? *Answer* me! For God's sake, Derek, the abortion wasn't a request for

The gentleman at the back. Yes, sir, with the blue tie. With regards to the representation of the workers concerned if the government's proposed proposal does not, as it was in the last government, as part of the conciliation programme of both sides in this dispute, would the panel agree that until such time as conciliation procedures are agreed on both sides they will not until the government does?Well

so the thousand metres are just a warm up for Dianne. Against the strong East German team

has provoked a strong reaction in America. Senator Kennedy

has thousands of little bubbles. *Hooray hooray, the bubbles shout, we will clean your inside out. Ping!* Yes , only with this new double-bubble action can

suppress women's artistic self-expression. Dr. Joan Sniff, you suggest in your book, do you not, that women are disadvantaged in the field of composing, in fact, by the fact that classical music is dominated in fact by male forms. If I understand it, a strong masculine subject *a* is always followed by a week feminine counter-subject *b*, although in fact true emotion should

bring the craft unions out. Nick Twinge reports

on the spread of incest in the suburbs. Has the in-breeding of the upper classes spread through the nation? Read Penny Thistleton's startling report of how an innocent-looking Act of Parliament which allowed Victorian widowers to marry their deceased wife's sister led to practices in Dulwich, Ealing, Islington and all over which will shock and amaze you. Plus the craze for nude fashion shows that is sweeping the Isle of Wight. Win a Rolls Royce and your own Caribbean island, just for naming a cat. All this and much more, only in toMORrow's

team for the vital match against his old club. Brian has always been a family man. He was born into a family and now has one of his own, relaxing in the lounge of his home. Brian has his head firmly on the ground, and he and Gladys made a few changes after the most expensive move in football history. Their three-piece suite is now two settees and a chair instead of a settee and two chairs, and there is a new telephone in the Merc, but otherwise the London home, conveniently near their son's school at Eton, is not very different from the one they left in Lancashire. Nor are there any language problems, since both Brian and Cheryl are both fluent in English. After a light breakfast

it was beer and sandwiches again for another round of these marathon talks with the craft unions. Chris Crossman, News at 3, ITV. Housewives in Bromley Kent had a surprise today when

good morning sir, I've come about your wife's complaint. Why, what's the matter with her, doctor? I'm not a doctor, I'm from the dairy. Oh, well what's the complaint? She said she's not getting it (*hahahahahahahahahaha*). Ah, I thought you looked like a milkman (*hahahahahahahahaha*). No, the cream, sir; the cream delivery is off on Monday. And the cream's off on Tuesday, eh? (*hahahahahahaha*) . . .

236

firemen were on the scene within minutes but there was little they could do. One of the survivors was on his honeymoon. How exactly do you feel, losing your bride in the fire and

what I have said all along is that no amount of tinkering with the money supply will

give you the highlights of tomorrow's viewing, Sunday the 19th. At 7.15, the Hairy Fairies, back from their sensational tour of Tasmania, live from London in a show called *The Biggest Victorian Round Hall In South Kensington*. At 8.15, an unusual documentary, *Vikings Up Everest*, made in sepia in 1927 by Sir Norman Ohlsson-Lundqvist, as he then was, sepia photographer to the ill-fated expedition in 1929 just before his death last year, showing what may be Viking goblets, runic stones and a complete longship, or some experts say the skeleton of a whale, at an altitude of 22,000 feet; or could they be sepia marks on the film? You can judge for yourself at 8.30. At 9.15, the start of a major 15-episode serial showing the adventures of a boy from the backwoods of America caught up in romantic intrigues and laudanum-smuggling in the exciting post-Napoleonic war period, *Huckleberry, Werther, Rouge et Noir*, a joint production of the BBC, *Time, Life, Ladies' Home Journal, Paris Match* and the *Frankfurter Allgemeine Zeitung*. This is followed by a special programme for the seventh Sunday of Lent, called *Don't Come Dancing*. And finally, *Highlights of Tomorrow's Viewing* – that is of course the day after tomorrow's – followed by *These You Have Missed*, highlights of today's viewing. A shortened version of Sir Norman Ohlssohn-Lundqvist's documentary is printed in this week's

strong opposition from the East Germans. But Dianne

naturally embarrassed if people draw away from your dog because he has bad breath. Aow yes, I couldn't understand why my friends all seemed, well to back away from Rex, then my dog's chemist, well, I asked him why you never seem to smell their breath at Cruft's or any of these shows, and he told me about Doggident, and now

the meteorite, which is about thirty times the size of our planet, will hit and destroy the earth at 11.33 Greenwich Mean Time on May 11th this year. At the United Nations

my goodness that was a close shave for Wally! But with that brilliant double 19, under such pressure, he can go on to the finals at Uttoxeter next month with

Roger. Of course he slept with Peter at Cambridge. My God, I thought Carol would have told you that at least. Olivia only married him as an objective correlative. That's why I married him. No, Roger, not Peter, don't you understand? I may not be a good novelist but I'm a good mistress, Charles, even though I slept with Carol at Cambridge. And there's something I must tell you. I miss having Peter's children more than I love being with you, you bastard. Sometimes I think those days at Cambridge.

would not have been acceptable to the craft unions

was discussed at the United Nations, with Russia's delegate dissenting. The wording of the vote was

of this we can be sure; she's approaching her peak. Or we are

Watch the Birdie

DR. JIM FLEGG, head of Zoology at the East Malling fruit research station, has clearly got rather desperate about bullfinches. In this of course he is not alone. He is in the company of anyone who has tried to grow apples, pears and blackcurrants, although his figures, as reported in the *Sunday Telegraph* story, are considerably below those of the Royal Society for the Protection of Fruit (of which I was Eastern Region secretary for some years). His estimate that bullfinches can eat fruit buds at 30 a minute is well below our figure, which ranges from 92 a minute, for apple buds, to 170 a minute for small fruit like blackcurrants.

With respect, for we in the RSPF are appreciative of much that has been pioneered at East Malling, I cannot help thinking he is on the wrong track in fitting the bullfinches with miniature leather braces with colour-coded tags so that scientists 'can study the movements of the bullfinches through binoculars' replacing the 'time-consuming and expensive' traditional method of ringing their legs.

He is reported as saying, 'I thought of putting braces on birds when I saw the leather pants and braces worn by men in Austria.' Since 'several pairs . . . fitted with the coloured tags have bred successfully this year' we must assume that he is correct in his statement that the braces do not harm the birds; indeed it is rumoured that leather skirts, or possibly very small gay dirndls, were made for the females, or cowfinches.

Clearly, no one, least of all the head of Zoology at a fruit research station, wants the bullfinches to produce calf-finches which will grow up to eat even more fruit buds. I am afraid it looks very much as though Dr. Flegg still has faith in the now discredited BASHORT system.

As all scientific fruit-growers know, this is the acronym for Bird Analog Simulator, Human Orchard Raiding Technique. It has been known for some time that the excited twittering and chirruping by which birds signal to each other that they have found a new stock of fruit buds is different from their song, and has a detectable sequence. When Eikopf evolved, for the Audubon Society of America, a computer programme in which these quasi-grammatical sequences were checked against a data bank containing all known details of the species, its home country and the structure of its language, the results, when fed through a translation unit, were hailed as a major break-through.

It all seemed so in keeping with the lyrical character (and, one now sees with hindsight, the long human poetic association) of birds that the HSE (Human Speech Equivalent) read-outs of BASHORT should be in verse, of a kind. One well-known blackbird experiment produced:–

> *Unripe fruit is not our scene*
> *To hell with pears or apples green*
> *But soft fruit! Currants, black or red!*
> *We'll eat them till we fall down dead,*
> *Sing trilliby, yummity, gurgle goo*
> *There's no bird net that we can't get through*
> *Gurgle gallopy gargle um goo.*

An equally famous bullfinch read-out was predictably short and to the point (bullfinches, with their 170 buds a minute, are much greedier and more busy eating than blackbirds and therefore do not have *time* to sing very much):–

> *Never mind summer, start in spring*
> *We'll eat any bloody thing*
> *Yum glub yum*

It was, curiously enough, a BASHORT experiment in the Eastern Region, where a long historical association of human invasion by Angles, Saxons, Danes etc. has perhaps caused most RSPF members to think of all fruit marauders as invaders from the Continent (not for nothing do we speak of the 'Plumgeld Line' passing from the Warwicks-Worcester borders up to the Lake District, east of which no plum tree can ever bear more than ten plums, if that), which showed the basic fallacy of BASHORT.

The experimenters, Wilson and Troutbeck, fell into the same trap that seems to have caught Dr. Flegg – that of treating bullfinches as Austrian birds. They got this HSE read-out:–

> *Wir trinken und tratschen*
> *Und fill up die Platschen*
> *Mit Plum-budden tasting so gut.*
> *So gobblen die Plummen*
> *Und die Englischer Bummen*
> *In Sommer will not have der Fruit*
> *Tritscherli tratscherli tree, tra-la*
> *Die champion Plum-budden Eaters we are.*

Wolstenholme of Cambridge pointed out that *the bullfinch is a native British bird*, without a scrap of Austrian blood, indeed in parts of our Region it is still known by its old name of bulldogfinch. It seems obvious now; yet how often is the elementary rule forgotten that in all computer work programming determines output.

It was the end of BASHORT (and, unfortunately, of Eikopf, who committed suicide). But we in Eastern Region have not been idle. At present three main lines of research are being followed.

One is *Laser Cat Projection*. It has been known for some time that the only thing bird fruit-eaters (even bullfinches) really fear is a cat. It is equally well known that a cat cannot be trained to catch (or even merely frighten by staring at) birds specifically designated by its owner, in so far as anyone can be said to 'own' a cat. A cat cannot be trained to catch mice, let alone birds. A cat put down by a mousehole from which the 'owner' has actually seen a mouse coming and going will walk away very angrily with its tail vertical. Chalmers of King's Lynn reported that on his taking a cat into an orchard containing 274 blackbirds, 392 starlings and 143 bullfinches, it killed only a nightingale, of which the presence had been undetected because the others were making such a noise. The modern laser technique, therefore, of projecting a 3-D 'holograph' cat seemed promising to Jackson of Wisbech and others, although the initial cost of the equipment (around £45,000) and the difficulty of getting a real cat to be the model for the projection make this scheme unpracticable except in the very largest orchard. Moreover, Jackson reports that after an initial success, some species not hitherto known as fruit eaters, such as owls, herons and seagulls, have been attracted by the light and formed new fruit-eating habits.

Area Camouflage has been practised by Aldous of Thetford with some success. Arguing, empirically, that just as no one knows why the Danes never went much west of Birmingham, no one knows why fruit-eaters respect the Plumgeld Line, unless there is something about the proximity of Wales, perhaps with eagles and other feared birds of prey in the mountains, he has therefore erected large panoramic views of distant blue hills on the western side of his orchard, with tape-recordings of Welsh hymns, male voice choirs and the sound of burning cottages. He reports an encouraging .002% decrease in fruit-eating.

Better Fruit Decoy involves, if you grow apples, having some tastier fruit, such as plums, to draw off the birds. If you grow plums, put out strawberries (tinned strawberries on sticks when the natural season is over). Statistical information is hard to come by. All I can say is that I have a tree from which I get one plum every year, but I get lots of apples. And at least it is less trouble than making little leather pants and braces and fitting them to bullfinches.

Simply Shattered

ONE MINUTE, WONDERFUL hum-along, come-along car I career in, carefree-content, semi-conscious of motion and otherwise-thinking, remote from the region I ride in, rapt in the reverie every driver alive is enveloped by, rhythmic I roll by unrealised reel-past-eyes vanishing vistas of mindfields, traffic in top-of-the-mind-attended-to transit-towns dreamt of at ease in a daze, in a lullaby-lay-by of life all so lazily soothed by the tyre-thrum and hum-throb –

Quickly, be wide-awake, check it and brake it and slack it, decelerate! For suddenly underneath, thundery rough-roaring surface, I've blundered unheralded on to the clatter-bang scatter of stonechips, a pattering tin-clank, brittle on metal and fatal to paint with its pebbledash pin-plonk percussion of stonelets, upside-down hailstorm and maelstrom, chrome-pitting, battering, scotching and scratching the coachwork. A murrain on mean, modern methods of road-mending, raw-rudimentary, rollerless, slovenly, slivers of gravel-grit grating and tinkling on mudguards!

A curse on the cost-cutting council, shovelling shingle so slapdash and then shoving off! They vanish, the mission half finished, the ratepayers robbed of the rolling that's really required for repairs. Once, reliable rollers steadily steamed up and down with a pulsing of pistons, a burnish of beautiful brassbound boilers, or diesels were easily, lazily passing, re-passing, compressing the mass into ready-made roadness.

Now my motor is menaced with macro-molecular malice, attacked by these tintack-like sticky-stone splinters that crash on the chassis and crack and excoriate paint.

So to parry the peril I dawdle and crawl and go solemnly-slow, to eradicate risk from the frisky flint fragments that fly, and counter their crepitant cutting with caution, with minimum motion.

Has nobody *noticed* this nuisance but me? All the traffic that faces me races regardless; no trace of awareness or fairness to me as they blind on the grinding and gravelly gritstone, they spatter and batter my car as they bucket and rock by unslacking, and back in the mirror I see them diminish and vanish in staggering aggregate-grapeshot aggression.

Come off it, cowboys – perhaps careless of cost because cosseted, cushioned in company cars, it's not *their* wear and tear. Oh chuck it, you're chipping *my* chariot, mauling *my* motor, maintained by mere *me*! Oh blast you, you dastard, you passed a deal faster than masters of driving (like me) think a pass to disaster. Confound you, you bounder! A pox on you, pockmarking pitter of paintwork! What about wind-shields when –

– BOK!

Oh, I'm blinded to grind-halt! I'm shut in all sightless in shatterglass shambles! Some dadgasted bastard has blasted my eyesight to blisters, a frosted-light criss-cross of stresslines, my clearpane opaque with a cat's-cradle complex of fractures and fissions, crazily interconnected in jagged-edge geometry, Euclid not lucid, I cannot see through it I knew they would do it, I knew it, I *knew* it!

I have heard recommended immediate, almost mandatory motion for motorists so incommoded. Sight is essential, they say; with your fist make a vista in urgent emergency, make your vehicle viable, veering already with steering unsighted. Such a deed I'll concede I'd be needing (my left hand all bleeding) if I had been speeding. But dash it, why smash it, why poke these precarious various pieces tucked tightly together in feathery fragile cohesion, when stopped, at a standstill and safe (and small thanks to the thug who so thoughtlessly threw up that flaming, that fracturing, that – any adjective prefaced with f – that fatal and fissuring flint)?

So, slowly I sidle at side of the road, and I enter a countryside cubist and cross-cut Picasso-wise, piecemeal, its puny perspectiveless stained-glass-like fragments and segments disbanding and bending at random;

242

a jumble and jigsaw, a jagged farrago of fractions that don't make a whole, a fly's-eye fantastic reflection of images damaged, imagined; a shifty surealist lunatic landscape . . .

I'd better decide, shall I drive on cross-eyed, by head-waggling juggling a new point of vision, a viewpoint so short it is reckoned in less than a second, and despairing of bearings, repairing my steering by staring with head out of window?

Ah no, for the cops will lay traps for such lapses. It's not lawful, they'll say, to trifle with life in this way. May we see your insurance . . .

The thing's past endurance. I've got to have clearance; I'll have to demolish, abolish this screen so obscure, obfuscated and scary. So, wary, I carefully stop – and with one timid tap there's a terrible tinkle and clank, a jangle as spangled triangular fragments collapse and collect in incredible corners of car. Too late I recall all the sockets and slots, all the gratings and grilles ungetatable, gritted with gobbets of glass undislodgeable, wreaking unknowable harm. They clash on the dashboard and cover the carpet with crackling collections of cullet*, and some smaller slivers, slyly inserted in segments of seat, painfully pricking me weeks after windshield-replacement.

Too late, as they clatter and clank, it occurs to me, *carry a blanket* to counter this clot-caused catastrophe, catch and contain the uncountable clutter. At last it is clear, I can fare without fear through the fresh unfamiliar air; but whoever the horrible hurrying hobbledehoy who hit me so hurtfully hard, I sure as hell hope that the whole thing will happen to *him*.

* Cullet, 1817 (Glass-blowing). Broken or refuse glass for remelting (OED).

Printer of Discontent

British Government and its Discontents. By Geoffrey Smith and
Nelson W. Polsby. Harper and Row. £7.95. A leading American
political scientist and a British journalist, have here set down the
outcome of their discussion with each other (sic) on the short unhappy
life of post-imperial Britain . . . those who know the work of Nelson
Polsby would relish a more detailed examination of the contents of
British government . . . *Times Literary Supplement*

O PAST, O history, O post-imperial Britain,
How many more vols are there to be written?
    What help to us will all these vols be
    Who do not know this Nelson Polsby?
Another great thick book of deep analysis
All about our land's alleged paralysis
    By – (recollection's rather wobbly)
    Benson (or was it Welton?) Spobley!
What *are* these discontents uniquely British
That get *critiques*, that make the Germans *kritisch*
    And get from – was it Wesley Hobson? –
    Social psychiatry with knobs on?
In 1878 a worldwide conference
At Washington decreed, the earth's circumference
    From north to south might very well be
    Zeroed on Greenwich, Polton Selby,
But dash it, even at that time of glory
The British never thought their famous island story
    Would simply be, O Wensley Poling
    Page on triumphal page unrolling;
Some artist from New Zealand, said Macaulay,
Would sketch St Paul's in ruins; outlook squally!
    Even if, O Pobsley Renton,
    Rome (as it always had done) went on.
The white man's burden (in the phrase of Kipling)
We did lay down, when it had got too crippling
    (As Roosevelt, ere you judge too glibly,
    Said we ought to, Belton Wibley,

Though why so soon the ship we should abandon
Might now be asked by more than one Ugandan;
    We never thought we'd keep a hold on
    All that Empire, Selsby Poldon –
And, while we're on the subject, surely Gandhi
Wouldn't have found a Russian *raj* so handy
    As responders to his nobly
    Passive resistance, Fenton Cobley).
But somehow, just because we were imperial,
We're subjects for this long, this endless serial
    As though we'd failed to pass some test on
    Staying up there, Holby Weston.
But Spengler's *Untergang des Abendlandes*
(*The West's Decline*) applied to *others* and us;
    We're all declining, more-or-lessly,
    All discontented, Holton Presley.
The loss of nerve, that Death of God of Nietzsche's,
And all industrial life's less lovely fietzsches,
    And doubt and fear, are troubles felt on
    All the earth now, Formsby Welton.
Our strikes? They strike from Katmandu to Shannon;
Our cops? In Amsterdam they've water-cannon;
    Unemployment? Race?Not solely
    Ours, such troubles, Belson Foley.
You've every right to say this verse I scribble
Is normal stuff for any British fribble;
    How more different could souls be
    Than yours and mine, (ah!) *Nelson Polsby?*
But still I beg, considering my views, you'll
Forgive such trifling with your name unusual –
    More apt for poesy and myths
    Than your co-author's, Geoffrey Smith's
But he *is* British. Learn, both, from these verses,
We're not dead yet, no need to order hearses;
    Though rather vague where Britain's goals be
    We'll reach them yet, you Smith and Polsby.

Notes From the Asylum

Poetry contest: Brentwood Poetry Group have launched a new poetry competition to be known as the John Clare Competition. Entrants must be born, bred, educated, or resident in Essex to qualify. The subject for 1981 is The Environment.

Daily Telegraph

CHELMSFORD

A<small>ND WHAT IS</small> Chelmsford? What untold renown
Made Essex choose it for a county town?
Is that small green-roofed church, that modest fane
Chelmsford *Cathedral*? O'er what civic pride
Do passengers in the Harwich-London train,
High-embankmented, uncaring ride?

Say, will they ever know what lies beyond
Those close allotments, that triangular pond?
This is the county town; and so down there
Can there be wretched felons trembling brought
'Fore red-robed judge and lawyers' cold-eyed stare,
The dread tribunal of the County Court?

Mysterious Chelmsford! 'Neath the railway line
You show, for those who care to read, a sign:
Where Crompton Parkinson once built fine trams,
Th'electric chariots of true urban life
Before swift cars, in snail-slow traffic jams,
Brought chaos, smell, noise, accidents and strife,

Marconi Radar, full of nameless skills
Now Chelmsford's air with complex wonder fills
Past nearby Writtle (where some years ago
The world's first broadcast leapt across the void)
To span the world (and space, for all we know)
And keep your boffins gainfully employed.

Chelmsford! Enigma to the travelling hosts
Who daily pass through you, electric ghosts,

We share your mystery; when th'electric spark
Flashes 'twixt body and the unknown soul
We, though it briefly lights the unknown dark,
Are ignorant yet of force we would control.

DUNMOW

From peaceful cornlands once came man and wife
To prove their marriage perfect, free of strife;
But now divorce so many doth unhitch,
Just staying married rates a Dunmow Flitch

CLACTON AND FRINTON

Sweet Essex Coast, how shall I sing of thee
That offerest to men of every sort
Vacation choices by the brown North Sea –
Plenty of seaside towns, though not one port
Save Harwich (which now sees more traffic go
From neighb'ring Suffolk's smarter Felixstowe)?

He who would banish care with social joys,
With pier and beer and fairs and lots of noise
To Clacton goes with others of his stamp,
Hears beach transistors 'neath th'East Anglian sun
Till night brings all, from digs or Butlin camp,
A vast, mechanical array of Fun.

Fair Frinton offers, on the other hand
Gentility on shores half mud, half sand:
Here, faded remnants of the middle class
Rent flats, read Tolkien, eat stewed prunes
And golfers, past the beach huts and the grass
Swing their sad mashies 'mid the salt sea dunes.

STANSTED

From many a cottage in the park-like scene
Where ten-foot rises give a view for miles,
From manor, new estate, pub, village green
Come Essex folk with hundreds of life styles
To band like Englishmen and fight the foe –
The faceless bosses of the B.A.A.
Who want a Stansted larger than Heathrow
And don't care tuppence what the locals say:

Men who from farming families descend
Which this stiff clay for centuries have ploughed
In Takeley, Wimbish Green or Howlett End,
Men who in speech are soft, but action loud;
From lovely Saffron Walden's timber-frames
Near Audley End, that English view of heaven
Commuters come, with residential claims,
Though linked to London by the M11;
Thaxted and Great Bardfield swell the queue
With those who ply the pen, or brush, or weave
Hand-woven fabrics of a natural hue
'Midst hand-bells, folk dance, song, from morn till eve;
Not only these, but ordinary folk
With ordinary jobs; the old, the young;
Locals for whom uprooting is no joke;
Londoners anxious for this vital lung.
See them all organise against the threat
Of B.A.A. with lawyers by the score;
They too some barristers will quickly get
(Whate'er the fee they guess, it's more).
With coffee morning, raffle, sponsored race
They raise the dough; and see, Miss Olive Cook
In *six weeks* pens th'unanswerable case,
With Betjeman foreword, in a new Pan book . . .

Lo! At the'Enquiry, when at last 'tis heard
The loathsome Plan is cast out as absurd!
So is this priceless bit of England saved
And greed, for once, denied the prize it craved?
Not on your life. From public purse well lined
The civil servants, each with one-track mind,
Revive, a decade gone, their cruel Plan
And once again we're back where we began –
Unlike the Duke of Wellington (let's say)
Whose Waterloo was final, no re-play.

SOUTHEND
To see Southend we missed our only chance;
'Twas there we took off with the car for France.

Books & Bookmen

PIERRE MENSONGE'S WORK is, unfortunately, known to English readers only through Kevin Edge's translation of *Qui?*, the book which established him as the leading exponent of the famous 'novel without a centre' and, incidentally, won him the Prix Unisex. At that stage, however, he was still half-committed to what he has since characterised as the *contrôleur bourgeois* role of the novelist as would-be godlike creator and manipulator of his puppets, and the story of Claudine, the blind Lesbian writer who meets a mysterious psychoanalyst who is writing a novel about a blind lesbian writer engaged on a novel about a psychoanalyst, is told by the 'I' (the *Qui?* of the title) who is sometimes Jean-Philippe, the latently homosexual husband of Claudine's partner Claudia (who may or may not be her alter ego), sometimes Claudine herself, sometimes by the chairman of a local writers' group at the 'real' village of Pissy-les-cerfs, where Mensonge was living at the time.

In *Le Passage de Monsieur Dieudonné* Mensonge goes a logical step further. The writers' commune at Pissy-les-cerfs, which has now come to comprise the entire population (*641, mérite un détour, caves, alt. 142m., musée pornographique, fermé 1.*), is writing a novel about the reactions of the imagined townsfolk – Paul Chirac the monumental mason, Claudine the baker's Lesbian wife, Henri Ennuyeux the bourgeois banker with his mysterious terrorist daughter whom he loves incestuously and other 'conventional' novel 'characters' – to the arrest of Dieudonné, a tramp who lives in the woods nearby, for the rape of a mysterious 12-year old girl, the *je* of a previous novel; the arrest is made by mysterious black-clad police who did not exist until Henri (persuaded by Claudine? Mensonge leaves this an open question) wrote them into the 'novel' which actually consists of 143 questions asked at the magistrates' preliminary hearing. It is not 'complete', says Mensonge, until the reader has filled in the answers on the dotted lines, if then. 'It is the most democratic book ever written,' Mensonge said in one of his rare interviews.

Some critics have seen Angela Wibley as the leading English exponent of the *noncentrisme* currently fashionable in France. However, I find her new novel *British Serial Rights* firmly rooted in NW1, though possibly none the worse for that. The main character, Delphinium

Sorley, gets married largely to annoy her mother, Dame Jason Sorley, CBE, Chairwoman of the Women's Anti-marriage League. She marries Knutsford Bridgeley, with whom she had lived when they were both at Cambridge. The marriage becomes a fierce battle of wills, since each is writing a novel about the other and about their marriage (is this also 'marriage'?). Both scorn the old novelist's bodying forth and 'creation' of character, both must find anchor in the social reality of their own lives, set of course in the context of Thatcherite consumerism.

Each therefore seeks every way of not providing the other with 'material'. Knutsford achieves this by total inactivity, doing nothing that Delphinium could possibly write about. She, who sees paternalism as the historic reason for women bearing children, has had three abortions. He is writing another novel, which he keeps secret from her (until a climactic point in the story) about the three children who might have been, called Foss, Roebuck and Equanimity; but he gives her 'nothing' to write about by this apparent total inactivity, indeed he stays in bed all the time, mostly with the mother's help, a mysterious ex-soldier who has an import business in Korean string vests and fasts for the IRA in his spare time.

The reality of the baby-sitter, referred to throughout as '704 Smith', obviously depends on whether the reader takes the viewpoint of Delphinium (we are never sure whether she sees him or not) or of Knutsford, who may or may not have created him as a character in his novel. Meanwhile Delphinium deprives her husband of his 'material' by never speaking to him, not living with him, and changing her name, significantly, to '704 Smith'. Ms Wibley's work continues to vibrate with creative doubt.

Duncan Peppiatt's *Zero Hour* (characteristically ironic-literary title) leaves us as uncertain at the beginning as at the end (since by now we have come to expect uncertainty at the mere 'end') whether Dennis Eggoe, the novelist who has 'failed through success' by pandering to bourgeois fiction values, is the creation of students in his university creative writing class or whether the students are 'characters' in the vast nonsense novel on which he is engaged. In this novel-within-a-novel, called *All Change*, he (Eggoe-Peppiatt, or, as he might say, Peppiatt-Eggoe) brilliantly suggests that all mental systems are equally useful (or worthless); the creative writing students desert *en masse* to attend chemistry lectures as a result of which they blow up the university (either inadvertently or on 'purpose') and the chemistry students attend the creative writing course with equally comic results. Although this happens in the first twenty pages the university is still 'there' (in Peppiatt's mind, in the minds of the students, or in reality? Peppiatt does of course himself teach a course which he impishly labels

250

Uncreative Writing), a background for his relentless sexual pursuit of his students of both sexes, many of whom have unisex names such as Evelyn, Kim, Robin, Sam, Deborah, etc. ('Fascism began when Eve was separated from Adam,' remarks Old Joe Scoggins the Securicor man to the Dean at the faculty wife-swapping). Alpha minus.

It might seem a far cry from metropolitan noncentrism to the conventional British northern-young-man novel, but it seems to me that Tony Bogmoss, in *How's My Father?*, has come within an ace, or at any rate a three no trumps, of doing so. Ted Crumpet passes a miserable childhood at the state school for novelists in his native Soddenmoor, where all the other boys have miners as fathers, whereas his has made a pile in cotton futures and lives comfortably at Alderley Edge in a Victorian mansion with a billiard room and a new woman every month from the Manchester firm of Rent-a-Mistress of which his brother (Ted's fastidiously amusing homosexual uncle) is managing director. His unhappiness only briefly relieved by an affair with Miss Hodjkin, his Lawrenceology tutor, Ted 'graduates' with a mere E in Atmosphere. Moving with one of his uncle's girls who has struck it rich to her luxury house in Sanderstead, he toils at a vast novel of proletarian life in which he himself is the son of a miner called Arthur Grodleigh in the pithead village of Hugglesby Undercote, with its mangy greyhounds, decaying pubs and get-rich-quick chiropodists. Taking the finished manuscript up in his motor-cycle combination he drives through an Alderley Edge unknown to him, perhaps after the crisis of identity after his nervous breakdown. When he enters the dark, primitive cottage of Hugglesby Undercote, Arthur Grodleigh turns briefly from the television. 'Happen thee nivver got thi hands dirty writin' that!' he sneers, leaving Ted filled with 'this huge unanswerable fire of hopeful rage'.

SHORTER NOTICES. *The first of June*, by Eileen O'Leary. June O'Grady, an Irish novelist, engaged on a novel about a sex maniac terrorising Irish dairies, has to interrupt it when she finds that the sexual experiences she has been relating to her mysterious psychoanalyst, Hugh, appear in a strange novel published under her own name. Marvellously ambivalent.

All God's Writers. Another 1000-pager by Alvin P. Conquest. Pearl Pigeon, a nymphomaniac best-seller, researching for a huge historical novel on the famous 100-year old writers' commune in Bogota, finds herself converted to its principles before she, with all its members, is massacred sadistically by Government writers supported by the CIA. Powerful, if you are strong enough.

Mate in One

MEDIUM (5ft 8in) PROFESSIONAL WRITER, looks fat when sees self sideways in mirror but can either pull in stomach with diaphragm strengthened by years of choral singing, or can sort of draw self up to look, well, not slim like many advertisers in *Select* (incorporating *Singles Magazine*), seeks further details.

Advertiser may not be slim, but not gross either, just reasonable for (O God) 62, own home, frightful overdraft, six children 16 to 28, rather awful cat that makes point of coming *in* to pee in upstairs lavatory, well not *in* it but on successive squares of coir matting (yes, only coir) which then have to be successively burnt, you just try washing coir matting, but he and wife can't bring themselves to have cat put down, seeks *sincere* (another v. common adjective, surely unnecessary, who would seek insincere mate?) person who can explain to him what seem contradictions in booming computer-dating business.

Obviously not advertising for wife, as stated already got perfectly good one and not through some magazine either, so this ad not directed at, e.g., Box 11805 (*Warm-hearted, extrovert female, tall, slim, would like to meet tall, educated business/professional gentleman 48–55ish, for friendship, outings. Beds, Herts Area. Interested in ballet, dining out, music, theatre, bridge, countryside*).

In first place, ads usually describe advertiser rather than kind of person advertiser wants to meet, well that's fair enough, but how come 80% of them are tall, slim, caring, sincere, and who *doesn't* like dining out, theatre, countryside, travel, etc? Surely they must keep meeting each other anyway in these professions and businesses so many of them seem to be in?

Of course can understand advertisers presenting selves in best light, no one likely to say Man, late forties, yellow teeth, hair growing out of ears, once thought of going to Australia but now stuck in middle management in insurance, redundancy in the air, stupid wife couldn't see anxiety about this was one reason for coming home sloshed some Friday nights after session with the boys in Claims, but not *every* Friday for God's sake, mind you bit of a temper too, e.g., threw china dog at TV during *That's Life*, seeks slim caring professional woman into Bartok, folk medicine, own TV set (preferably colour), view outings etc, Rugeley Area; photo appreciated . . .

252

Do computers, simply because they can deal with millions of people in ⅛ second (well, less than that, but ⅛ second is smallest fraction on advertiser's typewriter), know in ⅛ of ⅛ of a second where to locate some woman with exact qualities as specified in Box 11529 (*Intelligent, humorous, dark, handsome bachelor, 32, company director and workaholic, seeks sensuous, attractive lively female for fun and friendship. Interests include Mozart, Scotland, Woody Allen*)? Or does it do wide sweep, offering every female who doesn't actually say she hates Mozart, Scotland, Woody Allen etc? Perhaps even including Box 11541 (*Fattish but honest and attractive girl, 25, wonders if there's more to life than just work*)? (Don't we all?)

Suppose fattish but honest girl go up to intelligent etc bachelor's area for Scottish weekend (well, actually just Sunday afternoon, if he workaholic he running over company's books, oiling lathes, changing bulbs in men's lavatories in factory all Saturday, and got to be back at desk in Hexham or somewhere 8 a.m. Monday morning), what happen if she honestly admit she never heard of Woody Allen, her face fall when he quote Woody Allen interview in *Time* or somewhere where he say, 'If my film makes one person feel miserable I'll feel I've done my job'?

In second place, how hell does computer know, human nature being what it is (well, to answer own question, that's *how* it doesn't know) that miraculous friendship (to put it mildly) might not spring up between such unlikelies as Box 11577 (*Edinburgh male, 28, single, in rut and lonely, no specific likes or dislikes, seeks girl for companionship, or will correspond. Also has hankering to visit Iceland*) and Box 11582 (*Surrey, Hants. sincere professional female, 34, warm, humorous, childless divorcée, non-smoker, enjoys music, theatre, stimulating conversation. Seeks rapport with slim, amusing, intelligent, cleanshaven male, professional/managerial*)? She could be hostess of salon attracting all the brilliant young artists and intellectuals of Reykjavik, or they could give amusing cocktail parties in igloo just outside Liphook.

In third place (should have been first really, any computer could see that) what all these ads doing anyway in *magazine* run by computer-dating firm? No doubt ads cheaper than full computer treatment; but why magazine full of articles about how married people are suspicious of singles, young wife either does not ask single girlfriend to dinner because potential rival for husband (what, even if she fattish, hate Woody Allen, yawn at husband's slides of Iceland? Could be) – or does ask her but at same time asks single man, nudge wink got a mate for you, come and join us in marriage trap. What bosh, if readers think marriage is trap they can advertise and fill in forms till they're blue in face, won't do any good.

In fourth place, when it comes to full computer treatment, do

253

Dateline International (same address) agree with their 'eminent behavioural psychologist' Dr. Sharpe, who drew up questionnaire? He say, 'Whereas previous generations have tended to seek a life-long partner,' now people want one of four relationships: '*Soul Mates* . . . on which a sound marriage can be built. Research has shown that such partnerships provide mutual support and encouragement' (you need *research* to show that?); '*Soloists* . . . primarily concerned with aims and ambitions outside their dating relationships' (well, to hell with *them* then, who wants a date like that?); '*Catalysts* . . . look for a short affair with a partner who displays this alternative lifestyle . . . enabling the partner to change or adapt their way of life during the short period of their relationship' (then back to 33 Acacia Drive, eh, pity the old girl would never have appreciated the Mozart 39 at St John Smith Square, my God, what night that was with Yvonne Whatsit, still, can't live on Mozart, and the old girl does do a good lemon and meringue); and '*Network*', clearly just a euphemism for the promiscuous.

In fifth place, OK, so applicant fills in, or to be exact ticks Yes/No boxes, questionnaire with 213 questions. (. . . *most people consider me [19] Very Attractive, [20] Attractive, [21] Not Attractive . . . [91] Atheist, [92] Muslim, [93] Other major religious groups . . . [131] I like quiet subtle humour . . . [152] I think sex should be reserved for special relationships etc etc*). Well is there slightest evidence that somewhere there will be someone who wants that kind of person? Does anybody *know* the kind of person they are going to love before they have met him/her?

In the sixth place, does anyone ever say Yes to Question 21?

Chain Reaction

*F*RI. A.M. FINE October morning, usual weekend Gardener's Multiple Choice (which task has lowest priority, can theoretically even be left till next weekend?). Surely it ought to be at least down to single figures by this time of year. Not like, say, early summer, when GMC can be: 1. Mow lawn. 2. Get round veg garden with Merry Tiller (la la, la la, la la la LA la la, etc, very convenient machine and all that, fine in straight lines, but Schumann's Merry Peasant didn't have to turn lurching throbbing 2½ cwt thing round at end of each furrow). 3. Go out and see if *any* shop got seed potatoes left, how everybody else got them in during snow? 4. Dig sweet pea trench. 5. Buy sweet pea *plants*, too late for seeds now unless don't want sweet peas till August. 6. Sow lettuce, if veg bed raked as well as Merrytilled. 7. Weed rose beds. 8. Weed brick path. 9. Weed front path. 10. O God, thought some weedkiller left from last year, huge rusty tin just contain crumbly yellow sort of meteorite . . . on to 23, do *edges* of rose beds; though probably just 1 and 2 will take whole weekend.

But this lovely Fri. a.m., fine after gale, lovely obvious single task: 1. Hire chainsaw. Gale blew enormous piece of ash tree down. With apple-tree that blew down last year, perhaps not quite big enough to justify hire of chain-saw, this will make enough logs to last winter, or most of it. Load of logs, now £25, crazy to buy wood in country when it's all round. Find people actually billed as 'The Chain-saw Specialists' in *Yellow Pages*. Yes, I can have one, they close 12.30 Saturday, if I bring it back early Monday morning it will be £10. Gosh, I shall save £££££s, as the ads say.

Sat. 10.30. Drive seven miles to chain-saw people on industrial estate of town. Shed full of giant chromium walking sticks with little engines at one end, short nylon cord at other end which whizz round at 1 million rpm, cut grass in those awkward corners. Instructions all in Swedish, *net gøn 5 metre standeret* or something, general impression is Stand Well Clear. All chain-saws Swedish too, leaflets have pictures of amateur loggers in birch-woods, with woolly caps. *Ho, Sven, a littlet mør to mi, loek OET, TIMBERET!*, cries echo through frosty air of clearing . . .

Have you ever used chain-saw before, asks man at counter. No, I say, but first time for everything, live dangerously, gosh shouldn't have said that, he look doubtful, then explain *very* carefully how you press this catch on top when you have pulled this catch beneath, apparently simultaneously accelerator and clutch, up while squeezing other catch on top (otherwise it won't come, safety device, see? Don't, but nod) then that first catch stops it from going completely back again, just holds it there, see? Don't, but nod again.

Petroil must be 20 to 1 mixture otherwise it will seize up. Put chain oil in here. Avoid stones. Would you like to try? Here is choke, push in when it start. OK, I say. He pull starter rope with immense young-man violence I suspect I can't match. When it not start instantly, this is point at which should have remembered other GMC; 2. Get up bean poles, 3. Weed brick path again, 4. etc, bid him good-day, sorry I troubled him. But he take machine outside, give it really terrible pull, it scream into life, there you are, he shriek at me, use end nearest you, like this, as he cut through huge block of dense-looking red wood for demonstration, don't forget, stones wreck blades, petroil is 20 to 1. I give him cheque for £30 (£20 is deposit, fair enough, this thing cost, my God, £290). Good luck, he say. Resist, fairly easily, temptation to buy woolly cap on way back through town.

Sat. 11.15. At home, ready to start, pull starter rope. It go *bubbubbubb-bubbb*. Again. Again. Again. *Bubbubbubbb* sometimes just *bubb*. People always tell you it flooded at this stage. Oh well, get plug out, clean it.

Where hell plug spanner? Where hell 18 plug spanners bought since lived in this house, archaeologists will find them buried in year 5000, it will be famous site of Middle British garage. No good. Pull again. *Bubbubbubb.* And this time cord doesn't spring back, till fiddle with flywheel thing through grating with screwdriver, when *brrrrzonk*, spring suddenly catch. Ha. Once cord start doing that it get worse, and if 89 pulls so far any indication it going to get a lot of use to get worse with.

Sat. 11.59. Just time to get back to Chain-saw Specialists before they close, either sort this spring-pull out and lend me plug spanner or give me another chain-saw. Drive like maniac along road which make idiotic 90-degree bends every fifty yards in perfectly open cornland, get stuck behind zombies doubtless off to slow rustic drinking. Chain-saw rumble about in boot, falling over, smell of petroil, well just can't bring self to stop now.

Sat. 12.27. Chain-saw Specialist look as if closed for month, like entire industrial estate. *Ah, dagbladet en blivvering bløsted Gödbenikket soedding chainsawetteret.*

Drive from small town to large town, calling at every single garage, will at least buy 19th plug spanner. They look at me as if loony, imagine them roaring with laughter at local garage association dinner; you had

256

that geezer wanting a plug spanner too, ha ha ha, a *plug* spanner, Satdy lunchtime, and it was for 36 mil (or some damnfool thing) in a chain-saw, not even a car . . .

Do not actually discover this till

Sat. 4.45. After fruitless trips to two other small towns, resist temptation to buy, at one garage, Socket Set Bargain £7.95, surely one of them would fit. Then think, £17.95 for hire of chain-saw plus petroil plus petrol in all this driving about plus fact that diminishing amount of weekend left won't leave *time* to cut equivalent of £25 load even if it there, and even if eventually get perisher to start, is too much. Just as well; neighbour with socket set finds the only one that fits can't be used because idiotic plug too long for him to get other part of tool on. Ah, *drucket en flicken ok krokketet Svenska dogblikket sparketbougie, en skøppered et høll bloeddy woekend.*

Sat. 5.15. Other neighbour, well don't know him at all actually, know he on other side of village, reputation as having near-professional garage in garden, ring him up in desperation, he say yes of course come round, he pause from welding sub-frame, find *ring* spanner which actually fit plug, too true, it smothered in øl (well, what hell supposed to do then, perisher wouldn't start *without* choke either?), clean it, put back, perisher roar into maniacal life, fill garage of this saint with dense blue smoke. Resist temptation to drive home with it still ticking over in car, never mind dense blue smoke.

Sat. 5.45. Actually start cutting in gathering dusk. Marvellous, it go through as if butter, nothing to it. *En singet joelly woedman, in kleerings frisket är, en chainsaw klippet køtting, en singet tra lo la.*

Sun. 11 a.m. Make up for lost time. Pull start rope. *Bubbubb.* And this time, rope permanently out, no amount of jiggering will make spring pull it back. *Dag froeket, gadbastardet de frokkende bloeddy chainsaweretten, all det swet ond møney før nötting, grastet ond blikket en soedding ting . . .*

Mon. 9.30 a.m. Chain-saw Specialist, with weary I-thought-as-much look, say OK, will lend you another one, free. But will have to charge you for re-sharpening this one, you must have hit stone with it . . .

No bill yet. But one thing sure. Total a damn sight more than £25.

The Ballad of BP Tioxide

When Mr. Justice Goff, of the High Court, allowed an appeal by
BP Tioxide against an arbitrator's decision in favour of Pioneer
Shipping, owners of the *Nema*, a Greek Ship chartered by BPT,
Lord Diplock said leave to appeal against the arbitrator's award
should never have been given. Parliament's intention to promote
finality in arbitrators' awards would be defeated if judges were to grant
leave to appeal . . . Lord FRASER of TOLLYBELTON, Lord
RUSSELL of KILLOWEN, Lord KEITH of KINKEL and Lord
ROSKILL all agreed that the appeal should be dismissed.

Daily Telegraph

O N TOLLYBELTON'S rolling braes
　Where dauntless Wallace strove
Lord Fraser passed his pensive days
'Twixt library and grove.
'These woods, these fields, these burns,' quoth he
'Wi' mental joys are blent;
O, fairer is life here tae me
Than hours in Law Courts spent!'

'O, wad some Pow'r had laid it doon
That we could judge at hame!
What gars we sit in London Toun,
Wha'd judge here jist the same?
Aye, ilka case we wad decide
Wi' judgement muckle fair –
– And muckle clear, sith a' were tried
In Scotland's braw clear air.'

'By fair Killowen's lonely shore
Laird Russell keeps his hoose,
His heid nigh burstin' wi' its store
O' precedents an' use;
An' if we twa could nae agree
There's aye Laird Keith o' Kinkel
By silv'ry Tay (or is it Dee?),
We'd up an' gie'm a tinkle.'

258

'The Hoose o' Lairds, a gey fine place
The Sassenachs might feel,
Is whaur blind Justice shows her face
In ultimate appeal
Tae us, the finest, fairest brains
In Britain's legal system;
But London's *charms*? Ane look explains
Up here, why we've no missed 'em.'

He scarce had ceased, when o'er the mead
There came a rider hasting
Who leapt down from his foaming steed
No word in frivol wasting;
'I come frae Laird Roskill,' he cried,
'He thinks yon Goff is slipping
Else why should BP Tioxide
Appeal 'gainst Pioneer Shipping?'

A frown is wrinkling Fraser's face
And thunder clouds his brow;
'Though London is a fearfu' place,'
He cries, 'we'll gae there now.'
He's phoned Lord Russell, and the pair
In Kinkel find Lord Keith
Nor pause to ask 'Roskill of *where*?'
On the bonny ship at Leith.

It's up the Forth she swiftly sails,
It's south she sails past Berwick
Till London her arrival hails,
Beflagged each crane and derrick
And thousands cheer them from the Strand
Upon disembarcation
As cries are heard on every hand
Of 'Long Live Arbitration!'

So to the dread Tribunal come
Lords Fraser, Keith and Russell
With Roskill adding to the sum
Of intellectual muscle,
And barristers for BPT
And all the others in it
Who rub their hands, since costs could be
A hundred pounds a minute.

Five law lords now sit on high –
Lord Diplock's joined the forum
And this makes up, none could deny
A formidable quorum
To whom Tioxide's men must show
The Greek ship, SS *Nema*,
In spite of judgements months ago
Was not a tip-top steamer.

Lord Keith has asked them, stern of eye
'Whit profit are ye after?
Hae ye fresh arguments, forbye?
Or hopes ye'll find *us* safter?'
But they can only nod and blink
At Fraser's angry roar
'Then whit the de'il dae ye think
An arbitrator's *for*?'

'Tis quickly done, the case thrown out,
Diplock for all has spoken
And by the crowd's approving shout
Loud echoes are awoken.
Their task achieved, to Scotland fair
They all return rejoicing
To drink its drink, and breathe its air,
This last opinion voicing:

'Nae mair frae Bellytolton dear
Or any Scottish dockside
Will we depart, some case to hear
Like yon BP Tioxide.
Nae mair tae London wull we gae
Frae Bollykinkeltelton;
Le' them come here, whaur *every* brae
Is bonny as Maxwellton.'

Invenkion; buk necessiki?

PLOBABLI ONLI A celkain kinb of pepson – ze kinb of pepson zak likes closswolb puzzles anb wolb kanes in jenelal – will kake ze klouble ko bekin, lek alone finisk, an akkicle in wkick ak no poink can ze followink lekkeps appeap: d, g, h, m, r, t, y.

Bann ik all, zak's neakli a qualkel of ze enkipe alpkabek. Buk befole zou consikn zis akkicle ko ze well-known *New Jolkel* cakekoli of Akkicles We Nevel Finiskeb Leabink, please lek ne explain wky ik was absolukeli necessali fop ne ko akkenk ko neek zis ckallenje.

Ze fack is zak anonk all ze skuff wkick clukkeps up ze besk ak wkick I sik conposink zis akkicle is a wee (well, we nusk ckoose bekween *wee* anb *likkle*), a wee pencil-skanpenep, one of zose bevices for lenewink ze poink on a pencil. Anb zis pencil-skanpenep is so consklukkeb as ko look like a likkle pipewipen.

Pipewipen is as close as I can appnoxinake ko ze spellink of zc fanilial nackine useb eveli dai of ous lives bi us jounalisks, wiz iks space baa, iks kex fop CAPIKAL LEKKEPS LIKE ZIS, ekc. Coulb *zou* nanaje anikink bekkep wiz suck a nisenable seleckion of lekkeps? If ik's bekinnink ko senb zou klazi alweabi, fink wkak ik nusk be like fop ne. (I feel sonekow zak ze lekkep we'pe koink to niss nosk of all is ze one zak cones bekween q anb s in ze alpkabek.) Fop inskance, woulb *kipewkipep* be ani beppep zan *pipewipen* fop zak nackine? No, ik looks *wolse* ko ne.

Well, as I was kellink zou, I kave zis likkle pencil-skanpenep nabe in ze skape of a pipewipen. Ik was a plesenk flon ni son wken ke wenk on a skool klik ko Jeunani – Wesk Jeunani, I neeb kalbli poink ouk, nok ze 'Jeunan Benoklakic Pepublic'.

Ik is well-nabe, anb looks quike pealiskic. Ze ackual pencil-skanpenink bik is kibben awai in ze back of ze nackine. Wkak zou ackualli see looks fop all ze woklb like a veni snall pipewipen. Zou can see ze wolb REMINGTON on ik, anb ze likkle ciccles nepnesenkink ze nibbon-spools (wkak bliss ik was ko pipe zak wolb REMINGTON, I skall bo ik akain fop ze skeep pleasupe of ik. RRRRRRREMM-MMMMINGGGGGGGTTTTTON). Anb ik kas zis exklaolbinalili obb ckoice of lekkeps on iks kexboalb:

F S A L J K B V X Z
N C P O I U E W Q
. + 98765432

Anb zak's ze lok. So zou will see zak in fack I've nabe ik a bik easiek fop anione akkenkink ko nake sense of zis akkicle, bi ak leask usink connas inskeab of ze full skop, op peliob, wkick is ze only punkuakion nalk sklickli allowable; anb zou'll kave nokiceb I also use ze aposkopke, anb quokakion anb queskion nalks.

Now, I've nevel ackualli seen a Jeunan pipewipen, so I bon'k know kow ze kees (looks wlonk buk ackualli sounbs nole like ze wolb I'n ainink ak zan *kexs* woulb, ek?) ale lekkepeb. Buk I skoulbn'k be a bik sulpliseb if zei wele exackli ze sane as oul own – *qwertyuiop*, *asdfghjkl*, ekc., wiz of coulse a few funni finks of zeil (zou'll neeb an inspileb kuess fop *zeil*, op can I ckeak jusk fop once anb abnik zack's ze nealesk I can kek ko *their*?), a few funni finks of zeil own, suck as ze biaelesis accenk fop Jeunan wolbs like *sckön* (beaukiful), anb zak funni conjoineb f and s zei kave zak alwais nakes ne fink zak wkeleas ze lesk of ze woklb plais fookball, zei plai fussball.

Ik sais a lok fop oup jenelal abnikakion fop Keukonic efficienci zak we bo nok, fop one nonenk, inajine zak zese Jeunans, biscovelink zak zei kave zis linikakion ko 19 lekkeps inskeab of ze usual 26 on ze likkle wkike plaskic kexboalb (ze lesk of zis pseubo-pipewipen pencil-skanpenep is nabe of blonze-colouleb bun-nekal) sinpli puk on ik ze filsk 19 lekkeps zak cane inko zeil kcabs. We feel, knowink ze Jeunans as we bo, zak zele nusk be a kecknical leason fop ik.

One fink is celkain sule ko skalk wiz; zese likkle finks wele ceikainli nok nabe fop kone consunkion, wei wele nabe fop expolk. Zei woulb be no use in Jeunani ikself ak all. One kas onli ko fink of

Beucksklanb, Beucksklanb übel alles

ko see zak, op ze filsk lines of ze ckolus in Beekkoven's Ckolal Sinfoni

Fleube, sckönel Kökkelfunken
Kockkel aus Elisiun.

Ik neans 'Joi, Elisian baupep' (O Lolb, I skall have ko ckeak akain. I can't kek aniwkele neap 'daughter' in zis kekkible lankuaje, in wkick one can weep buk nok lauf, unless zou counk *aka ka ka, ko ko ko* anb appnoxinakions like zak) 'of ze skalli keavens.' Obviousli ze Jeunans coulbn'k use suck a pipewipen even fop olbinali, evelidai, connonklace convelsakion, lek alone ze likelali explessions of zeil poeks anb novelisks, flon Koecke ko Kkonas Nann op Kunkkel Klass.

In fack wiz all zese zs, ze jenelal implession one leceives is of sone solk of skaje Flencknan, like Helcule Poilok, ze fanous fickional defeckive in ze novels of (O Kob!) Akava Kliski – onli a Helcule Poilok evibenkli

262

suffelink flon a clefk palake anb also wiz a Ckinese bifficulki wiz zak blaskeb lekkep bekween q anb s inko ze balkain. Vietnanese, pelkaps?

Ik is bifficulk ko inajine zen all sikkink bown ko a sales confelence, in sone spankink new inbusklial eskake on ze oukskilks of Busselbolf, op Flankfulk, anb finalli concullink wiz ze views of ze sales nanajel:

'Jenklenen, ik is oup ploub boask zak Jeunan fanci koobs, pelkaps especialli Jeunan pencil-skankeneps, kave an unlivalleb lepukakion all ovel ze woklb fop leliabiliki anb solibiki of nanufakkule. Buk people nowabais neeb ze elenenk of novelki as well. Now, oup lesealck depalknenk kave cone up wiz a nunbel of biskuises unbel wkick we coulb conkinue ko sell oup fanous pencil-skankeneps, anb I pepsonalli fink zak one of ze nosk successful is zis likkle nobel pipewipen, ov wkick zou kave ze plokopipe op nock-up befole zou. Unfolkunakeli, as zou see, zele is only space fop 19 lekkups. Now, wkak lankuaje is sinulkaneousli ze nosk wibeli skoken in ze woklb anb ze one in wkick ze lekkeps d, g, h, m, r, t anb y woulb leask be nisseb?'

Well, if zei fink ik's Enklisk, I've kok news fop zen. Back to ze blawink-boalb, jenklenen.

HOMOMOMONUKUNUKAUGUK!

IT IS A hard life for us lexicographers. Decisions, decisions, decisions. How much longer are we going to keep *firlot* in the Shorter Oxford English Dictionary, for instance? It is actually a measure of corn, the fourth part of a boll if you want to know. At least, it was in 1573, the kind of date a lot of these OED words seem to go back to. I am pretty sure bolls and firlots went out even before we were into metres and kilos. And who was the last poet to write *rhopalic* verse? This is (or was in 1682) verse in which each word contains one more syllable than the one immediately preceding it. I am willing to bet not many poets were writing it in 1682 (just had a quick look at Dryden and Vaughan; not a sign of it).

Meanwhile all sorts of words are having to be left out (they do actually have *pogy*, although all they say is that it is a 'menhaden' and you have to look in the other volume, A to M, to find that this is 'a U.S. fish of the herring family, *Brevoortia tyrannus*, much used for manure and producing a valuable oil'). But by including all those words dating back to 1682, they are forced to leave out, for instance, the information that a large fish in Hawaii is *ō* and a very small fish is known as homomomonu-kunukauguk.

What I mean is that modern life is constantly throwing up experiences and things which are crying out for dictionary status, things far more real than obsolete verse forms and corn measures. For instance:

Aggro-Saxon: n. English football hooligan abroad (see *Aston Villan*).

Aston Villan: n. English football hooligan at home (see *Aggro-Saxon*).

Backeye: vb. To look at, be aware of, even with the back turned, esp. of cats (see *subeye*).

Bennefictor: n. One who makes large promises of peace, prosperity etc. which assume the co-operation of large social groups or entire other nations.

Bewarehouse: n. The abandoned warehouse and/or yard with piles of crates, tyres, or rows of pillars, behind which armed villain lurks, at end of all television police serials. Often referred to simply as BWH.

Biturgy: n. Any local church service of which the form has been locally devised (see *postscripture*).

Bleaktide: n. Traditionally the period between the four Sundays following the feast of St Blearicus (April 4), a 6th-century hermit whose cave in Northumbria was miraculously surrounded by snow throughout the year. The first of these was known as 'Shivering Sunday.'

Britic: n. A person of British birth who thinks that everything Britain does is wrong and talks about 'the British' as though he were of some other nationality.

Bumplunker: n. One who makes the playing of simple chords, or even single notes, on an electric guitar look difficult by waggling his hips and bottom (see also *organisma* and *pelvist*).

Crastics: n.pl. (From Latin *cras*, tomorrow). Obsession with, and ever increasing showing of ever-longer extracts from, tomorrow's television programmes.

Drumble: n. Basic low sound, not part of its normal running noise, in a car (see *squigget*).

Euphonia: n. State of artificial merriment, accompanied by permanent smile, of people in commercials, esp. those for cornflakes (see also *rigor electronicus*).

Hypnogogue: n. Modern educationist who believes that all learning is a passive process requiring no effort (i.e. memorising multiplication tables, verbs etc.), but can be passed on by mechanical and electronic methods.

Jamdoodle: vb. To improvise music which starts and ends in the same key in a once-only, aleatory fashion, usu. with piano and double bass.

Kissteria: n. Ritual emotion shown by footballers after the scoring of a goal.

Lakerage: n. (1) The swamping of a place, usu. a resort, by tourists without enough money to leave it. (2)Travel for travel's sake rather than interest in the places visited.

Mummerum: n. A theatrical piece not written by one author but developed by improvising actors.

Neolist: n. One who always has a new car, a new television set, new video machine, new furniture, new everything, and has *never* had anything old from the moment of setting up house.

Nipotism: n. Tendency of the offspring of well-known actors and actresses to become well-known actors and actresses.

Organisma: n. Affliction of keyboard musicians who, at an instrument which is best played in a sitting position (organ, harmonium, piano, vibraphone etc.) have uncontrollable urge to stand up and dance about, often wearing sleeveless leather waistcoats (see *bumplunker* and *pelvist*).

Oscalation: n. The uncontrolled spread of television shows in which actors, actresses, writers, producers, etc. keep handing each other awards.

Parkolepsy: n. Potentially lethal mental condition of motorist unable to find anywhere to put his car, or even to get out of it (see *saturdation*).

Pelvist: n. A bumplunker (q.v.) who sings as well.

Phobately: n. Fear or dislike of large new postage stamps celebrating obscure anniversaries, e.g. Great British Herbalists.

Postscripture: n. Any translation of the Bible after the Authorised Version (C. of E.) or Douai (R.C.) (vulg.) 'Holy Babel' (see *biturgy*).

Rectocrat: n. A public official who insists on the letter of the law, e.g. electricity board inspector who turns off mains supply of pensioner with hypothermia, or ticket inspector who will not allow 2nd-class ticket-holders standing in corridor to sit in empty 1st-class carriages.

Rigor electronicus: n. (L.) Terminal stage of euphonia (q.v.) in which sufferer, off camera, smiles or laughs himself to death.

Sabbato-nimbus: n. Cloud formation which takes shape about 11a.m. on bright Sundays, after most motorists have left for seaside, and turns to fine drenching rain by 3p.m.

Saturdation: n. The complete filling-up of seaside or other resort at weekends, so that no one can get in or out (see *parkolepsy*).

Simulact: n. The representation of sexual intercourse on stage.

Squigget: n. Basic high sound, not part of its normal running noise, in a car (see *drumble*).

Subeye: vb. To look at a person while the eyes are apparently closed (of cats) (see *backeye*).

Telipsism: n. Tendency of television to regard *itself* as reality, e.g. taking for granted that satire on television must necessarily be about television programmes and personalities.

Yavair: n. Any popular tune, but esp. in 'Eurovision' contests, where backing group sings *ay yay yay* or similar refrain.

The Bank Beautiful?

DEEP DOWN – NO, not deep down, with the top part of my mind as well – I have always felt that nobody can afford anything, unless he is the kind of farmer-baron who inherits lots of land and cows and pigs and hens, and is strong enough to kill anyone who tries to take them away from him.

The rest of us, who do not grow or make any entire thing ourselves, only have these bathrooms and television sets and cars and armchairs and the rest if it because of banks. Banks are the mysterious, magic point at which unreal money from unreal jobs makes contact with the real world.

Sometimes we are (or, in my own case, were) mysteriously 'in credit'. More often we are 'in the red', and you can tell how utterly unquestioning is people's belief that this state of affairs is magic and unreal from the way they all solemnly say to one another, 'Oh, but that's how the banks make their money. They *like* you to have an overdraft, with you paying them all that interest.'

But look here, that is not real money you are paying them the interest with. You have not got any real money. Presumably it is true that in certain extreme cases the banks send men in heavy brown boots to take away your carpet and television set. But even if they sell it at some huge bankers' auction rooms, doubtless in Leadenhall Street, it will only fetch a fleabite compared with what you owe them.

In our case it would not even be that, because the only carpet it would remotely profit them to take has a huge irremovable stain where a four-year-old dropped a bottle of wine on it (oh, you can live it up on an overdraft, with drunken children and everything).

Yet there it is. I read somewhere that Lloyds' Bank made £385.6m. in 1981, and I dare say my bank (which shall be nameless in case the men in brown boots read this) made even more. And in my nearest town they have started spending it in a most spectacular way. *They are turning the branch into a drawing-room.*

Until a year ago it was just like any other town bank. The only modernisation had been in the sixties style of Functional Inconvenience – or FI as it is known to architecture and engineering (same thing nowadays) students. At the time, this was hailed as an elegant paradox: the 'functionality' of any public service – the ease of operation for those working in it – increased in direct ratio to the inconvenience felt by the public using it.

Hence the replacement, for instance, of the old public telephone with its courteous money-returning Button B, by the FI model of today (in an imitation space helmet nailed to the wall too high for you to write down numbers, instead of in a proper kiosk). Hence British Rail's building the new platform at Colchester in such a way that old ladies have to walk 300 yards on a high windswept embankment out over the Essex fields instead of, as before, getting straight into the London train from the main station entrance. Hence the noxious, fume-laden claustrophobic taxi tunnel at Euston Station (with its FI total absence of anywhere to sit down, or tiny cafeteria). Hence any billing by computer.

Hence in banks the counter made too narrow for writing of any kind, such as of paying-in slips, or indeed anything remembered too late when one has left the table where the chained-up, non-working pens are.

My local branch (which is very nice to me and has not sent the men in brown boots around yet) is designed like that still. But in this town nearby suddenly all has been changed.

It is full of fitted carpets and settees and climbing plants and round tables with glass tops. You would think the board of the bank had telephoned their manager from London and said 'Let yourself go, Henderson' (if that indeed is his name). 'Go to Heals or Habitat, order anything you want; the sky's the limit, we've had a hell of a good year and your branch has done as well as any. Warm browns and cerises are probably the thing just now. And those big Lalique ashtrays . . .'

I get the feeling they only just stopped short of tropical fish and a drinks cabinet. They have a lot of alcoves, with soft chairs and those

267

glass-topped tables, which often seem to be occupied by a trio consisting of a girl from the bank and a couple talking earnestly but amicably over documents, like people in an architect's drawing. It would not be all that surprising if the chief cashier sounded some kind of electronic *ta-raa* on his computer, two major-domos rolled back the central carpet to reveal a stage floor, there was a roll of drums, and all those trios turned their chairs inwards to watch the adagio dancers.

No, come on, banks are serious places, there is some perfectly serious explanation. The bank realising that a strong home economy and a strong export position are somehow magically interlinked, is trying to get the sluggish retail trade of the high streets moving. Those girls are qualified interior decorators hired to persuade those couples to be devils, have an overdraft for the first time in their lives and splash out with rainbow-unit settees, module bookcases, pinewood loft conversion with spiral staircase, black bath, Bauhaus chairs, the lot. They are finding it rather difficult; the couples have the air of starting out seriously on married life around 30. He is a smallholder or tractor rep., doing well, she a farmer's daughter. They had a church wedding – none of your teenage town register-office, irresponsible rush jobs.

One of the men, pausing at an illustration of a bidet in a catalogue, says suspiciously 'Who would want one of them?' The bank girl whispers something to his fiancée and says hurriedly 'no, the next page, Mr. Sneezum. It's an exciting new concept called the Studio Bathroom. For just under £1,000 you can . . .'

Or perhaps it is that there have always been two polarities in English banking, a kind of Cavalier/Roundhead dichotomy. On the one hand all those serious East Anglian families with surnames like Gurney or Lloyd and Christian names like Abel, very often Quaker, disapproving of ostentation and display. On the other, people, like Henry Hoare (1705–1785), known as Henry the Magnificent, the banker who laid out Stourhead, one of the most beautiful gardens in the world; or some of the wilder Rothschilds. There is a periodic swing from one extreme to the other, and just now the latter party is in the ascendant, so that . . .

. . . No, of course, *I* see why they have done it. It is nothing to do with consumerism or even money. It is, in fact, the unlikely but effective response to the rising violence of our time.

It is designed to foil bank robbers. In the old bank the robber would know which window to go to for the money. But if he tried that here he would trip backwards over a pouffe or bang his knee against one of the glass-topped tables. You can hold up a bank but you cannot hold up a cocktail party.

In this new decor the robber would be visually confused the moment he got into the place. His way to the mosaic-floored Encashment Area obscured by a huge arrangement of bamboo and trailing indoor plant, he would blunder into one of those alcoves where a hostess, greeting him courteously, would motion him to a chair and say 'What *type* of robbery were you considering, sir? Basically the distinction is between bonds and specie, as you probably know . . .'

Even if she did not say that, but just fled with a scream, he would know from the mellow three-tone hooters which suddenly sounded that the couples who appeared on the floor between him and wherever the money was were not ordinary couples, but swiftly-summoned Securicor karate experts whose skills, however, were rendered unnecessary as the armchair automatically tipped back into the reclining position, nerve gas disguised with the odour of jasmine hissed gently from the great bowl of flowers, and an elegantly-designed steel cage dropped over him from the ceiling.

And all without a hint of FI anywhere.